Yankee Cavalrymen

Yankee

BY JOHN W. ROWELL

THE UNIVERSITY OF TENNESSEE PRESS

KNOXVILLE

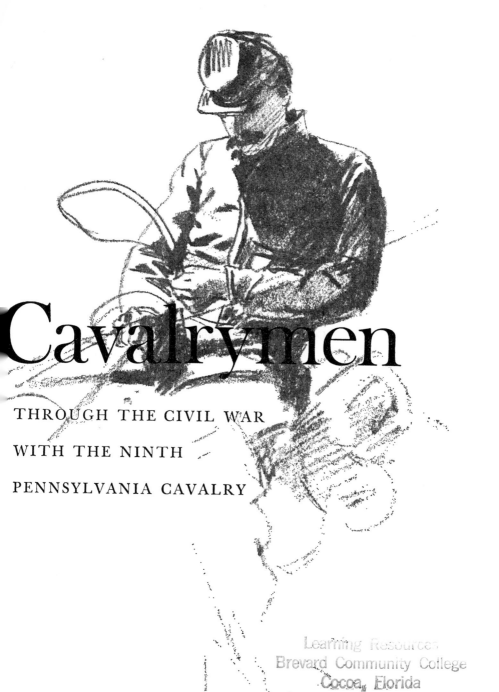

Cavalrymen

THROUGH THE CIVIL WAR
WITH THE NINTH
PENNSYLVANIA CAVALRY

Library of Congress Catalog Card Number 70–126939
Standard Book Number 87049–125–3
Copyright © 1971 by The University of Tennessee Press.
Manufactured in the United States of America.
All Rights Reserved. First Edition.

Preface

If they expected that war would be adventure, excitement, and glory, the Yankee cavalrymen who served with the Western armies during the Civil War were not disappointed. Theirs was a war of movement with frequent scouting and foraging expeditions, skirmishes, and raids. While the bored infantry remained in camp for long periods, the cavalry was out raising havoc with enemy communications or chasing Rebels intent on destroying Union rail and telegraph lines. When the infantry did march, the troopers rode ahead and were the first to meet the enemy.

In contrast to the Eastern soldiers, whose campaigning was limited to northern Virginia, the Western troopers ranged widely through Kentucky, Tennessee, northern Alabama, Georgia, and the Carolinas. More than any other soldiers, they observed the remarkable contrasts of the South—the poor, remote mountain cabins of Kentucky and the rich plantations of Georgia; pro-Union East Tennessee and solidly secessionist South Carolina.

The cavalrymen paid for the excitement of their service through more frequent exposure to danger and hardship. Although losses usually were light in individual skirmishes, casualties through four years took a high toll. Sleeping unsheltered on wet or frozen earth and marching in rain or snow led to sickness and additional deaths. Fewer than half of the men who enlisted in cavalry regiments in 1861 were on the rolls in 1865.

The Ninth Pennsylvania Cavalry was one of the few Eastern regiments to serve from 1861 to 1865 with the Western armies and the only cavalry from the East to make the final campaigns through Georgia and the Carolinas. They may have traveled farther and have seen more of the South than any other group in the Federal army. Upholding the honor of Pennsylvania among the Western soldiers, the Ninth became one of the most respected units of the Army of the Cumberland. Even early in the war, when the Southern cavalry was generally superior to that of the Union, the Ninth fought successfully against such Rebel leaders as Forrest, Wheeler, and Morgan. Because they consistently won their fights and were never routed or captured, the morale of the men remained high throughout the war.

Although scouting, raiding, and skirmishing with enemy cavalry was the principal work of the cavalry, the Ninth Pennsylvania performed honorable service at the Battles of Perryville, Chickamauga, and Averasboro and often was in the van as the Union armies marched through Tennessee, Georgia, and the Carolinas. Their guns were the last to fire in the main war east of the Mississippi.

Surprisingly, no history of this exceptional body of cavalry was written during the late years of the nineteenth century when regimental histories were written about many less distinguished and less active units. Perhaps the officers and men believed their record did not require recounting or embellishment.

My interest in developing this story of the Ninth Pennsylvania Cavalry began in 1962 when I read the diary kept by my grandfather, Cornelius Baker, an enlisted man in Company C. Because his entries were brief and told only what he saw, I began to research other sources to learn how his daily records related to the campaigns and strategy of the war. Officers' reports from *The War of the Rebellion: A Compilation of the Official Records of the Union and Confederate Armies,* materials on file in the National Archives about the regiment and the individual soldiers, and information from other sources confirmed that this regiment had consistently been where there was action. Combined with Baker's diary, this material gave a complete record from the time of the regiment's furlough in 1864 until their discharge. However, there were gaps in the story for the early years because the officers' reports covered only the most significant actions. Then the lucky break occurred.

The column "Events 100 Years Ago" in the April 1964 issue of *Civil War Times Illustrated* contained this sentence: "A Union cavalryman journeys north by train and boat from Tennessee to his Pennsylvania home for the 30-day furlough which is his reward for re-enlistment." Knowing that the Ninth was the only Pennsylvania cavalry in Tennessee to be furloughed at the time, I thought, "This fellow knows something." I wrote the editor of the column, Mr. Robert D. Hoffsommer of Harrisburg, Pennsylvania, who also happens to be the Executive Director of Gettysburg Battlefield Preservation Association.

He not only knew something; he had in his possession the diary of William Thomas of Company B of the Ninth Pennsylvania that Mr. LeRoy Robert Matter, great-grandson of the soldier, had loaned him. Mr. Hoffsommer most kindly typed the entire diary to give me a copy and also obtained Mr. Matter's consent to use it in this history. In addition, Mr. Hoffsommer offered to give me his opinion and editorial comment as the story developed, an offer most eagerly accepted.

Beginning on the day of his enlistment in 1861, the Thomas record complemented the Baker diary. Although Thomas discontinued his daily entries at the end of 1864, Baker's record continued until muster-out. Between them, there is a soldier's notation for every day of the war. Fortunately the two soldiers seem to have been cast from the same mold, and a change from one diary to the other did not change the feeling or sense of the story. Both men obviously liked soldiering, and both fought four years because of patriotism. Both reflected pride in their regiment.

Before learning of the Thomas diary, I had begun a travelogue of the soldiers' route. Upon reading that places mentioned in Baker's diary, such as the Bennett Place at Durham, North Carolina, and Midway Church, Georgia, could still be seen, I photographed the old homes and public buildings that were seen by the troopers as they marched through the South. These pictures were supplemented by photographs from the National Archives of places as they were at the time.

The reader will notice that an occasional person or place mentioned in the quoted material has not been fully identified by the author. Unfortunately, extensive research of all likely sources revealed no helpful information.

Much credit for historical value of this endeavor belongs to Grace Baker Rowell, my mother, who kept Cornelius Baker's souvenirs, including his diary, his Testament, his discharge papers, and other items that he, a common soldier, prized most highly. Some of the unique mementos may have historical interest and are included among the illustrations.

JOHN W. ROWELL

Columbus, Indiana
April, 1970

Acknowledgments

The late Roy H. and Laura Baker, Blain, Pennsylvania; Colonel Campbell H. Brown, Civil War Centennial Commission, Nashville, Tennessee; Mr. Ted Campbell, Campbell Studios, Columbus, Indiana; Mrs. Catherine Chinn, Columbus, Indiana; Dorothy J. Clark, Vigo County Historical Society, Terre Haute, Indiana; Mrs. Frances Dietz, Columbus, Indiana; Caroline Dunn, William Henry Smith Memorial Library, Indianapolis, Indiana; Elizabeth Eisenhart, American Bible Society, New York, New York; Mr. Harold S. Fink, History Department, The University of Tennessee, Knoxville, Tennessee; Mr. Victor Gondos, Jr., chief, Army and Air Corps Branch, National Archives and Records Service, Washington, D. C.; Mr. Bob Heilman, Hill Studios, Harrisburg, Pennsylvania; Mr. Robert D. Hoffsommer, Harrisburg, Pennsylvania; Staff of Indiana State Library, Indianapolis, Indiana; Staff of Indiana University Library, Bloomington, Indiana.

Colonel Allen P. Julian, Atlanta Historical Society, Atlanta, Georgia; Mr. LeRoy Robert Matter, Harrisburg, Pennsylvania; Staffs of Military Records, Pension Records, and Photograph Records Divisions of the National Archives, Washington, D. C.; Mr. Clayton L. Peters, Lykens, Pennsylvania; Mr. Irwin Richman, Pennsylvania Historical and Museum Commission, Harrisburg, Pennsylvania; Staff of the Cleo Rogers Memorial Library, Columbus, Indiana; Mrs. Grace

BAKER ROWELL, Yonkers, New York; MRS. CORNELIA F. TILLMAN, The Historical Society of Dauphin County, Harrisburg, Pennsylvania; MR. DONALD E. THOMPSON, Lilly Library, Wabash College, Crawfordsville, Indiana; MR. NICHOLAS B. WAINWRIGHT, The Historical Society of Pennsylvania, Philadelphia; MRS. EMELYN ROWELL WEBSTER, Yonkers, New York; The HONORABLE EARL WILSON, Bedford, Indiana.

The Pennsylvania Historical and Museum Commission, Harrisburg, Pennsylvania, helped to support publication of this book.

Contents

Contents

Illustrations

MAPS

Yankee Cavalrymen

Mr. Lincoln's Plain People

Many families sent two, three, four, five, and even six sons to defend the flag. From a little house one mile east of Blain on the Ickesburg road went six stalwart sons of Cornelius Baker and wife. A younger brother – a mere lad – went to Harrisburg to enlist but was rejected on account of his age.[1]

This quotation tells how the people of Perry County, Pennsylvania, answered the crisis of civil war. The statement might equally have been written about any other Northern county except that few had families with as many as six men who had the youth, health, and inclination to serve. From Maine to Iowa, people responded with an enthusiasm and a determination that exceeded any demonstration of patriotism before or since. The response reflected what President Lincoln termed "the patriotic instinct of the plain people."[2]

Because of their patriotic instinct, the plain people supported their government through four years of bitter, expensive, and bloody war. They did not require coercion, sophisticated reasons, or propaganda. "They understand, without an argument," wrote Lincoln, "that destroying the government that was made by Washington means no good to them."[3]

Abraham Lincoln understood the plain people and had faith in their moral strength and determination. "The people will save their government if the government will do its part only indifferently well,"

[1] H. H. Hain, *History of Perry County, Pennsylvania* (Harrisburg: Hain-Moore Co., 1922), p. 553.
[2] From "Message to Congress in Special Session, July 4, 1861," Abraham Lincoln, *Literary Works*, selected and with an introduction by Carl Van Doren (New York: The Heritage Press, 1942), p. 202.
[3] *Ibid.*, p. 202.

he told Congress at the beginning of the conflict.[4] And in spite of political bickering and often inept generalship, the plain people and the common soldiers did win the victory.

Perhaps the county history should have said, "*one* family even sent six sons" because the Cornelius Baker family was honored during the Civil War Centennial as the only one in the county to send this many men.

The people of Perry County generally and the Baker family specifically were representative of Mr. Lincoln's plain people. Like most Americans of that era, they were rural people. However, Cornelius and his three oldest sons were craftsmen and, thus, were typical of people who were beginning to move toward an industrial economy.

Perry County lies northwest of Harrisburg. The crest of Blue Mountain, also called Kittatinny, forms the southern boundary of the county. The northern boundary of the county is the crest of Tuscarora Mountain, which trends in a more southwesterly direction from the Susquehanna River than does Blue Mountain. Thus, the county is pennant shaped; along the Susquehanna it is wide, but the western end comes nearly to a point. Except along the Susquehanna, the county is enclosed in mountain walls that rise 600 feet to 1,200 feet above the valley floor. The valley is drained by Sherman Creek near the base of Blue Mountain and Buffalo Creek along the base of Tuscarora.

The Juniata River cuts across the northeast corner of the county and empties into the Susquehanna. This feature gave the eastern part of the county a different character from the rest since the Susquehanna-Juniata waterway was an important link in the Pennsylvania canal system during the days before railroads. Newport on the Juniata was the principal point for the transshipment of cargoes from the east to Pittsburgh. In the late 1840's, the first track of the Pennsylvania Railroad was laid along the Susquehanna from Harrisburg to Newport.[5] Thus, the economy of the eastern part of the county was based on commerce while the western end was dependent on agriculture.

The town of Blain, where the Cornelius Baker family lived, lies far up the valley of Sherman Creek and deep in the rural part of the county.

[4] *Ibid.*, p. 197.
[5] Hain, p. 421.

4

Here the converging mountains narrow the valley to a width of only a few miles. The neat, cultivated, green and gold appearance of the valley contrasted with wild, forested mountain slopes in the mid-1800's, as it does today.

The valley did not have this cultivated appearance when the elder Cornelius Baker settled there in the 1830's. Although a gristmill had been built on the upper Sherman Creek in 1778, few settlers came to this remote area.[6] Cornelius was born in Germany in 1808 and, by the time he emigrated to Pennsylvania in the late 1820's, was a journeyman cobbler, a skill needed in the new country. He also had learned to read and write in his native language, an ability not shared by many Americans of the same class and generation.

In the early 1830's, Cornelius was established as a shoemaker in Harrisburg. Each spring, he packed his awls, lasts, and leather and set out through the mountain valleys making and mending shoes for the country people. Usually the peddler and the shoemaker were the first people to reach the settlements after the winter.[7] Cornelius kept his eyes and his ears open on his trips through the country, and when he settled, he selected land in an area reported to have some of the most productive soil in Pennsylvania.[8]

A young man, Cornelius found attractions other than land. During one of these journeys, he met Mary Ann Mumper, who lived near New Germantown in the most westerly part of the Sherman Valley. Soon afterwards Cornelius and Mary Ann were wed.

Mary Ann was the daughter of Henry and Elizabeth Mumper, native-born Americans. A biographical sketch tells that Henry Mumper was "a prominent distiller and farmer."[9] Most likely, he was one of those Pennsylvania farmers who found that the only way to transport a cash crop to market from remote areas was to distill the grain into whiskey. In Henry's day, there were no good wagon roads across the mountain from Blain to the markets of Carlisle and Harrisburg.

[6] Hain, p. 927. The gristmill was built by the Blain family, the ancestors of James G. Blaine, Republican candidate for President in 1884.

[7] John Newton Culbertson, "A Pennsylvania Boyhood," *American Heritage*, XVIII, No. 1 (Dec. 1966), pp. 80–85.

[8] Hain, p. 864.

[9] Samuel P. Bates, *History of Cumberland and Adams Counties, Pennsylvania* (Chicago: Warner, Beers and Co., 1886), p. 487.

Henry Mumper died in 1835 at the age of forty-seven.[10] This was a short time after Cornelius and Mary Ann settled on their own land. Henry may have succumbed at this relatively early age to the hardships of frontier life or, perhaps, he drank too much of his own whiskey. Succeeding generations were teetotalers and nearly all lived their allotted three score and ten years.

Cornelius and Mary Ann moved onto the farm that has been known as "The Baker Homestead" ever since. Their first home was a log house that was built by Cornelius and his neighbors in a house-raising, which was customary in sparsely settled areas. The house was solidly built, and the foundation was still used a century later as the base for a large corn crib.

The 110 acres that formed the homestead lay on the northwest side of a high ridge that extends northeast from the present town of Blain. Thus, the farm faced Tuscarora Mountain. A large, free-flowing spring about one-third of the distance up the ridge provided a plentiful water supply for people and animals and also cooled the perishables stored in the springhouse.

The principal crops grown were wheat, oats, corn, and hay. In addition, a patch of flax was grown. When woven with wool, flax made the homespun cloth known as "linsey-woolsey," from which most clothing was made during the early years. Soon after coming to the farm, Cornelius planted an orchard high on the ridge. Of course, a garden was grown to provide fresh vegetables during the summer and potatoes for the winter. Livestock included horses for work, cows for milk, sheep for wool, and hogs for meat. Farms were nearly self-sufficient then.[11]

Farming was hard work. During some seasons, Cornelius arose at dawn and was in the fields until dark. Manpower and horsepower did all the work. During the winters Cornelius continued his trade, making shoes for neighbors. Mary Ann's days seemed even longer. In addition to cooking, baking, and washing, she made the cloth and the clothing for the family. She churned the butter, made tallow candles, and cared for the chickens and geese. Cooking and baking was done in the fireplace itself or in a Dutch oven that was placed on the hearth.[12] When

[10] Gravestone, Union Cemetery, Blain, Pa.
[11] Culbertson, pp. 80–85.
[12] *Ibid.*

Mary Ann did finish her work, she often relaxed by the fire, smoking her clay pipe.

Through such hard work, Cornelius and Mary Ann prospered. The 1860 Census listed eleven children and showed that they owned $4,000 in real estate and $1,800 in personal property.[13] The absence of children's or infants' graves in the family plot of the Blain Union Cemetery suggests that all children born to Cornelius and Mary Ann grew to adulthood, a remarkable achievement during that era.

The children were put to work as soon as their hands were large enough to hold a tool. In the rural life of the 1800's, every hand helped. Part of the work of the three oldest boys, Samuel, Henry, and Cornelius, was to help build the "little house" during the 1850's. This work made a deep impression, and all three boys became carpenters. They built well on this first job, and the house was occupied continuously by the Baker family for more than 100 years.

The town of Blain had not even been platted when Cornelius and Mary Ann moved to the farm; and the area remained sparsely settled during the years when Samuel, Henry, and young Cornelius were growing up. As late as 1846, the town had only three houses.[14] This region remained remote until 1845, when a good wagon road was finally built across Blue Mountain and connected to roads that led to Carlisle.[15]

East of the Susquehanna River another valley lies between the same mountain ridges. This valley, sometimes called Wiconisco for its stream and Lykens for its earliest settler, also was wild and sparsely settled in the 1830's. When people moved into this valley in the following decade, development was in a different direction from that of rural Blain and Sherman Valley. The reason was that outcroppings of anthracite coal were found on Short Mountain, which extends several miles into the head of Lykens Valley.[16]

Although coal was discovered in 1825, development of the mines

13 National Archives, 1860 Census, Jackson Twp., Perry Co., Pa. Baker children listed: Samuel, 24; Henry, 22; Cornelius, 19; John, 18; Frederick, 17; Jeremiah, 15; David, 10; Sarah E. (Ella), 8; Anna M. (Annie), 6; Charles, 5; and James, 3. The oldest child, Elizabeth, was married in 1855.
14 Hain, p. 497.
15 *Ibid.*, p. 242.
16 William Henry Egle, *History of the Counties of Dauphin and Lebanon* (Philadelphia: Everts and Peck, 1883), p. 450.

was slow because the coal had to be hauled the sixteen miles to Millersburg in wagons for transshipment by canal barges. In 1832, shrewd Simon Gratz, a Philadelphia financier, acquired all the coal-bearing land in the area, enlarged operations, and built a crude railroad on which cars were hauled by horses. However, large-scale development did not come until the railroad was rebuilt with steel rails in 1848 and steam locomotives were placed in operation. From this time, production expanded rapidly, and 848,781 tons had been shipped from the Lykens Valley mines by 1858.[17] In the decade from 1840 to 1850, the population of Wiconisco township, where the mines were located, increased from 488 persons to 1,316.[18]

Among the settlers who arrived in the middle 1840's were John A. Thomas, a Welsh miner, his wife, son William, and three daughters.[19] John Thomas was one of the thousands of skilled workmen brought to Pennsylvania from Britain and Germany in that period to develop the mines. Native Americans had neither the skill nor the inclination to work below the ground. Because of scarcity of the required skills, men like John Thomas earned more than other workmen. Often they were contract miners, hiring laborers, providing equipment, supervising work at the face, measuring and placing the blasting charges, and directing the placement of supporting timbers. They were paid on the basis of tonnage mined.[20] The hours were long and the work hard, dangerous, and dirty.

When the Thomas family arrived, the valley was relatively unspoiled,[21] although a pile of coal dirt had already been burning "for many years" near the townsite of Lykens.[22] The mountains had not yet been denuded of trees to provide timbers for the mines and the streams

----

[17] *Ibid.*

[18] Luther Reily Kelker, *History of Dauphin County* (New York: Lewis Publishing Co., 1907), I, 488; Daniel Rupp, *The History and Topography of Dauphin, Cumberland, Franklin, Bedford, Adams, and Perry Counties* (Lancaster: Gilbert Hills, 1846), pp. 216–17.

[19] National Archives, 1850 Census, Wiconisco Twp., Dauphin Co., Pa., lists Thomas family: John A., 37; Mary Ann, 32; William, 11; Mary, 10; Elizabeth, 8; and Martha, 6; all born in Wales; and Margaret, 3, and Sarah, 1, born in Pennsylvania. 1860 Census lists three additional sons: John F., 9; George W., 7; and James, 5.

[20] Peter Roberts, *Anthracite Coal Communities* (New York: Macmillan, 1904), p. 91.

[21] *Ibid.*, p. 5.

[22] Egle, p. 456.

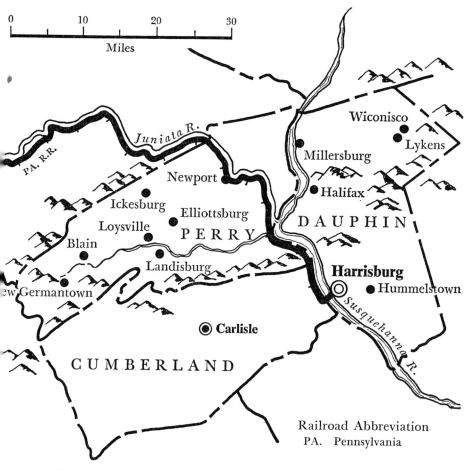

Railroad Abbreviation
PA. Pennsylvania

PERRY, DAUPHIN, AND CUMBERLAND COUNTIES, PENNSYLVANIA

had not become polluted with mine wastes. Thus, young William Thomas was able to hunt, fish, and enjoy other rural activities.

Although originally platted in 1832, the town of Lykens failed to develop until Edward Gratz acquired the site and replatted it in 1847. By 1860, the town could boast of two churches, a newspaper, a hotel, the "company" store, and a stone school house, in addition to the homes of the merchants who served the miners.[23] Miners and their families usually lived away from Lykens in "clusters," or "patches," of houses near the mines. Most Welsh miners lived in a cluster named Hickory-

[23] Egle, pp. 456–57; Clayton L. Peters, Lykens, to the author, Dec. 28, 1969.

town, where the coal company mule stable also was located.[24] Although some company houses stood in this cluster, the Welsh usually built and owned their homes.[25]

As in most sparsely populated areas, the church was the center of social life and a clearing house for news. While the Baker family attended the Union Church in Blain where the Lutheran and Reformed congregations shared the same building, as they did in many areas of Pennsylvania, the Thomas family belonged to the Grace Methodist Episcopal Church of Lykens. William Thomas's diary mentions attending his Sunday School class, where he was given a Bible when he went to war. Young Cornelius Baker carried a Testament for most of the war. Both men possessed the strong religious convictions of right and wrong held by the plain people of that generation. Moral standards of the era were such, even in the mining towns, that boys under eighteen would not think of using tobacco.[26] A share of the righteousness of the people during the Civil War may be attributed to the church.

The schools attended for about four months a year were simple, one-room structures, and the education was as simple as the school-houses.[27] The first free-school act in Pennsylvania had been passed in 1834,[28] so public schools were still in their infancy when the Civil War generation grew up. In rural areas such as Blain and Lykens, the facilities and quality of education were poorer than in more settled areas. Although the school year was short, children from age six to eighteen attended.[29]

The subjects taught were reading, 'riting, and 'rithmetic. The New Testament was the usual reader.[30] The soldiers' diaries indicate that the children were taught to write neatly but that spelling was entirely phonetic. Punctuation was not taught at all. However, some accounts

24 Clayton L. Peters, Lykens, to the author, Dec. 28, 1969.

25 Roberts, pp. 89–91.

26 *Ibid.*, p. 118.

27 Silas Wright, *History of Perry County* (Lancaster: Wylie and Griest, 1873), p. 150; Culbertson, pp. 80–85.

28 Commonwealth of Pennsylvania, Dept. of Public Instruction, *Pennsylvania Today* (Harrisburg, 1962), p. 44.

29 National Archives, 1860 Census, Jackson Twp., Perry Co., Pa., Cornelius Baker family.

30 Culbertson, pp. 80–85.

in the back of Cornelius Baker's diary indicate that the arithmetic taught was adequate for the needs of future craftsmen.

When compared to twentieth-century standards, this education appears poor. However, if compared to other standards, the public schools of the North in the mid-nineteenth century may be seen as a major educational advance. The schooling was far better and more universal than that received by the preceding generation; and it was far superior to the education given to the ordinary people of the Southern states. During the war, an illiterate Union soldier was a rarity. On the other side, one sampling of the rolls of a number of Confederate companies showed that 40 percent of the soldiers signed with an X.[31]

The men were proud of their ability to write. Cornelius Baker and William Thomas kept diaries of their war service in which they recorded their daily activities.

During the eight months when they were not attending schools, the boys were not allowed to loaf. The Bakers helped with the planting, cultivation, and harvesting of crops and cared for the stock on the farm. As they grew up, they spent time learning and working at their trade. William Thomas, like other boys in mining towns, began working at the coal breaker picking slate from the coal when he was thirteen or fourteen.[32] However, the hard life of a coal miner did not appeal to William. By 1860 he had left his father's house, moved to Lykens, and had become a tinsmith.[33]

Becoming a journeyman in any of the industrial trades required the serving of an apprenticeship and the acceptance of discipline. Thus, the carpenters, the tinsmiths, the shoemakers, the blacksmiths, and the other Pennsylvania craftsmen were able to adapt more easily to the training and discipline of army life than were Southern farm boys who often were too independent to obey their officers.[34]

Most important of all, these men learned to be responsible, law-

[31] Bell Irvin Wiley, *The Life of Billy Yank* (Indianapolis: Bobbs-Merrill, 1952), pp. 305–306.

[32] Roberts, pp. 168–79.

[33] National Archives, 1860 Census, Wiconisco Twp., Dauphin Co., Pa.; National Archives, "Co. B, 9th Pa. Cav., Descriptive Roll."

[34] J. K. Herr and E. S. Wallace, *The Story of the U.S. Cavalry* (New York: Little-Brown, 1953), p. 117.

abiding citizens who believed that they should support their government in critical times. The Bakers' neighbors were intensely patriotic; and the first known offer of volunteer troops for the impending conflict came from the Washington Artillery of Blain on January 21, 1861, in a letter to President James Buchanan. The company tendered their services "to suppress the Southern fire-eating disunionists."[35] President Buchanan did not call up these men or any others. Strongly influenced by Southern members of his cabinet, Buchanan believed that he could not lawfully stop the secession of the states, although President Andrew Jackson had set a precedent by meeting a similar threat with stern action nearly thirty years earlier. Thus, the country was allowed to drift and divide until the strong hand of Abraham Lincoln took the helm.

Although the plain people were ready to do their duty at an early date, they lacked leadership. Even after his inauguration, Lincoln moved slowly, hoping to resolve the issue without war. After Fort Sumter fell in April, he called up only 75,000 militiamen for three months' service. Only when events had moved beyond the capabilities of this force did he call on the Congress and the people for their full effort and support. When the time came for them to act, the people responded by contributing more than their assigned totals of both men and money..

During the summer of 1861 when patriotism in the North reached a fever pitch, young Cornelius Baker built a tall Liberty pole on the farm, and his mother made a huge American flag in proportion to the height of the pole. Then Cornelius arranged a dedication service to which people came from miles around.[36] In Lykens, the *Farmers and Miners Journal*, published continuously since 1856, was forced to suspend operations when all four of its employees marched off to war.[37]

The people of the Sherman Valley did not lose their patriotism or determination while the war progressed. In 1863, when Lee's Confederate army invaded Pennsylvania, they gave refuge to the people of Chambersburg and Carlisle who fled across Blue Mountain. When Confederate cavalry was observed at the foot of the mountain, the old men,

[35] Hain, p. 546.
[36] George C. Baker, typewritten copy of manuscript, "War Record of Cornelius Baker," written Sept. 23, 1923. George Baker was a son of Cornelius.
[37] Egle, p. 457.

the women, and the clergy fortified and prepared to defend the gaps over the mountain.[38]

Although people at home had the courage to support the government they had elected through four years of war, the plain people who became the common soldiers were the real heroes. Especially was this true of some 200,000 men, including Cornelius Baker, William Thomas, and Henry Baker, who enlisted at the first call for volunteers and reenlisted for a second three-year term when their first expired. The following pages tell the story of these men and their regiment from enlistment until their discharge.

[38] Hain, p. 548.

II

Volunteers All

*Had to leave home and all That was
near and dear to us and go forth in
defense of our countrys Flag That
Has been trampled in the Dust by
traitors.*

In these few words William Thomas told why he enlisted and marched
off to war. His feelings were the same as those of most early Northern
volunteers. They enlisted to preserve the Union and to support their
government. The flag was the symbol, patriotism was the motivating
force, and with some men, there was a degree of righteous indignation.

On July 4, 1861, President Lincoln asked Congress to authorize the
calling up of 400,000 volunteers for three years' service.[1] Congress requested him to recruit 500,000 men, but the people themselves increased
this figure. So many turned out that 714,000 were accepted by the end
of the year,[2] and unknown thousands were sent home because neither
the Federal government nor the states were prepared to arm, clothe,
and train so many. "One of the greatest perplexities of the government
is to avoid receiving troops faster than it can provide for them," President Lincoln said of this situation.[3] When the government called for
300,000 additional volunteers in 1862, 431,000 enlisted. Thus, over a
million men from a nation of only twenty million people volunteered
to fight for three years.[4] These events occurred before there was a draft,
and President Lincoln could truthfully say, "So large an army as the

[1] Lincoln, p. 197.
[2] A. H. Guernsey and H. M. Alden, *Harper's Pictorial History of the Civil War*
(Chicago: The Puritan Press, 1894) II, 789.
[3] Lincoln, p. 197.
[4] Guernsey and Alden, I, 123; II, 789.

government has now on foot was never before known, without a soldier in it but who has taken his place there of his own free choice."[5]

The soldiers' songs give a clue to their patriotic sentiments. "John Brown's Body" was far and away the most popular tune. Although Julia Ward Howe wrote words in 1861 that made "The Battle Hymn of the Republic" the powerful and dignified hymn we know today, the soldiers continued to sing, "John Brown's body lies a-mouldering in his grave but his soul is marching on." They varied this rendition with innumerable parodies, the most popular of which began, "We'll hang Jeff Davis on a sour apple tree. . . . "[6]

Generally considered to have been next in popularity was "The Battle-Cry of Freedom," which the soldiers called "Rally 'Round the Flag." The chorus tells why the Union soldiers fought:

The Union forever, Hurrah! boys, Hurrah!
Down with the traitor, up with the star;
While we rally round the flag boys, rally once again,
Shouting the battle cry of freedom.[7]

Reasons other than patriotism existed for enlisting. Some men went to war "to see the elephant," their expression for a wondrous thing that had to be experienced to be believed. Others volunteered because all their friends were doing so. Many saw an opportunity to see the world beyond their home counties. Also, the attitude of the general population influenced some men to sign the rolls. However, there had to be a reason stronger than these to draw large numbers of mature, married men into the army. President Lincoln expressed their purpose when he remarked that they enlisted "to prove to the world that those who can fairly carry an election can also suppress a rebellion."[8]

A private's pay of $13 a month was not a great inducement to the skilled craftsmen of Pennsylvania, nor was the $100 bounty for a three-year enlistment.[9] The money, however, may have brought in some unskilled laborers because there was a depression in 1861. This money also

[5] Lincoln, p. 201.
[6] Wiley, *Billy Yank*, pp. 32, 158–61.
[7] *Ibid.*
[8] Lincoln, p. 202.
[9] Wiley, *Billy Yank*, p. 49; National Archives, service record of Cornelius Baker and others (unpublished).

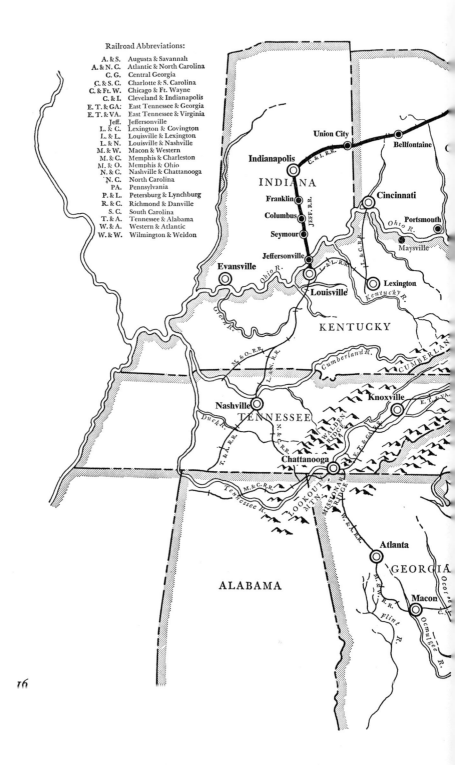

Railroad Abbreviations:

A. & S.   Augusta & Savannah
A. & N. C.   Atlantic & North Carolina
C. G.   Central Georgia
C. & S. C.   Charlotte & S. Carolina
C. & Ft. W. Chicago & Ft. Wayne
C. & I.   Cleveland & Indianapolis
E. T. & GA: East Tennessee & Georgia
E. T. & VA. East Tennessee & Virginia
Jeff.   Jeffersonville
L. & C.   Lexington & Covington
L. & L.   Louisville & Lexington
L. & N.   Louisville & Nashville
M. & W.   Macon & Western
M. & C.   Memphis & Charleston
M. & O.   Memphis & Ohio
N. C.   Nashville & Chattanooga
N. C.   North Carolina
PA.   Pennsylvania
P. & L.   Petersburg & Lynchburg
R. & C.   Richmond & Danville
S. C.   South Carolina
T. & A.   Tennessee & Alabama
W. & A.   Western & Atlantic
W. & W.   Wilmington & Weldon

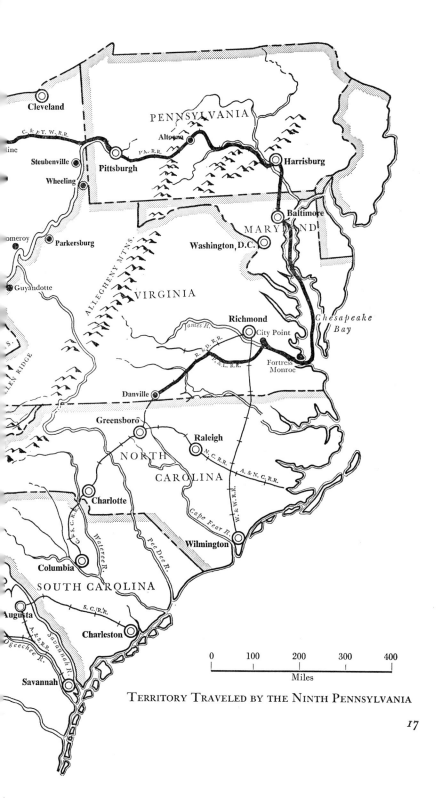

Cleveland

PENNSYLVANIA

Altoona

C. & P. T. W. R.R.

ine

PA. R.R.

Steubenville

Pittsburgh

Harrisburg

Wheeling

Baltimore

MARYLAND

omeroy

Parkersburg

Washington, D.C.

Guyandotte

ALLEGHENY MTNS.

VIRGINIA

James R.

Richmond

Chesapeake
Bay

R. & D. R.R.

City Point

S.

LEN RIDGE

P. & L. R.R.

Fortress
Monroe

Danville

Greensboro

Raleigh

NORTH

N. C. R.R.

A. & N. C. R.R.

CAROLINA

Charlotte

C. & S. C. R.R.

Wateree R.

Cape Fear R.

W. & W. R.R.

Pee Dee R.

Wilmington

Columbia

SOUTH CAROLINA

Augusta

S. C. R.R.

A. & S. R.R.

Ogeechee R.

Savannah R.

Charleston

| 0 | 100 | 200 | 300 | 400 |

Miles

Savannah

TERRITORY TRAVELED BY THE NINTH PENNSYLVANIA

may have been attractive to many young farm boys and to some newly arrived immigrants.[10]

Although their efforts resulted in ending slavery, those who enlisted in 1861 to accomplish this objective were rare. Abolitionists made up as small a proportion of the army as they did of the general population.[11] Many from Western states fought to keep the Mississippi River in one country from source to mouth. For Pennsylvanians who had little interest in freeing the black man or in an open Mississippi, the general principle of an indivisible Union was sufficient reason for enlisting.

After the National draft act was passed in 1863, the ranks still were filled largely with volunteers. There is no way of knowing how many of these men enlisted for the same patriotic reasons as the earlier volunteers and how many enlisted to avoid being drafted. By volunteering, they could get a bounty and also could choose their service and regiment. The government did obtain an additional 650,000 three-year enlistments in 1863 and 1864. Among these were over 200,000 of the 1861 veterans who reenlisted.[12] They, at least, did not have to worry about the draft. They had already done their part.

For the entire war, the Federal government obtained over 2,700,000 enlistments. Of these fewer than 250,000 were draftees and substitutes.[13] Many of the latter never did report to their regiments, and those who did were considered to be utterly worthless by the veterans. Thus, it seems fair to conclude that the volunteers were the men who saw the task through from start to finish and that they would have completed the work just as soon if there had not been a draft.

Except for the Regular Army, which was a very small part of the total, the responsibility for raising the regiments rested with the states. The Federal government called upon the states to raise numbers of regiments in proportion to their population. The states, in turn, assigned quotas to the counties. The governors of the states also authorized certain individuals to recruit these regiments. These men appointed recruiting officers to go into specific counties. As a reward the recruiters became the officers of the regiments raised.

10 Wiley, *Billy Yank*, pp. 37–38.
11 *Ibid.*, pp. 40–42.
12 Guernsey and Alden, II, 789; Wiley, *Billy Yank*, p. 343.
13 Guernsey and Alden, II, 789; Wiley, *Billy Yank*, p. 319.

The system had the fault of making officers of politicians who had no military qualifications. However, the appointment method used by Pennsylvania generally found better officers than did the procedure of some other states which allowed the soldiers to elect their officers. The politician, looking at the men as a group of voters, failed to enforce discipline and usually was a failure as an officer.

The Ninth Pennsylvania Cavalry was one of the regiments whose politically appointed officers were above average in military knowledge and ability. At the request of Secretary of War Simon Cameron, the most powerful Pennsylvania politician, Governor Andrew Curtin appointed Edward C. Williams of Harrisburg to recruit twenty-four companies of cavalry. Twelve of these companies, recruited as the Ninety-second Regiment, became known first as the "Lochiel Cavalry" and then as the Ninth Pennsylvania Cavalry, with Williams as colonel.[14]

Williams was the best known soldier in central Pennsylvania, where the new regiment was recruited. A Harrisburg bookbinder, he had been active in the Pennsylvania militia for twenty years. Williams had been one of the heroes of the Mexican War, and had achieved statewide fame when he marched his company from Chambersburg to Pittsburgh in the dead of winter in 1846. He pushed his men so hard they completed this 150-mile march in four days in spite of fifteen inches of snow along the route through the mountains.[15]

Upon their arrival in Mexico, Williams and his company fought at Vera Cruz, Cerro Gordo, and Chapultepec. At the latter place, Williams, along with a Captain Samuel Montgomery, raised the first American flag above the Citadel when this building was stormed.[16] For its time and place, this was as dramatic as the action of the marines who raised the colors on Iwo Jima in World War II.

Following the Mexican War, Williams continued to be active in the militia and by 1860 was brigadier general. He was the first man mustered into service by Governor Curtin at the start of the Civil War. He

[14] Samuel P. Bates, *History of the Pennsylvania Volunteers 1861–1865* (Harrisburg: B. Singerly—State Printer, 1870), III, 234.
[15] *Commemorative Biographical Encyclopedia of Dauphin County, Pennsylvania* (Chambersburg: J. M. Runk & Co., 1896), p. 244.
[16] Kelker, I, 166–69.

organized Camps Curtin in Harrisburg and Slifer in Chambersburg and then commanded a brigade of Pennsylvanians in the Shenandoah Valley during the "three months' war."[17] Upon his discharge from the three months' militia service, Williams was ordered to recruit the new companies of three-year volunteers.[18]

Williams's reputation attracted excellent subordinate officers to his regiment, and they, in turn, were able to be more selective in the recruiting of enlisted men. From the large numbers who sought to enlist under a soldier with the reputation of Colonel Williams, the recruiters could choose those they thought had the intelligence and energy to become good cavalrymen. Intelligence was more important to a cavalryman than to the other soldiers of this war. They had to learn to fight effectively both on foot and on horseback, to care properly for their mounts, and to maintain both horse equipments and a variety of weapons.[19]

For lieutenant colonel, Williams selected Thomas C. James of Philadelphia. James had served as captain of one of the most honorable and distinguished military organizations in the country, the First Troop of Philadelphia City Cavalry. This troop had been in continuous organization from the time of the Revolutionary War, and at the time of the Civil War, was the second oldest military group in the country. Only the Ancient Artillerists of Boston antedated them. The First Troop was one of the very few cavalry units called up immediately after Fort Sumter fell. The men served in the vicinity of Harpers Ferry, Virginia, until the end of their three months' enlistment.[20]

With this background, Lieutenant Colonel James brought a superior knowledge of cavalry organization, drill, and tactics. From his service at Harpers Ferry, he brought an understanding of the changed role that the cavalry would play in this American war. As a result, he drilled

[17] The three months' war refers to the initial period of the Civil War following the fall of Fort Sumter in which militia called up by Lincoln served for a term of three months. During this three months, Union forces successfully campaigned in west Virginia but lost the Battle of Bull Run in northern Virginia. These troops were disbanded at the end of their three months' term and replaced with new regiments of three-year volunters.

[18] Kelker, I, 166–69; *Commemorative Encyclopedia*, p. 244.

[19] Herr and Wallace, p. 118.

[20] Frank H. Taylor, *Philadelphia in the Civil War* (Philadelphia: the City, 1913), pp. 261–62.

the men in those skills most necessary for this service and not in the text-book theories based on European wars.

The third officer was Thomas Jefferson Jordan, the senior major, who was the only high-ranking officer identified with the regiment from muster-in to discharge. At the start of the war, he was a forty-year-old Harrisburg lawyer with no military experience. He was a friend of Governor Curtin, who respected his intelligence and administrative ability. The day after Fort Sumter fell, Jordan was mustered into the state service by the governor as an aide to General William H. Keim, then the head of the Pennsylvania military organization.[21] In the capacity of aide, Jordan carried dispatches to Washington and happened to be passing through Baltimore on the day when rioters of that city attacked the Sixth Massachusetts Regiment passing through the city to Washington. Jordan was the first man to bring the news of this infamous action to Lieutenant General Winfield Scott and Secretary Cameron.[22]

A short while later, Jordan accompanied General Keim on a campaign into Virginia. In this campaign, the Pennsylvanians met and defeated Confederates commanded by a Colonel Jackson at the Battle of Falling Waters.[23]

At the conclusion of this campaign, Jordan was mustered out and assigned to assist Williams in recruiting the new regiment. Jordan adapted to the military life quickly and well. He became colonel of the Ninth in early 1863, and commanded it through 1864. In 1865, he became brigadier general, but because the Ninth was one of the regiments in his brigade, his association with the regiment continued to the end of the war.

The prospective captains and lieutenants were sent into the various counties to recruit the twelve companies of 100 men each that would make up the regiment. Captain William H. Harris, for example, was in Blain on September 4, 1861, and enlisted John Berrier, John Boyd, and Jeremiah Sheibley. Not only was there competition for the men among

[21] *Commemorative Encyclopedia*, p. 1194.

[22] Thomas Jefferson Jordan, "The Battle of Thompson's Station and the Trial of the Spies at Franklin, Tenn.," *The United Service* (Mar. 1890), p. 310. General Scott, hero of the War of 1812 and the Mexican War, was the ranking officer and head of the U. S. Army at the beginning of the Civil War.

[23] *Commemorative Encyclopedia*, p. 1195. The defeated colonel rose in stature to become General Thomas Jonathan "Stonewall" Jackson.

the various regiments being organized at this time, but a few men did not make up their minds so quickly. Therefore, Captain Harris, who was recruiting for Company C, returned to Blain on September 11 to enlist Cornelius Baker, Henry Baker, and Samuel Snyder.[24]

A review of the records of Company C indicates that most of the men enlisted at Harrisburg, giving the impression that the company was made up of Harrisburg men.[25] However, this impression is misleading because many men from the Sherman Valley in Perry County went to Harrisburg to volunteer. Cornelius Baker's records show that James Anderson and Samuel Gutshall from Blain, William Stump of New Germantown, Samuel Duncan of Landisburg, and George Shuman of Carrol were among those enlisted at Harrisburg. Samuel Spohn is buried at Elliottsburg and Joseph Chestnut at Loysville, indicating that they also were Perry County men. There must have been many more, and Company C may well have been made up predominantly of men from southern Perry County.

Company A was recruited in the northern part of Perry County. Company B was largely recruited in Dauphin County, outside of Harrisburg, by Captain Edward G. Savage. However, a part of this company was recruited in Scranton by Lieutenant Lewis A. Gratz. So the statements in the histories that various companies were recruited in certain areas should be accepted only as generalities. However, with some exceptions, Company D was recruited in Luzerne County (Scranton), Company E in Dauphin and Susquehanna Counties, Companies F and G in Lancaster County, Companies H and I in Cumberland County (Carlisle), and Company M in Huntingdon County. Companies K and L seem to have been a mixture of men from Dauphin, Luzerne, Mifflin, and Northampton counties.[26] Lost in these generalities is a contingent that Lieutenant Colonel James brought from Philadelphia.

The first entry in William Thomas's diary, dated September 16, gives only the briefest idea of the recruiting procedures. He wrote, "I was this morning sworn into the services of the U.S.A. into Co B 9th

24 National Archives, "Co. C, 9th Pa. Cav., Descriptive Roll."
25 *Ibid.*
26 Bates, *Pennsylvania Volunteers*, III, 242–83.

Pa. Cav under command of Capt. E. G. Savage   The transaction
took place at Hoffmans Hotel Lykens town." Captain Savage used his
new recruits to help enlist others and took his Lykens recruits to Millersburg to assist him. They "Had a jolly time of it."

The recruits were from a large geographical area and from many
occupations. They were the type of men that President Lincoln had
in mind when he said, "There are many single regiments whose members, one and another, possess full practical knowledge of all the arts,
sciences, professions, and whatever else, whether useful or elegant, is
known in the world."[27]

Company C was typical of the regiment. The 156 enlisted men who
served in this company during the war represented thirty-six occupations: artist, blacksmith, bookkeeper, boatman, boatbuilder, brick-
maker, carpenter, chairmaker, chemist, cigarmaker, civil engineer,
clerk, cooper, engineer, engraver, farmer, farrier, gunsmith, laborer,
machinist, mason, merchant, miller, miner, painter, physician, plas-
terer, printer, railroader, saddler, shoemaker, soldier, tailor, teacher,
teamster, and weaver. Over 60 percent of the men in the company were
tradesmen or specialists, and 20 percent were farmers.[28] This figure
compares to 50 percent farmers in the average Union regiment.[29]

If Company C was typical of the regiment as a whole, and there is no
reason to think otherwise, the men were predominantly Pennsylvanians. Of the 156 men on Company C's descriptive roll, all but seventeen
were born in Pennsylvania. Four of the remainder were born in other
states, while seven were German, three were Irish, two were English,
and one was Welsh.

In the first flush of the martial ardor of the North, the people were
proud of those who were going to defend their country. On the Sunday
following his enlistment, William Thomas attended Sunday School and
"received a Beautiful Testament as a token of respect from the School."
The next morning when the recruits left for camp there was "a great
crowd at the Depot to see us going in defense of our country" and, when

27 Lincoln, p. 201.
28 National Archives, "Co. C, Descriptive Roll."
29 Wiley, *Billy Yank*, pp. 303–304.

the train halted briefly at Halifax on the way to Harrisburg, Thomas "got a bundle of grapes from miss Sarah Noblets & a boquet from miss Angeline Bordner."

At the same time, the recruits from Blain, from Scranton, from Carlisle, from Newport, from Lancaster, and other towns were given enthusiastic farewells from their homes. The enlistees of the Ninth Pennsylvania were all headed toward Harrisburg, and all hoped that they would see the elephant very soon.

Boot Camp
1861 Model

arrived in Harrisburg at 1 pm. We were mustered Into ranks and marched to camp Cameron 2 miles outside of Harrisburg   We then separated into messes   i went into mess with Hen Feindt France Feindt H.H. Hoffman C.Spangler   Received a Blanket a pice at 10 pm and then Laid down to rest   But we did not sleep much as sleeping on the ground was not quite so nice As Laying in Bed.

In this manner, William Thomas and the other recruits reached the training camp. Neither the Federal nor the state governments were prepared for the tremendous numbers of men who came into the various camps during the late summer and fall of 1861. This country had been peaceful a few months before with only enough military equipment to supply the small standing army that was required to control and punish, from time to time, a few unruly tribes of Plains Indians. Now, the government was suddenly called upon to equip and train an army larger than the combined armies that had fought in all previous wars. Perhaps the soldiers were fortunate to get even a blanket on their first day.

At this particular time, Camp Cameron was crowded. Four new regiments were at some stage of assembly and training there. These men were merely civilians at drill, a fact that was reflected in manner and dress. Drills began on the first full day in camp, and it was not until a week later that the men got their first bit of uniform—"a pair of stockings from the U.S."

When the recruits returned from their first day's drill, they found that tents had been put up and that rations had been prepared for them. However, "it did not quite suit some of the Boys   They allowed if This is Soaldering i want to go Home again." It was still "rations scarce and Hard grub" a few days later. However, conditions either improved thereafter or the men got used to army life, because the complaints ceased.

William Thomas, and probably most others, learned some military duty the hard way. He stood guard, in civilian clothes, of course, on his third evening in camp. "rain pouring down in torrents got all wet the first night of my standing gaurd," he wrote. He remained on guard until three o'clock the next afternoon. Most of the work of the new cavalrymen was close-order drill on foot. They had neither horses nor weapons.

The men had been in camp for two weeks when the doctor gave them a physical examination. This examination must have been only a quick look because one doctor apparently examined more than a thousand men in a couple of days. Generally, if a man could stand up in 1861, he was pronounced fit for the service.[1]

On Sunday, October 6, Thomas reported, "the Whole company [was] meausered for uniforms by Col Williams and major Jordan preaching in camp and a general fight at dress parade   3 or 4 companies arrested   Quarter Master also arested." The next day, the regiment was sworn into the United States service, each company being sworn in as a group.

The regiment was made up of twelve companies. Each company had a captain, a first lieutenant, and a second lieutenant as commissioned officers. These officers were supported by eight sergeants and eight corporals. Heading the sergeants was a master sergeant and a commissary sergeant. The men called the latter "the orderly sergeant." Each company had a blacksmith, a farrier, a saddler, a wagoner, and two buglers.[2]

When the regiment was organized, the captains of the various companies were:

Company A	Griffith Jones	Company G	Jacob K. Waltman
Company B	Edward G. Savage	Company H	David H. Kimmel
Company C	William H. Harris	Company I	Hugh W. McCullough
Company D	Jacob Bertles	Company K	Joseph Phillips
Company E	John S. Detweiler	Company L	George G. Hand
Company F	John Wise	Company M	George W. Patterson

Of these twelve men, only Kimmel remained with the regiment until

[1] Wiley, *Billy Yank*, p. 125.
[2] National Archives, "Co. C, 9th Pa. Cav., Muster Roll, Apr. 30, 1865."

the end of the war. He became colonel in 1865. Jones and Savage were promoted to major and resigned with that rank. McCullough was killed in action, and the others resigned from the regiment for various reasons.[3]

The companies were grouped into three battalions of four companies each under Majors Thomas J. Jordan, George B. Brown, and Roswell M. Russell. Colonel Williams and Lieutenant Colonel James were assisted by a large regimental staff which included an adjutant, a quartermaster, a surgeon, an assistant surgeon, and a veterinary surgeon. Enlisted men on the regimental staff were a sergeant major, a quartermaster sergeant, a commissary sergeant, a wagonmaster, a saddler, a chief bugler, and a hospital steward. A chaplain also was assigned to the regiment.[4] Several of these men deserve special mention.

Edmund McKinney was called "our worthy chaplain" by William Thomas. McKinney apparently was of the "Praise the Lord and pass the ammunition" school and was cited for meritorious service at the Battles of Perryville and Thompson's Station.[5]

Surgeon Oscar Robbins was termed "a splendid physian" by Thomas, who may have had reason to think otherwise. At the time he used this expression, perhaps sarcastically, Thomas was crippled from having been kicked in the thigh by a horse. He could hardly walk, and skipped dress parade. For this absence, the captain reprimanded him and told him that he had to see the doctor to be excused from duty. "I hobbled up to the doctors quarters the best way i could," wrote Thomas, "the doctor reported me fit for duty without looking at me." Even so, Surgeon Robbins was cited for his efficient care of both Union and Confederate wounded following the Battle of Mossy Creek, Tennessee, in December 1863.[6]

A colorful assistant surgeon joined the regiment in 1864. His name was James B. Moore. Instead of remaining at the rear with his bandages, Moore liked the thrill of being at the head of cavalry charges.

---

[3] Bates, *Pennsylvania Volunteers*, III, 243–79.

[4] *Ibid.*, pp. 242–43.

[5] U. S. War Department, *The War of the Rebellion: a Compilation of the Official Records of the Union and Confederate Armies* (Washington, D. C.: Government Printing Office, 1880–1901), Ser. 1, XXIII, pt. 1, p. 83 (hereafter referred to as O. R.); O. R., Ser. 1, XVI, pt. 1, p. 1038.

[6] O. R., Ser. 1, XXXI, pt. 1, p. 656.

Several times in the Carolina Campaign he was among the first to get at the Rebels. His military adventures ended when he was shot through the lung during one of these charges. He survived and later wrote a book entitled *Kilpatrick and Our Cavalry* and a general history of the war entitled *A Complete History of the Great Rebellion*.

When organized, the regiment had a sixteen-piece brass band. The leader had the classical-sounding name of Louis Praetorious. The band was discharged in Kentucky in August 1862 when the army ruled that no units smaller than brigades could have a band.[7] Praetorious was made a second lieutenant in one of the line companies but resigned after a couple of months. William Keiser, one of the musicians, went into Company B as a sergeant and served the rest of the war with the Ninth Pennsylvania. Eventually he was commissioned. The other bandmen were discharged and given transportation home.[8]

The recruits of the Ninth Pennsylvania finally received their uniforms on October 8 and began to look more like soldiers. The basic cavalry uniform consisted of cavalry jacket, shirt, long trousers, cavalry boots, drawers (long underwear), and the familiar peaked forage cap. The pants were tucked into the boots when the men were mounted but worn outside when on foot. A 1½-inch-wide stripe of yellow, red, and yellow ran down the pants seam from top to bottom. The dress trousers were dark blue, matching the jacket.[9] Photos indicate that lighter summer pants were issued as well. The waist-length cavalry jacket was made of a durable whipcord and fastened with a row of brass buttons, embossed with the National eagle and shield, down the front.[10]

In addition to the basic uniform, the cavalrymen were issued "gum coats," which were waterproof ponchos that kept the wearer relatively dry whether mounted or on foot. The ponchos were issued to the Ninth on November 1 after most of the men had their new uniforms thoroughly soaked by the October rains. For winter wear, the men also had overcoats.

This clothing was not given to the soldiers. The cost was deducted

[7] Wiley, *Billy Yank*, p. 157.
[8] Bates, *Pennsylvania Volunteers*, III, 243.
[9] Herr and Wallace, p. 133; Wiley, *Billy Yank*, pp. 59–60.
[10] The author has a remnant of a cavalry jacket that belonged to John Rowell, Co. E, 12th Ky. Cav.

from the soldier's pay. A clothing account was carried on the company records and was settled at infrequent intervals. Cornelius Baker's account for the last period of the war ran from reenlistment in January 1864 until discharge in July 1865 and amounted to $64.61. Part of the clothing drawn during this period was itemized in the back of Cornelius's diary and gives the values of the various items:

```
List of Clothing Drawing in the year 1865
Comencing on January the 1st 1865
1 Cavalry Jacket      9.25
1 Pair of Pants       5.90
1 Shirt               2.32
1 Pair of Drawers     1.60
1 Pair of Socks        .48
1 Pair of Pants       5.90
1 Pair of Boots       4.65
                     30.10
```

The men also had to pay for equipment that was lost or broken, and the service records of Henry and Cornelius Baker list such items as: surcingle, $1.12; spurs and straps, $.52; curry comb, $.26; horsebrush, $.75; screw driver, $.40.[11]

The new cavalrymen spent their days at Camp Cameron drilling on foot since they did not have horses. Neither did they have weapons until November 4, when sabers were issued. They then proceeded to exercise with the sabers, but it is difficult to believe that they could learn much of this weapon's use while drilling on foot. This curved weapon was designed for maximum effectiveness by mounted men. The saber was a slashing weapon and not made for thrusting, as is a sword.

October had been a pleasant month for the new soldiers in spite of the rains. Friends from their home towns and relatives frequently came to visit them, and people from Harrisburg often came to watch them during dress parade. On these occasions, the soldiers mentioned the ladies especially. Sometimes the men got passes in the evening and were able to sightsee in the city. As they had not yet received any pay, few were able to do more than look. In fact, the soldiers were not paid for their first thirty days service until 1863, although they were paid reg-

[11] National Archives, individual service records and muster rolls show amounts chargeable to soldiers for clothing and equipment.

ularly for the time after their muster into the U. S. service.[12] Apparently, it took over a year for the Federal government and the State of Pennsylvania to decide who should pay for the thirty days between recruiting and muster-in.

In early November, most of the men received furloughs of a few days to go home for the last time. William Thomas was one of them. When he got home he found Lykens very dull. He went to Sunday School on Sunday afternoon but "found our Bible class vacant   all in the army." In the evening, however, things became livelier when he and Francis Feindt went to church in Wiconisco, half a mile away. They met many friends and "Had quite a crowd of girls to take home." He had so many invitations on Monday that he found he just could not respond to all. He finally "Spent the Evening at a Party at Hoffmans   me and France Had a Pleasant time of it   Kept the party up late." These men returned to camp on Tuesday.

On November 14, Governor Curtin received the following telegram from Secretary of War Edwin M. Stanton, who had replaced Simon Cameron:

> Send Williams Cavalry regiment by rail and water to Covington, Kentucky. Regiment will be furnished with horses by Capt. Hastings from horses now in Harrisburg.[13]

Three days elapsed before the enlisted men learned of the order. For a few more days camp life went on normally, except for the added excitement in anticipation of their trip. On November 23 they were issued six days' rations, and the next day Thomas wrote, "coocking rations to leave tomorrow   all in great glee." His diary describes the trip to Kentucky:

> Monday 25th
> We packed up and Left camp Cameron at 10 a.m. and marched to Harrisburg   The Regt were then marched To the residence of Gov Curtin where He Delivered A Speech to the regt and presented the regt with Colors and each company with a Small marker   We were then marched up to the round House above Harrisburg and waited there till 4 o clock P.M. and then got on the train for pittsburg   it took 21 passenger cars to convey our regt to pittsburg   Slow ride in the cars

12 National Archives, service records of Cornelius Baker and others.
13 National Archives, "9th Pa. Cav. Regimental Order Book."

Tuesday 26th
After a dark and Slow ride we arrived in Altoona At 5 A.M. and laid over
till day light after which time passed more pleasantly gazing on the Mt
Senery of the alleganeys   we arrived in Pittsburg at 4 P.M. when we
marched Down to the Wharf and got a board the Boats that were waiting
to convey us down the Ohio   We were treated with every thing that
showed Respect to a Soldier But Something good to eat   but Hold the citizens got us a free supper in the city Hall for the regt   the regt were then
marched of[f] the Boats and went up to the Hall ware we partook of supper
And each tried to do justice to it   each company Gave three Hearty
Cheers for the citizens   me and 2 others walked around the city till late
And went back to the Boat when i had to Go on gaurd again

Wensday 27th
Still the good things go on for this is market morning & the Soldiers
carried of[f] nearly Everything in the Market House free of charge   one
lady Bought $15.00 worth of provision for us   quite a confusion to re-
move Co. B from the Arago to the Ida ma[n]y orders countermanded
Capt Savage Had to Leave and go aboard the Anglo Saxon with the other
Halv of our Company   Great trouble to get the Soldiers aboard
Started Out of the wharf at 4 P.M. and comenced Sailing down the river to
Louisville   the Poe Run a ground and Detained us about 2 Hours
It took 7 boats to convey our regt and Horses Down the river   We an-
chored opposite worster for the night   Cheering on both sides of the
river

Thursday 28th
Started again at day light   passed weeling, Va   They run up their Colors
and cheered us Heartily A beautiful suspension bridge across the ohio river
at this place   the bridge was crowded with people and Cheered us Heartily as we passed under the bridge   The anglo Saxon run aground   we
run all night   The westmoreland run aground during the night   It
rained from 8 P.M until daylight   the mt. Are white with frost on both
sides of the river

Friday 29th
All the Boats tied up this morning at pomroy a Town about 6 miles Long
in the ohio river to take in coal for the balance of the trip   we Lashed the
Decotah to us for a bout 5 miles   unlashed Her and Lashed the Clara poe
for 10 or 12 miles   we unlashed And run race with the westmoreland and
Left her astern   passed the town Guyandotte all Destroyed   Passed
portsmouth a town on the ohio bank Beautiful illimuned at 9. P.M.
Passed Cincinatti in the morning about 3. A.M.

Saturday 30th
In the morning about 4 A.M. another excitement On board the Arago
owing to a report that Isaac Messner was kicked over board by one of the
Horses on board the Anglo Saxon   one of Co. B   Both sides of the river
bank is quite white Resulting from one of these cold Atumnul frosts Which

So often [follow] a long & Heavy rain   General Jollefication among the young Lykens town Boys   We had word inspection on board the boat   all the boats Tied up at Louisville Ky[14] in the Evening But a gaurd with Strict order Leaves No one Ashore   the report of Mr. Messner proves True the[y] could not recover his body so he found a watery grave in the ohio a great crowd of people Gathered on the wharf as we run in at 4 PM The crowd did not Disperce until Dark   Soldiers never was in better glee than we are Tonight   no one can Hear His own voice   it is a general Hum from one end of the deck to the other

Sunday 1st
We crossed the river this morning to Jeffersonville Indiana   went to camp Joe Bright located On the Confiscated property of Jessie Bright About a ½ mile east of town[15]   we drawed new Sibley tents[16]   5 tents for each company   Some of the boys are fetching in the Horses from The boat   The ground all wet and mud   We seperated into Bunks again i went into Bunk no.3. name of it Savage tribe   name of the boys that are in the bunk Seargt Wm. Keiser John Kerstster George Shreffler Wm. Kreiger Hen Feindt James Witman John L Matter D. I. Erb P Messner Hen Pell Cyrus Mark Frances Feindt H.H. Hoffman Rich. Martz and myself Wm. Thomas   Disagreeable camp

[14] Evidently, the regiment had received a change of orders to continue to Louisville rather than stop in Covington as originally ordered by Secretary of War Stanton, although the author could not verify this assumption in the records.

[15] The name of the camp was changed to Andy Johnson, in honor of Andrew Johnson, senator from Tennessee and the only southerner who remained in the U. S. Senate after Secession. Jesse Bright, a Democratic senator from Indiana, had become disreputable. A short while before the Ninth reached Jeffersonville, the U. S. Army arrested an arms peddler with a letter of introduction to Jefferson Davis signed by Bright. This letter led to Bright's expulsion from the Senate (Guernsey and Alden, I, 188).

[16] The Sibley tent was a bell-shaped structure supported with a center pole that rested on a tripod. It was designed to accommodate twelve men sleeping in the manner of wheel spokes with their feet to the center, but usually more than twelve were assigned to one tent (Wiley, *Billy Yank*, p. 55).

IV

Camp
Andy Johnson

*A more miserable lot of horses could
not again be gathered together –
some were blind, lame, string-halted,
spavined, ring-boned, with heaves and
mares with foal. The ages of the horses
varied from 25 to less than 3 years. At
least a fourth, even if sound, were
unfit for cavalry service. A large number had distemper, and many with
very defective and deformed feet.*[1]

This was Colonel Williams's appraisal of the horses that were given to
the regiment at Harrisburg and that had been transported at considerable trouble and effort to Kentucky, an enterprise that seems somewhat
of the same order as carrying coals to Newcastle. The procurement and
shipment of these horses seems to have been just one of many instances
whereby Secretary of War Simon Cameron rewarded his political sup-
porters in Pennsylvania. This specific contract became a part of the
evidence presented to the House of Representatives by the Committee
on Government Contracts during their investigation of corruption in
materiel procurement while Cameron held office.

On January 13, 1862, Congressman Henry Laurens Dawes of Massachusetts, a member of the Committee on Government Contracts, told
the House of the arrival of the regiment in Louisville and said that a
board of Army officers had condemned over four hundred of the thousand horses as unfit for service. Dawes mentioned that the officers had
sworn that none of the condemned horses was worth $20, yet the Gov-
ernment had paid $58,200 for them and had added $10,000 for transportation before finding them unsound.[2]

[1] National Archives, "9th Cav., Order Book," Jan. 1, 1862 entry.
[2] Carl Sandburg, *Abraham Lincoln: The War Years* (New York: Harcourt, Brace,
1939), I, 428.

Colonel Williams had expected that his own men would take possession of the horses in Harrisburg and load them on the train. However, he was told that this was not his responsibility and that men at the depot would attend to it. Thus, neither Williams nor his men saw the horses until they reached Pittsburgh. Only then did Williams learn that they had been loaded without being fed or watered.

He did learn, however, that the horses were being loaded without halters and were loose in the cars. He managed to obtain 300 rope halters, which he shipped with the horses. When the railroad employees in Pittsburgh unloaded the cars, they put these halters on the first 300 horses, which were led away and secured without incident. The remaining 700, thirsty and hungry, were quite uncontrollable when let out of the cars without halters or other means to hold them. Many bolted and ran away. Some were finally recaptured seven or eight miles from town. Twenty-four were not recovered.[3]

After this experience, Williams had his soldiers take over the care of the horses. They fed and watered the animals and then loaded them onto the boats for the trip down the Ohio. On board, the horses were fed and watered morning and evening.

When the cavalry inspector from Louisville visited the regiment, which he called "The Lochiel Cavalry Pennsylvania Militia," he condemned 411 of the remaining horses and had them replaced with fresh animals from the Louisville depot. The report of the inspector, who spent four days with the regiment, December 5 through 8, gives information about the men and equipment. He wrote that the horses were being shod but that this work would take about three weeks with the facilities available. He also reported: "no horse medicines; arms—sabers only; accoutrements—complete; horse equipments—good and complete; clothing—good; appearance—recruits."[4]

The soldiers did not let the poor quality of their mounts interfere with their own ideas of proper appearances. They began trading horses on their first day at Camp Andy Johnson. "We traded our Horses of[f] for Black ones   Co. B has all Black Horses and Co. H All Gray

[3] National Archives, "9th Cav., Order Book," Jan. 1, 1862 entry.
[4] National Archives, "Inspector's Report, Dec. 8, 1861," unbound paper in 9th Pa. Cav. records.

Horses," wrote William Thomas. The men also put up horse lines and generally improved the camp to make it more livable. Company B paved their quarters with bricks.

The quality of the animals was improved rapidly. In May, when the regiment visited South Union, Kentucky, Eldress Nancy Moore of the Shaker colony remarked that Colonel Williams's men were "mounted upon better looking horses than is common to be seen passing here." Eldress Nancy was an experienced observer, since many large and small contingents of both Confederate and Union cavalry had stopped at South Union during the preceding year.[5]

In the two weeks after this visit to South Union, the regiment was called upon for some hard campaigning, and when the cavalry inspector from Nashville visited them on June 16, he reported, "Found horses generally well groomed but in need of rest. Co. A in best order; Co. C and E horses need shoeing; Co. D and H badly groomed. Condemned 74 horses as totally unserviceable and will require 6 to 8 weeks rest." The inspector recommended that these horses be turned over to the convalescent yards in Nashville. Most of the horses condemned had sore backs, some had unsound hooves, and a few were "too old and used up." Fresh horses were immediately made available from Nashville.[6] William Thomas recorded, "Turned over 30 of our Horses and Drawed new ones in their place   all good Horses Now."

The "good and complete" horse equipments mentioned by the Louisville inspector meant that the Ninth had McClellan saddles.[7] The earliest of these saddles had been covered with rawhide, which often split on the seat and was the reason why some Union cavalrymen early in the war were observed riding on pillows. By the time the Ninth drew their equipment, leather was being used, and there were no complaints of split saddle coverings.

[5] Mary Julia Neal, ed., *The Journal of Eldress Nancy* (Nashville: Parthenon, 1963), p. 43.
[6] National Archives, "Inspector's Report, June 16, 1862."
[7] The McClellan saddle, named for Major General George B. McClellan, ranking officer in the U. S. Army during late 1861 and early 1862 and commander of the Army of the Potomac, was the standard saddle of the Civil War. A modification of the Mexican saddle, it was so satisfactory that it remained the regulation U. S. Army saddle until the horse cavalry was disbanded in 1942 (Charles D. Rhoades, *Photographic History of the Civil War* [New York: Review of Reviews], IV, 58).

Other horse equipments issued to the new soldiers included articles such as reins and bits, saddle bags, nose bag, lariat and picket pin, curry comb, and horse brush.[8]

Soon after arriving at Camp Andy Johnson, the men began to drill on horseback. On December 16, William Thomas wrote, "First Drill on Horseback in Sabre exercises in the morning." December 17, "First Drill by the sound of the Bugle in the Forenoon." December 19, "drill in the morning   the major ordered [us] to jump the fence with our Horses   Thomas Griffith was the first man to jump   He was Thrown out of the Sadle on the ground but not hurt   Grand Review in the evening by Gen Buehl."[9] On December 26, Thomas reported, "pleasant time on drill jumping our horses" and, on January 14, he wrote, "the Companys A & B Had Squadron drill This morning under Capt Savage   5 of us Had a Squad of our own trying to catch an old mule."

The first Christmas was spent at Camp Andy Johnson. "Drilled in the forenoon   we Had a very poor Christmas but as good as a Solder Could Expect   pleasant day." The troopers did not know it, but this would be the most pleasant of the four Christmases that they would celebrate in the army.

The weather was especially important to these men who drilled and marched in the open and who had only tents for shelter. From their observations, we learn that December of 1861 was generally pleasant, but some days were "Cold and rainy," "Cold and gloomy," and "Cold and Rough winds all day." Consecutive diary entries in early January recorded, "No drill on account of the rain," "raining all day," "Cold day," and "Cold and Snowy." Then another day of rain was followed by two cold days and then by a "very cold day   the ground Froze Hard and Slipy   Horses can Hardly Walk." Two days later, "Had a Thunder storm in the night and pretty near all our tents Drowned out with the rain."

Exposed to the variable weather, marching in mud, and often soaked to the skin, large numbers of the men were soon in the hospital.

8 Rhoades, IV, 62.

9 Maj. Gen. Don Carlos Buell, then in command of the Department of the Ohio, was organizing the Army of the Ohio (subsequently of the Cumberland), the principal Union army in the 1862–63 campaigns in central Kentucky and Tennessee.

Deaths occurred frequently. On December 20, William Thomas wrote, "Solemn prossesion in the afternoon after the corpes of H. H. Weaver of Co. B with our Black Horses to the station w[h]ere he was sent home to his frends in Millersburg." On December 31, Thomas reported, "We Buried one of our comrades to day out of Co B in Jeffersonville   His name johnathan Hoke From Lykens Valley   Died in the hospital at Jeffersonville."

Through the rest of the winter, after the regiment left Camp Andy Johnson, sickness and death continued to follow the regiment. In March, "Old Daniel Bitterman Died in the hospital During the night." During April, Thomas recorded the deaths of two men of Company D and on May 5, a sergeant of Company B died. Company C's returns record eight men who died of sickness during 1862. The regimental returns, however, show no "ordinary deaths" during 1861 and only three in 1862.[10] Probably most of the 110 men shown as "discharged on surgeon's certificate" actually had died. Discharge papers were made out for the dead as well as the invalids.

The men learned better how to care for themselves as the war progressed. Only three men of Company C died of sickness after 1862, and no "ordinary deaths" were recorded after October 1864. Deaths of five men of Company C were due to typhoid fever, two to chronic diarrhea, and one each to brain fever, general debility, pneumonia, and typhoid pneumonia.[11]

The men began to learn about military discipline at Camp Andy Johnson. The first serious incident occurred on December 11 when "Co. H refussed to drill until paid   put to labor at Digging a road on the river bank to water Horses." On January 3, Thomas wrote, "Dress parade in the Evening w[h]ere we wits ned the Drumming Out of a man out of Co. G with half His Head Shaved and the Rouge [Rogues'] march played after him." This was the usual punishment for desertion, and Thomas recorded several later instances of drumming out from his regiment and others. Sometimes, in addition to the half-shaved head, the culprit was made to wear a sign reading "Deserter and Sneak."

[10] National Archives, "9th Pa. Cav., Quarterly and Annual Returns."
[11] *Ibid.*

William Thomas did not record any instances of cruel punishments. The punishments seemed to fit the crime. For example:

> When returning to camp George Hoober drawed his Sabre on the Capt He was put in the gaurd House For a day and night

> They Had Henry Miller out of Co.C and a Women that staid with Him on the Bull ring [horse corral] All day

> Corp D Hoober was redused for going out to town to Play the fiddle at a party   Disobeying the Capt Orders

> 2 Seargt and 2 Corp marched to Louisville jail for disobeying orders out of Co F Capt Wise

> Martin Snooks under arrest for Stealing the Capt whiskey

> Had to go on gaurd in the evening for cuting a pice of my Horse tail off By order of Capt E. G. Savage Double Duty

> Corporal Lehman was redused   Having a fuss with Wm Kreiger

> Hen Messner Shot His Horse in the neck acidently   He got tied up to a post for it

> Corp Homes redused for intoxication

> stood gaurd to day when a man slept On my beat when i was ordered on 4 hours Extra Duty by the Officer of the day

> Hoover and robison made to Stand on a Board across a ½ barrel for a couple Hours for fighting   Commenced fighting While on the barrel both upset of[f]

Sometimes a threat of punishment could stop disobedience. When the Ninth Pennsylvania stopped at South Union, Eldress Nancy Moore recorded in her journal, "Some of the men disobeyed orders by going to the different families for milk, bread &c, The Officers said they should walk and lead their horses to B. Green [Bowling Green] for mortification."[12]

The death penalty was ordered by courts martial very rarely, when the size of the army is considered. Fewer than 300 executions were found in one examination of records.[13] The Ninth went through the war without seeing any soldiers executed, but did witness the maximum penalty immediately after the peace. Cornelius Baker recorded the incident on May 13, 1865:

[12] Neal, p. 43.
[13] Wiley, *Billy Yank*, p. 205.

We remaind in camp in the foarnoon and in the afternoon at half past 2 o clock we were orderd out to see a man out of the 9th Mishigan shot
We marched out 2 miles from town to w[h]ere he was to bee shot and formed our lines pasing his grave and he was brot out in a ambulance on his coffin and the band playing the ded march and the coffin was plased 3 pases from his grave and a chapter was red and a prair oferd up for him by the chaplin of his regiment and after the men were in line and his eyes were tied shut and a voly was fired and the prisner droped   15 balls passed threw his body and was a instant corps   he was shot for kiling a sitisan for his money at Goalsborough No. Caroliny.

V

Campaigning
in Kentucky

*Still raining   Struck tents this morn-
ing and up To our knees in mud
Started out of Camp Andy Johnson
at 9 A.M. and marched to the ferry in
Jeffersonville and crossed the ferry to
Louisville where we had to sit in The
sadle in the streets of Louisville until
the whole regt was ferried across
which took till 4 P.M. Then we
marched 4 miles back of Louisville
and camped in a corn feild in the mud
and slept out in the open air   We
sat in the sadle from 9 A.M. untill
8 P.M. in the Evening Without Dismounting once   our first march on
Horseback   Tough one*

The Ninth Pennsylvania Cavalry began their first campaign on January 19, 1862, under the conditions described by William Thomas. For recruits, this was a hard march. Before many months, the men would be riding day and night, and the march described above would be considered routine.

Major General Don Carlos Buell was assembling all his forces at Munfordville in south central Kentucky in the hope of striking a blow at the center of the Confederate line in the west. The center and strong point of the line was at Bowling Green. To the east, the line was anchored at Cumberland Gap. It extended westward to Columbus, Kentucky, on the Mississippi. The Ninth was just one of many new regiments that was ordered to join Buell's growing army. The men marched in adverse winter weather.

"Slept on the wet ground   Soft bed," was Thomas's comment about conditions during his first night in Kentucky. He continued, "Had no cover but the canopy of Heaven and was Awakened by the rain falling in Torrents   Pitched tents in the morning and fixed to stay a few days."

Fortunately, these half-trained soldiers did not encounter any of the enemy during the next few months. Not only were they half trained, they were poorly armed as well. They had their sabers, of course, and at

Louisville were issued Belgian rifles, which were smooth bore muskets converted from flintlock firing to percussion caps. Colonel Williams called the Belgian rifle "the most ineffective arms ever placed in the hands of men." On April 22 he reported, "Some companies of my regiment have been compelled to turn them all over. Nipples blowing out and cast iron hammers [breaking] render them unfit for any service. We have loaded them and attempted to fire by companies. Sometimes three would go off out of sixty or seventy. Many have to be snapped four or five times before the cap will explode."[1]

A few days before writing this report, Williams had requested that the regiment be furnished Sharps carbines, but it was nearly one year before the men received good carbines. Williams's April 22 report did state, "We have Colts Holster Revolvers, all in first rate condition."[2]

As late as October, Colonel James wrote to Governor Curtin asking that Pennsylvania furnish proper weapons because he could not get them from the army through either Louisville or Washington. He reported that the entire regiment had only forty-one Sharps and thirteen Maynard carbines.[3] Colonel Jordan wrote that carbines for the regiment were finally received in March 1863.[4] Thus, most of the men were armed only with saber and revolver during their 1862 campaigns.

The men did not seem concerned about their poor arms on January 23, when they marched out of Louisville on the Bardstown Road. They reached Bardstown two days later and camped two miles beyond. This was reported to be "fine camp   Full of rabits the Boys have fine sport chasing rabits." Here, for the first time, they went "out foraging from a Secesh." The changeable weather caught the soldiers, and four inches of snow caused most of the tents to collapse. Two mornings later, at New Haven, Thomas reported, "woke up this morning and found Ourselves Laying in the water."

1 National Archives, "9th Cav., Order Book," Apr. 22, 1862, entry.
2 *Ibid.*
3 *Ibid.*, Oct. 27, 1862, entry; the Sharps and Maynard were breech-loading carbines. The Sharps, using a paper cartridge, was the most popular cavalry carbine early in the war prior to the introduction of the Spencer repeater. The Maynard was one of the first weapons to use a brass cartridge. For more information on Civil War firearms, see Andrew F. Lustyck, "Civil War Carbines," *World Wide Gun Report* (1962) and Spencer Wilson, "How Soldiers Rated Carbines," *Civil War Times Illustrated*, V, No. 2 (May 1966), pp. 40–44.
4 Jordan, "The Battle of Thompson's Station," p. 303.

"Struck tents and marched to Hodgensville," continued Thomas on this same day, "Turned off from the pike To day   Teams sticking in the mud up to the Hub   Had to pry them out with Hand spikes Our Blankets and Clothes all wet." They remained in camp at Hodgenville for the next two days. It continued to rain and the men were "up to our knees in mud."

On February 1 they managed to march ten miles on the muddy roads and "Passed through a creeck up to the Horse Middle." The following day, they were able to make seven miles with the teams sticking in the mud. That evening it was "Muddy water for us and our Horses." They did not even attempt to march on February 3 because of the mud and continuing rain.

They marched at daylight on the fourth. "Reached Mumfordsville at noon," reported William Thomas, "Camped on the bank of Green river in a fine woods   Lots of camps in sight as far as the eye can reach about 40 thousand camped Around Here." The troopers spent the next few days in camp cleaning up their arms, clothing, horses, and themselves after their muddy march.

"in The Evening we were all called out By Major Jordan to give 9 Hearty Cheers for Smiths Victory in Tennessee," wrote Thomas on February 7. Well might they cheer because Fort Henry was captured on the sixth, opening the Tennessee River for Union gunboats and causing the Confederates to evacuate the strong point of Bowling Green without a fight.[5]

On the tenth, Thomas reported, "Sixteen Thousand troops Passed through Here today   Gen Mitchell Division went through to Bowling Green   First troops across the river." People in the area reported that Mitchell's men swam across Green River.[6]

When Fort Donelson surrendered to General Grant on February 16, the Confederate defense line in the West collapsed. The Rebels were forced to abandon Nashville as well as Bowling Green and to move their army nearly to the Mississippi line. The role of the Pennsylvania

[5] "Smith's Victory" was the fall of Fort Henry. Brig. Gen. Charles F. Smith was second in command to Gen. Grant at both Forts Henry and Donelson, captured a few days later. Grant was not well known until his "unconditional surrender" terms at the latter place captured the nation's imagination.
[6] Neal, p. 31; the reference is to Brig. Gen. Ormsby M. Mitchell.

cavalrymen changed from possible action against the enemy army to that of maintaining law and order behind the lines.

Except for a regiment of infantry left to guard the bridge at Munfordville and Williams's cavalry, the entire army had marched south by February 14. The following day, the Ninth Pennsylvania Cavalry marched in the opposite direction. A few miles north of Munfordville, Major Jordan's battalion took up duty guarding the railroad bridge at Bacon Creek. The rest of the regiment moved on toward Leitchfield.

By March 1, Jordan was writing to Colonel Fry, Buell's chief of staff, and complaining about this duty. He said that there was no corn or hay available because the area had been foraged extensively for the past three months and the quartermaster at Munfordville refused to supply horse feed. He noted that the job of guarding the bridge could be done just as well by a company of infantry. Within a couple of weeks, Jordan, with Companies C and I, was moved to Gallatin, Tennessee.[7]

The rest of the regiment marched north through Priceville, forded the Nolin River, and again had to pry their wagons along through the mud. On February 18, they camped at Grayson Springs. "In the yard there are 24 Sulphur Springs   All different kinds of water   a regular Summer resort for Big Bugs   the House is Used as a Hospital and full of Ky Soldiers Sick and Convalesant," is the way William Thomas described the place. They lay over for a day here and then marched on to Leitchfield.

At Leitchfield, Lieutenant Colonel James's battalion left the regiment and the remaining battalion set up a good camp, began to have inspections and dress parades again, and had visitors to watch their activities. Captain Savage took twenty men of Company B to church in town on Sunday evening. "Some of the Boys out deer hunting for the Col" wrote Thomas of a different type of activity.

On March 1, the men had their first experience with one of the enemy. William Thomas wrote, "a rebel Soldier brought Into camp to day   The Col gave him in Charge of Our Capt   He appointed a gaurd over Him and Lodged him in the coocks tent." The prisoner spent the

[7] National Archives, letter from T. J. Jordan to Col. James B. Fry, Mar. 1, 1862 and letter from E. C. Williams to Col. Fry, Mar. 22, 1862, unbound papers in 9th Pa. Cav. records.

43

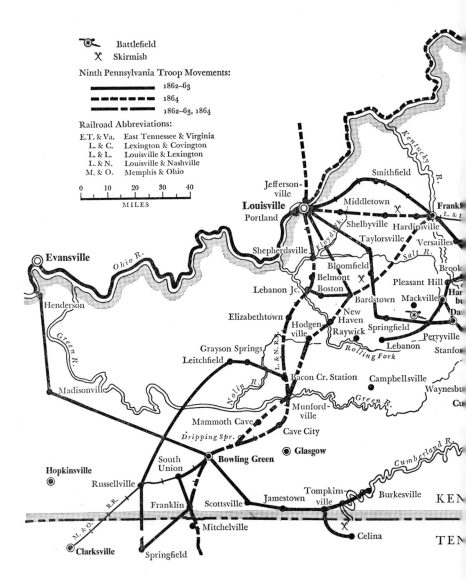

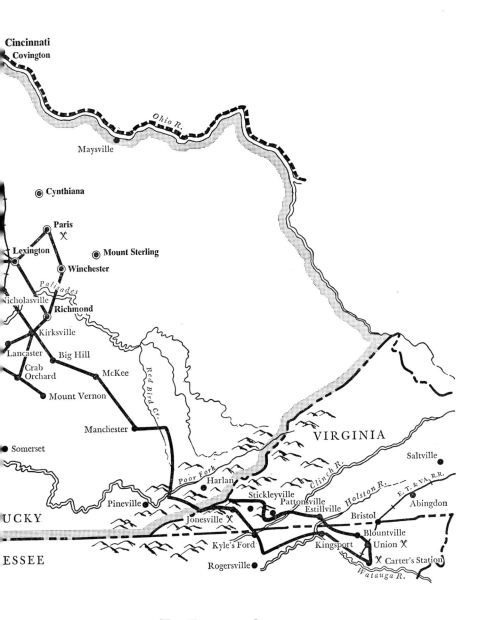

Cincinnati
Covington

Ohio R.

Maysville

Cynthiana

Paris
Lexington
Mount Sterling
Winchester
Palisades
Nicholasville
Richmond
Kirksville
Lancaster   Big Hill
Crab
Orchard   McKee
Mount Vernon
Manchester
Red Bird Cr.

Somerset

VIRGINIA

Saltville

Poor Fork   Harlan
Pineville
Clinch R.
Stickleyville
Pattonsville   *Holston R.*   *E. T. & VA. R.R.*
Estillville   Abingdon
Jonesville
Bristol
UCKY
Kyle's Ford   Kingsport   Blountville
ESSEE   Union
                            Carter's Station
Rogersville   *Watauga R.*

THE KENTUCKY CAMPAIGNS

45

next day in Thomas's tent, and then was taken to Louisville by Captain Jones.

Here also, rations became so bad that the men had to find other fare.[8] Thomas reported, "A Squad of twenty of us was out in the country Foraging for corn for us and our horses   We have to take the corn to a mill and get it Ground and make mush   The boys all sick of rations

Dont agree." At Leitchfield, the men received their revolvers and "Disposed of some of our old muskets   30 in number yet in the Company   sent the rest to Louisville."

Williams's battalion struck tents on March 16 and began another march on the muddy roads. "Had to carry our tents on Horseback traveling arabian style," wrote Thomas. They reached the Green River the next day and found the water over the banks. They began to build flatboats that could carry nine men and nine horses. This construction took until noon of the following day, and then the wagons and teams were ferried across. Company A ferried across the next morning, and Companies B and D in the afternoon. Thomas reported, "after we were across we Had to Swim our Horses through Some Back Water on the Bank of the river." On the twentieth, Company L and the band were ferried across and the battalion began to march again.

On March 21, "Passed out of Butler Co Into Logan   Lost one Horse on the road   Had to Shoot Him." On the twenty-third, they passed through Russellville. William Thomas wrote, "seen the motto on the market House Jeff Davis now and Forever   Camped at a Union mans House   passed an old secesh camp today   were ordered to Load our arms and have them in rediness." The following day, the unit went on to Springfield, Tennessee, and "Camped on a Hill Looking over the town   name of Hill pull tight." On March 25, Thomas recorded that the Ninth Pennsylvania "Hoisted the Stars and Stripes in Springfield." This was an achievement of note because "The people around Here are all Secesh."

---

[8] George Worthington Adams, *Doctors in Blue: The Medical History of the Union Army in the Civil War* (New York: Henry Shuman, 1952), pp. 206–207, states that the daily ration at the start of the war was 12 oz. of salt pork or 1 lb. of salt beef; 1 lb. 2 oz. of flour or 12 oz. of hard bread; and one vegetable, usually navy beans, peas, or rice. Coffee, sugar, salt, vinegar, candles, and soap were also part of the ration.

During this time the regiment remained split into small detachments. On March 22, Colonel Williams reported that he was at Springfield with Companies A, B, D, and L; Lieutenant Colonel James was at Clarksville with Companies H and F; Major Jordan was at Gallatin with Companies C and I; Major Brown was at Bowling Green with Companies G and K; Captain Detweiler, with Company E, was at Russellville; and Captain James Bell, with Company M, was at Edgefield, across the river from Nashville.[9]

For about one month the men at Springfield had little activity. For the first time Thomas mentioned, "Lots of Darkeys around Camp to day." As the men moved farther south, the Negroes coming into camp became an increasingly serious problem for the Union army. Theoretically, their owners could still claim them, but neither the Union officers nor the soldiers permitted the owners to take their slaves back. So the Negroes flocked into the camps and became an added burden on the Federal quartermasters. "Had cheering news," wrote William Thomas on April 11, "Another great victory at Corinth [Shiloh]   the companys were all called out to give 12 cheers and a Tiger for it."

A few days later the men began to improve their living quarters. "was out in the country Foraging after boards   tore down some Houses that was uesed by the Secesh for Commisary and Hospital   uesed the boards to floor our tents," Thomas recorded. He continued, "Tramped in a nail and Have a sore Foot   name of Secesh camp Camp Cheatham." Thomas's foot became worse the next day and he was sent to the hospital in town. He spent a couple of days there "sitting at The door waching the Secesh citizens." When the sun began to get hot in early May, the men used some of the boards collected to erect an arbor, or shed, to shield their horses from the sun.

The easy days of camp life ended abruptly when Colonel John Hunt Morgan,[10] the Rebel raider, struck at Cave City, Kentucky, north of Bowling Green. Colonel Williams's men saddled up and left Springfield in a hurry at 10:00 P.M. on May 11 and rode all night to Franklin. Here, early in the morning, "Had our Horses unsaddled and commenced to

[9] National Archives, letter from E. C. Williams to Col. J. B. Fry, Mar. 22, 1862, unbound paper in 9th Pa. Cav. records.
[10] Morgan captured a train on the L & N Railroad during his Cave City raid.

Feed when the Bugle went for us to saddle up   Started off again for
Bowling Green Ky   Marched through clouds of dust and reached
Bowling Green in the afternoon   Halted there And fed our Horses
and laid down an Slept."

At Bowling Green, Companies G and K joined the battalion and
the combined groups marched again on the following morning. They
reached Scottsville that evening. They started early again the next
morning, stopped to feed at Jamestown (now Fountain Run) and
marched until midnight to reach Tompkinsville. "Slept till morning," wrote Thomas, "All tired and weary." They were in the saddle
again in the morning and headed for Burkesville. "we marched along
the Macaac Creeck for 8 miles   a beautiful stream of Spring Water
and rock bottom and full of fishes," Thomas continued. In the evening,
they crossed a "Very High mountain" and reached Burkesville at sunset. They had marched a remarkable total of 140 miles in four days,
only to find that Morgan had beat them through Burkesville.

Colonel Williams's men returned to camp at Springfield but only
long enough to pack up to move to Bowling Green to provide better
protection for the Louisville & Nashville Railroad. According to William Thomas, June 1, their second day in the Bowling Green camp, was
unfortunate. "Fred Metzer of our company was shot Through the Head
by a pistol while Lieut Gratz was cleaning it   He expired in few moments After he was shot.   a man out of Company D was Bruttaly mur-
dred in town by a citizen."

VI

The Shakers
of South Union

*Started early and marched through a
very pleasant country turned into a
wood at South Union a Shaker village
where about 350 men women and
children live on 6500 acres of land
They are very kind and Simple Sect of
people very kind   They are all one
family and live in 3 Large Houses
Splendid Buildings   the women live
alone and the men the same   they do
not marry With one another and they
call Themselves Shakers.*

South Union was one of the two Kentucky and nineteen American colonies of The United Society of Believers in Christ's Second Appearance,
commonly called "Shakers." The Society was an offshoot of the Quaker
religion and possessed many of the same beliefs, including nonviolence
and conscientious objection to war. The sentiments of the people were
antislavery and pro-Union. For many years before the Civil War, the
Kentucky colonies had purchased slaves and then given them their freedom. Although excused from serving in the Federal army, a number of
entries in Shaker records tell of men leaving "to enlist in the U. S.
Army."[1]

The Shaker settlements were communal in structure, with the society owning all property. Elders and eldresses, in equal number, saw
to the spiritual affairs and discipline of the people. Deacons and deacon-
esses were in charge of the material affairs. Trustees handled the necessary contacts with "the world," such as legal documents, contracts, and
the like.[2]

As told by William Thomas in the opening quotation, the Shakers
did not marry. Men and women lived as "families" in the large buildings, with the men living in one side of the house and the women in the

[1] Daniel M. Hutton, *Old Shakertown and the Shakers*, 4th ed. (Harrodsburg:
Harrodsburg Herald Press, 1936), pp. 11–20, 61–63.
[2] *Ibid.*, pp. 13–15.

49

other. Separate work shops and different tasks kept the sexes apart during daytime activities. As there were no children, the membership was sustained by converts and by orphans, whom the Shakers adopted frequently.[3]

The industry and intelligence of the Shakers made the colonies extremely prosperous. Always located on fertile land, the colonies also possessed the best animals, the best equipment, and the most wealth in their neighborhoods. Their workshops produced nearly all the implements needed by rural people of that era. Thus, the Shakers became leading manufacturers as well as agriculturists, with the products of the Kentucky colonies being sold throughout that state and Tennessee.[4]

The Shakers' prosperity not only caused jealousy among many of their less well-to-do neighbors but, combined with their Union sentiments, led to persecution by their "secesh" neighbors when war came. Located between Bowling Green and Russellville, geography contributed to their problems because they were in territory occupied by the Confederate army until early 1862. The neighbors directed army agents to locations where the Shakers had hidden their best animals and wagons and encouraged guerrillas and stragglers to steal their goods and damage their property. Large bodies of Confederate soldiers often ate the Shakers' food without paying. Even when paid, the Shakers felt cheated because, as early as 1861, a Confederate dollar brought only seventy-five cents in gold in Bowling Green. In addition to this persecution, the Confederates were preparing to draft some of the brethren.[5]

Their situation changed in February 1862, when the Confederates were forced to evacuate Bowling Green and the surrounding areas. On February 16, Eldress Nancy Moore told in her journal of the first visit by Federal cavalry and related the sentiments of the Shakers. "All at first glance were persuaded in their minds, that they were union Cavalry. They looked very different from the secesh, both in their apparel and manners. Joy began to increase throughout . . . The Brethren and Sisters came around, with hearts full of thankfulness to God, for the pleasure of even beholding Union soldiers whom they viewed as their

3 *Ibid.*, pp. 13, 48–49.
4 *Ibid.*, pp. 26–29.
5 Neal, Intro. pp. v–viii, 3–31.

protectors and friends. God had sent them, was the sense, and this was manifested by strong expressions of true friendship and respect that flowed from the heart."[6]

For several months after this visit the Shakers fed the small parties of Federal soldiers who passed through South Union without charge. Later, the burden became too heavy, and they began to ask payment for their food. Even so, their menus told something about their true sentiments. The "secesh" were served sassafras tea and rye coffee. Union soldiers had "bought coffee" with their meals.

By May 29, when Colonel Williams and his Pennsylvania troopers rode into South Union, the novelty of seeing Union soldiers had worn off. The Shakers had seen enough of them to have become expert judges of the men. Eldress Nancy wrote of the visit of the Ninth Pennsylvania in her journal:

> About two O'clock in the afternoon, four hundred union Cavalry arrived here from Springfield, Tenn. They were moving on their way to B. Green. They camped at the head of our Mill pond. They conducted themselves in a quiet orderly manner. We have had a fair opportunity this evening for observing them, as they came in groups to the well for water, to the kitchen to get bread, to the milk house for milk. After supper they honored us with a splendid serenade from the brass band. They first stopped in front of the Office and made the music ring with drums beating. Then moved on in front of the Center house and there played several airs. From thence to the East family and honored them likewise. When they returned, our sisters in the center had prepared some supper for the musicians, while they were serenading the town. The brethren invited them to partake, they appeared well pleased with the invitation, and eat quite heartily. Immediately after they left the supper table, they struck up the music again, in honor & thanks for what they had received. They then retired for the night in a quiet and orderly manner. Some of the brethren & Sisters were up, pretty much all night, baking and preparing other things as it is intended to give the whole Battallion a free breakfast.[7]

William Thomas told of the breakfast briefly: "the Shakers got up a Splendid Breakfast for us this morning Which mostely consisted of Strawberries and Cream and all the other necessarys of life   The women waited on us and when the Boys talked to them they would not answer but they would fetch you any thing you wanted."

6 *Ibid.*, pp. 32–33.
7 *Ibid.*, pp. 42–43.

Eldress Nancy gave much more detail about the menu. She also wrote an opinion of the spirit and discipline of the regiment and of Colonel Williams's character:

> A most clear and beautiful morning, the dining room tables were all car- ried out into the door yard, west of the kitchen and placed under the sugar trees, and the victuals were placed thereon for the soldiers breakfast. They marched up from the camping ground to the Center and North fam- ilies in nice order, and depend on it there was a long line of them. We had for their breakfast good fresh coffee, fresh loaf and biscuit, boiled beef and fresh ham, sweet and Irish potatoes, canned Peaches and fresh strawberries, butter and corn bread. The officers eat at the Office. Colonel Williams said he could not sit down to his breakfast till he would go over and see his men, seated at the table, and see their fare. The Colonel seemed to be more anxious to see his men accommodated than himself. He appeared delighted with the table, and then went over to his breakfast ... About half after seven O'clock they mounted upon better looking horses than is common to be seen passing here. As they came near, the martial band, who went before, stopped in front of the Center house and played two tunes. They then took off their hats and waved them high in the air and gave three vociferous cheers; each company as they passed gave the same salute, for the Citizens of South Union for their kind hospitalities.[8]

A few days later, Lieutenant Colonel James and his battalion of the Ninth rode into South Union. Eldress Nancy said they were "in search of John Morgan and his band of guerrillas." Actually, they were riding to join Colonel Williams and Major Jordan in trying to catch a band of guerrillas near Tompkinsville. James had not sent word ahead, and as the men arrived just when the Shakers were finishing lunch, all they got were leftovers. However, Eldress Nancy wrote, "They soon discovered where the victuals came from and they flocked around the kitchen doors, they appeared very hungry for vegetables, they devoured the raw let- tuce with avidity and appeared thankful for all they got. When the bugle sounded they were off in a hurry. They had no time to tarry for cooking to be done."[9]

Obviously, these men had been living on army rations, which did not include antiscorbutics or vitamins; hence, the desire for vegetables. Although there is no record of scurvy occurring in the Ninth Pennsyl- vania, it was common among troops whose only food for extended pe-

[8] *Ibid.*, pp. 43–44.
[9] *Ibid.*, p. 44.

riods was rations.[10] The cavalry, foraging over a wide area, had more opportunity for variety in their diet than was possible for the infantry and, thus, had less sickness.

"Six hundred of Colonel Williams Cavalry and upwards of twenty wagons passed thro' our village in a drenching rain. They stopped at the head of our pond and camped for the night," wrote Eldress Nancy on June 26. The regiment was moving from Bowling Green to Hopkinsville and Madisonville to protect the citizens from guerrillas. William Thomas confirmed that the weather was wet. He wrote, "Raining all day   Struck tents this morning and left Bowling green and marched to South Union the Shaker village   Halted in a woods in the evening   the Shakers treated us with 3 wagonloads of apples   mud up to our knees."

Colonel Williams had decided not to impose on the graciousness of the Shakers again. "Colonel Williams said our kindness was calculated to destroy all military rule & discipline with the soldiers, for when they hear of fresh bread & milk being on hand, they will risk all & break thro' their orders to get it, and the Sisters cannot refuse them," wrote Eldress Nancy. She confirms that the brethren gave them apples and "accommodated them as well as they could by carrying milk to their camp both morning and evening."[11]

Late in July, a Russellville tavern keeper named George Gray and a friend killed two Federal officers who were in the act of confiscating a horse with the Confederate States' brand from Gray's stable. On July 31, Eldress Nancy wrote that "about seventy of Colonel Williams' brigade passed by here about ten O'clock A.M. going to Russellville to be in readiness there if they should be needed when the trial of George Gray & Company comes on tomorrow." These seventy men were from Captain Detweiler's Company E. Gray and friend were found guilty and executed and the "secesh" of Russellville were demoralized for some time.[12]

Eldress Nancy recorded one last visit by men of the Ninth Pennsylvania on August 5: "Captain Waltham [Jacob K. Waltman, Com-

[10] Wiley, *Billy Yank*, p. 135, lists 46,931 cases of and 771 deaths from scurvy during the war.
[11] Neal, p. 44.
[12] *Ibid.*, pp. 46–47.

pany G] sent a courier here about 8 O'clock in the morning to speak for breakfast to be prepared for one hundred and twenty Cavalry. Said they were very hungry they had eat nothing since they left Clarksville. Said the people of Russelville would give them nothing." The Center and North families working together had a large breakfast in place under cedar trees in the office yard by the time the soldiers arrived.

The eldress wrote that the soldiers looked sorrowful because they had been ordered to leave Hopkinsville before they were able to capture or drive some guerrilla bands out of that area. The captain had left ninety men at Hopkinsville to protect the citizens.

"They had cannon along with them, which had been hid in a corn-field ever since last winter," Eldress Nancy continued, "It was hid by a union party. They said they had a real hunt for it. Finally they formed in line & swept over the field by the corn rows & at last they found it in a thicket of sasafras bushes. They pressed six mules to draw the cannon. The artillerist took a good deal of pains, in showing us how it was loaded and fired. He said they could load and fire it off every minute in the hour."

The Shakers may have decided, by this time, that they should be paid for feeding Union soldiers. Eldress Nancy commented, "They said nothing about pay, neither did we, so we got nothing but thanky."[13]

[13] *Ibid.*, pp. 47–49.

VII

Guerrilla War

We were surprised in camp this morning About 2.0.clock A.M. by a party of Guerillas   They came up behind the camp and shot down the gaurd and then fired into the tentes   Our tent is riddled with balls   Henry Feindt who was sleeping by my side Had a Ball to graze the top of His head But not dangerous   the gaurd Had 14 Buckshots Shot in His Leg and thigh   The guerillas then fled into the woods and made their escape.

The July 6 entry in William Thomas's diary told of one of the Ninth Pennsylvania's many encounters with guerrilla bands during the late spring and early summer of 1862. Thomas continued this particular episode by telling that the attack was made "Comanche style" and that "What saved the most of us was because we were Laying down Sleeping The balls passed over us." Of course, the troopers started after the guerrillas at once but could not catch them. They scouted for several days and did arrest some "suspicious" men. However, Thomas related, "as there is no proof they are Released by taking the oath of Allegiance." After this, the regiment was more careful, and every man in the camp was assigned to either guard or picket duty. The pickets were posted at fence corners around the camps, and the soldiers were not surprised in camp again.

The first serious encounter between the Ninth Pennsylvania Cavalry and the guerrilla bands of Kentucky occurred in the middle of May after they had pursued John Hunt Morgan and his raiders to Burkesville. After finding that Morgan had crossed the Cumberland River into Tennessee, the 430 men of Colonel Williams's battalion marched back to Tompkinsville where they "received the news that the marauders [Captain O. P.] Hamilton and his band were at Celina 26 miles Back from Burkesville."

On May 18, the Pennsylvania cavalrymen marched from Tompkinsville to the Cumberland River opposite Celina, Tennessee. They found "Hamilton and his gang on the opposite shore." Thomas told what happened next:

> the Ferry boat was rather Small So we could not land a force Large enough to take the town   Two Seargt out of Co. A Potter and Lowe Took some Ladies across   When they were coming back they were fired upon by two men on Horsback   one of the Balls struck one of the boys on His pistol   we fired several inefectual shots after them but they fled into the river Bluffs

Colonel Williams's men then rode back to Tompkinsville. Thomas wrote, "our horses giving out very fast   Col Williams allowed it is time to get out of this when the Shots were fired on the Boys." The next day they started back to their camp at Springfield, Tennessee, passing through "Jimtown," Scottsville, Franklin, and "Black Jack."

A few days after their return to Springfield, Colonel Williams's command was ordered to move to Bowling Green; and Major Jordan's battalion was ordered to march from Lebanon, Tennessee, to Glasgow, Kentucky. Jordan's assignment was to watch the roads from eastern Tennessee, where two large Confederate armies were being organized.[1]

When he reached Scottsville, Major Jordan received orders to send one company on a scout toward Tompkinsville, where Hamilton's guerrillas were reported to be killing citizens and burning houses. Jordan sent Company I, commanded by Captain Hugh W. McCullough, on this scout and continued to Glasgow with Companies C, E, and M.[2]

On the night of June 5, Captain McCullough encamped at Moore's Hill, about eight miles south of Tompkinsville. Just as he was about to break camp in the morning, his pickets were driven in by a party of men under Captain Hamilton. This guerrilla band, estimated by different officers to be from 125 to 180 men, was drawn up in line in a deep woods with dense bushes and trees. As the Yankees, about sixty in number, were armed only with sabers and revolvers, much courage and discipline was required for them to attack the enemy hidden in the bushes.

---

[1] Thomas Jefferson Jordan, "Some Military Reminiscances of the Rebellion," *The United Service* (March 1889), p. 508.
[2] *Ibid.*, p. 508.

However, they did charge and were met by a volley of ball and buck-shot fired from shotguns. In spite of this defensive action, they main-tained their charge up to the dense underbrush. There they routed the guerrillas with their Colt revolvers. Captain McCullough was mortally wounded while leading the charge, and the command devolved on Lieu-tenant William H. Longsdorf. He pursued the guerrillas for half a mile where "a professed Union man" told him that the enemy were re-forming two miles down the road. As four men, in addition to the cap-tain, had been seriously wounded and Longsdorf's strength was only about fifty men, he decided to fall back to Tompkinsville, send a dis-patch to Major Jordan, and await reinforcements.[3]

Major Jordan's three companies were just getting into camp at Glasgow during the evening of June 6 when Lieutenant Longsdorf's courier rode into camp. Jordan immediately ordered boots and saddles to be blown. In spite of their hard march during the day, the troopers were soon on the road again. They marched all night and reached Tompkinsville at 7 A.M.[4]

Major Jordan, with his entire command, rode at once to Bennett's Ferry on the Cumberland River intending to drive the enemy from their stronghold in Celina. When he reached the river he found that high water made fording impossible, and all the flat boats were on the opposite bank. He called to some people on the other side to bring the boats over. He was answered by a volley of gunfire. Because his men had only a few carbines and no spare ammunition, Jordan decided not to engage in a senseless shooting match across the water. He returned to Tompkinsville to wait until the water receded or until he could find some other means of crossing the river.[5]

That evening, Colonel Williams and his six companies reached Tompkinsville. They had ridden the fifty-eight miles from Bowling Green in twenty-four hours. The ride caused a number of horses to drop dead while others had to be left along the way because of complete exhaustion.[6]

[3] O. R., Ser. 1, X, pt. 1, pp. 914–17.
[4] Jordan, "Some Military Reminiscences," p. 508.
[5] O. R., Ser. 1, X, pt. 1, pp. 914–17.
[6] *Ibid.*

On June 8, the combined force marched to McMillan's Ferry on Turkey Neck Bend of the Cumberland. Because only ten men and horses could be ferried across at a time, most of the day was spent in crossing the river. Company B appears to have been among the first across. William Thomas wrote that upon landing, they marched a mile and "surrounded a Church and kept the inmates prisoners all Day We then took supper at the guerilla Capt [Lieutenant J. M.] McMillans House   after our command were all over we released the citizens out of the Church and Started on a march down the river   camped at a Union man house all night."

The regiment started for Celina early on the ninth. High water forced them to cross the Obey River six miles from its mouth, and they did not reach Celina until four in the afternoon. Then Williams designated three companies to charge into town and deployed the rest of his force in the river bluffs to cut off the retreat of the Rebels in the town.[7]

William Thomas wrote, "marched through the river bluffs all day   captured a horse and equipments   made a charge into Celina in the evening   Ransacked the Houses and searched them   we took 4 prisoners and captured 8 horses and severall Rifles and pistols   Hamilton had left before we got in   Stood gaurd with the Boys over the prisoners at night in a liquor shop"

The four prisoners were Samuel Granville, Smith Butler, T. C. Settle, and William Henry Harrison Peterman. About these men, Colonel Williams wrote, "Against the last of these there is an indictment in Monroe County [Kentucky] for murder, and he has been the dread of the whole neighborhood, and next to Hamilton is the most important and dangerous man in that region. The others are very bad men, and were recognized as active men of Hamilton's band through the whole route to this place [Bowling Green]. There were no men in Celina except those we captured, and they made desperate attempts to escape."[8]

On June 10, while the main body recrossed into Kentucky, "Magor Jordan and His 2 Companies went down the river to Hamilton House and destroyed His commisary," according to William Thomas. Actu-

---

[7] *Ibid.*, pp. 914–15.
[8] *Ibid.*, p. 915.

ally, the goods which this detachment found were the remainder of stores captured from a steamboat by the guerrillas. Major Jordan reported that these stores consisted of 20 boxes of army bread, 10 barrels of the same, 2 barrels of sugar, 100 bags of wheat, and 23 hogsheads of tobacco. The troopers destroyed these goods by dumping them into the river because they had no way to transport them. Jordan also captured "Hamilton's celebrated race horse."⁹

On returning to Tompkinsville, Colonel Williams "found the citizens much in dread of attack from predatory bands said to be marching from Overton" and ordered Major Jordan and three companies to remain there and patrol the area to the Cumberland River. Colonel Williams wrote to Brigadier General Jeremiah T. Boyle,¹⁰ "If I were sent with my whole regiment after I get carbines and horses into the neighborhood of Tompkinsville, I feel that I could be of great service in driving out the robbers and restoring peace and quiet to that afflicted district."¹¹

William Thomas was a member of a scout that rode from Bowling Green to Scottsville and Jamestown. He reported, "Reached Jimtown at noon   a squad of ten men under corp [Henry] Hoffman went outside of Jimtown to arrest some Rebel Soldiers that deserted from the Army   took dinner at a Union man House   arrested 3 men Lieut arested 2 In town   great crowd of people there when we arrived very kind to us." The following day they arrested another man in Scottsville, and Thomas and nine other men escorted the prisoners to Bowling Green.

Contrary to expectations, Jordan was not troubled by guerrillas. However, the main body of the regiment ran into guerrillas in early July when they moved camp from Bowling Green to Madisonville. While marching through "a thick and swampy forrest," the advance guard was fired on by two horsemen. The troopers chased them, but they escaped into the thickets. The soldiers did capture one of their horses.

At Madisonville, on the Fourth of July, the regiment "prepared a

⁹ *Ibid.*, pp. 915, 917.
¹⁰ Boyle commanded the Department of Kentucky, with headquarters in Louisville.
¹¹ O. R., Ser. 1, X, pt. 1, p. 915.

barbecue to celebrate this great Birthday of american Independence in the morning   at noon we were marched out to Hear the Declaration of independence read by Magor Russel and a few short speeches by the other officers   the camp was thronged by Ladies and citizens   at noon we had a splendid dinner brought in by the Citizens   We had a fine time."

It was two days later that the attack mentioned in this chapter's opening quotation took place. After this surprise, Colonel Williams had one company camped at his headquarters at night. The harassment seems to have made some of the men jittery. "pickets comenced firing this morning   firing at the Head Stones in a graveyard," wrote William Thomas a few days later.

Guerrillas and bushwhackers were encountered by the regiment from time to time for the remainder of the war. For example, the First East Tennessee Cavalry and a part of the Ninth Pennsylvania encountered Captain O. P. Hamilton and his gang at Yankeetown, near Sparta, Tennessee, in November 1863. One man of the Ninth and four of the Tennessee regiment were killed. Colonel James P. Brownlow, of the Tennessee regiment, reported that the Union troopers drove the guerrillas eight miles following the attack, killing nine and wounding fifteen or twenty.[12]

On December 9, a few days after Colonel Brownlow's encounter, guerrillas attacked and robbed the sutler train that was following the cavalry brigade from Sparta to Crossville. William Thomas recorded, "The 9th Pa Sutler was Killed and 8 men out of Co G 9th Pa."

Guerrillas remained active even in the Louisville area as late as the summer of 1864. Troopers riding courier service or performing other detached service had to be especially alert. On July 26, 1864, Thomas reported, "George Burkle came into camp this morning   He was taken prisoner near Taylorsville on Our Last Scout by Guerillas   They took His Horse and arms and parolled him   He saved his money By throwing it away and after Being paroled found it again After the Guerillas Left Him   He Had to Walk to Louisville."

Andrew Robinson was less fortunate. He fell into the hands of true bushwhackers, men who were outlaws. On August 4 of this same year,

[12] O. R., Ser. 1, XXXI, pt. 2, p. 92.

William Thomas recorded, "Andrew Robison of our company was Brought Dead into the City to day   He was along with the Scout   it is supposed That He was shot by Guerrillas on His road Back to the City with a Dispatch   He was Shot through the Heart and Drawed up to a tree 7 miles from the city on the Salt river pike."

VIII

Hurrah for Morgan!

July 9, 1862, Morgan's Raiders coming from Tenn. on first raid into Ky., attacked force of 9th Pa. Cav. at USA garrison. Raiders captured 30 of the retreating enemy and destroyed tents and stores. They took 20 wagons, 50 mules, 40 horses, sugar and coffee supplies. At Glasgow they burned supplies, then went north, raiding 16 other towns before returning to Tenn.

A historical marker south of Tompkinsville, Kentucky, on the road to Celina, Tennessee, tells about the first action of the campaign that became known as Morgan's First Kentucky Raid. The force of the Ninth Pennsylvania Cavalry involved in this affair was the Third Battalion, made up of Companies C, E, I, and M, Major Jordan commanding.[1]

This was not the first time that Major Jordan's men had encountered Colonel John Hunt Morgan, who already had established a reputation as one of the most colorful and successful cavalry raiders of the war. The first encounter had taken place during the night of May 4 at Lebanon, Tennessee, where Morgan was bivouacked after capturing a train of Union wagons and convalescent soldiers near Pulaski.

On May 4, General Ebenezer Dumont, with contingents of Colonel Frank Wolford's First Kentucky and Colonel George C. Wynecoop's Seventh Pennsylvania cavalries, passed through Gallatin, Tennessee, where Jordan's battalion was serving as garrison. Dumont ordered Jordan to accompany his force in an attempt to surprise and capture Morgan at Lebanon.[2] They nearly succeeded. During the dark, rainy night, Morgan's pickets on the Gallatin road had taken shelter in a house some distance from the road. They did not observe the Union column until it was nearly past their post. The Confederates in the town were

---

[1] O. R., Ser. 1, XVI, pt. 1, p. 754.
[2] Jordan, "Some Military Reminiscances," p. 508.

unaware of the Federal approach until the Union troopers were entering the town.[3]

Most of the Rebels aroused in time to seize weapons, but they were unable to organize into units. After some hand-to-hand fighting by small groups, the Confederate force was routed. Nearly 300 of Morgan's men were captured, but the rest escaped in the darkness and confusion to nearby woods. Morgan himself barely managed to escape. He rode out of town toward the Cumberland River, twenty miles away, with a small party that became smaller at an increasing rate as the race to the river wore the horses down. The Federal troopers were in close pursuit in a chase that became known as "The Lebanon Races." Fortunately for Morgan, the ferry was on his side of the river, and he and a few of his men embarked before his pursuers reached the river bank.[4]

Within a few days, Morgan had rebuilt his regiment with stragglers who drifted into camp and new recruits. With this force, he made his famous raid on the Louisville & Nashville Railroad at Cave City, Kentucky. Here he captured a train and destroyed some track.[5] The nearest Union force was Colonel Williams's six companies of the Ninth Pennsylvania Cavalry at Springfield, Tennessee. Although Williams's cavalry was several days march behind Morgan at the start, they tried hard to catch him and covered the 140 miles from Springfield to Burkesville, Kentucky, in four days. However, they found that Morgan had already passed through Burkesville and into Tennessee. Furthermore, Morgan had taken all the horses in the area, and Williams was unable to replace his worn-out mounts.

However, Major Jordan and his battalion had marched from Lebanon to Livingston and were in a position to take up the chase. On May 14, they caught Morgan's rear guard at Spring Creek and captured it.[6] Now intent on reaching Knoxville, Morgan did not turn back with his main body to protect his rear guard. Jordan continued the chase as far as Sparta. By this time, his men had ridden for twenty-four hours with-

---

[3] Henry M. Cist, *The Army of the Cumberland* (New York: Scribners, 1898), p. 35.

[4] Basil W. Duke, *A History of Morgan's Cavalry* (Bloomington: Indiana University Press, 1960), pp. 159–63, 167.

[5] *Ibid.*, pp. 163–66.

[6] Frederick Henry Dyer, *A Compendium of the War of the Rebellion* (New York: Thomas Yoseloff, 1959) III, 1562; Bates, *Pennsylvania Volunteers*, III, 235.

out food, and Jordan asked the people of Sparta to feed them so they would not have to forage. The citizens consented, and the soldiers dismounted in the street with each man standing at his horse's head. Soon the people brought food. After eating, the cavalrymen began their march back to Lebanon. Jordan later was accused by the Confederates of coercing the citizens of the town.[7]

Jordan's battalion had marched to Tompkinsville, Kentucky, in early June, as related in the preceding chapter, and remained there through the month to protect the citizens from the guerrilla bands operating in that area. Meanwhile, Morgan was assembling a brigade in Knoxville for a longer and more destructive raid into Kentucky. The brigade included his own Kentucky regiment, a regiment of Georgians, a squadron of Texas Rangers, and two howitzers. The force totaled 900 men. Morgan knew of the battalion of Union cavalry at Tompkinsville and made the capture of this garrison his first objective. He left Knoxville on July 4.[8]

Jordan soon learned of Morgan's approach from loyal citizens. When he heard that Morgan was planning to camp at Celina, Tennessee, on the night of July 7, Jordan decided that he would become the aggressor. He planned a dawn attack on Morgan's camp for the eighth, believing that Morgan's men would be sleeping soundly after their long, hard march. With 200 men, Jordan marched all night, crossed the Cumberland River twelve miles north of Celina, and charged into town at dawn.[9] Morgan was not there. He had camped at Livingston, about twelve miles southeast of Celina.[10] Probably Jordan's battalion was fortunate that Morgan was not at Celina. Jordan was unaware of or misinformed about the strength of Morgan's force.

From Celina, Jordan sent scouting parties down the roads south of town. When these parties returned without seeing any sign of the enemy, the major decided to ride back to Tompkinsville.[11] While the battalion marched, the rear guard felled trees across the road, and Mor-

---

7 Jordan, "Some Military Reminiscences," p. 518.
8 Duke, p. 183.
9 Jordan, "Some Military Reminiscences," p. 509.
10 Duke, p. 183.
11 O. R., Ser. 1, XVI, pt. 1, p. 755.

gan's timetable was set back during the next night because of the need to remove these obstacles.[12]

Morgan reached Celina in the afternoon, a couple of hours after the Federals had left. Here he was joined by the local guerrillas under the notorious O. P. Hamilton, W. S. Bledsoe, J. M. McMillan, and Champe Ferguson. This brought his force to over 1,100 men, which should have been enough to surround and capture the 230 Union troopers in Tompkinsville. Morgan began his march to Tompkinsville after dark. At dawn, while still five miles from the Union position, he sent the Tennessee guerrillas and his squadron of Texas Rangers to the left for the purpose of blocking the Glasgow road and cutting off the garrison's escape.[13]

Morgan had planned a dawn attack on the Union camp, but reveille had already sounded in the camp and the Federal troopers were grooming and feeding their horses when they heard the first sharp reports of cavalry carbines on the Celina road. By the time the pickets came in, the cavalrymen had saddled their horses and formed a line-of-battle in the nearby woods.[14]

Still under the illusion that he was facing Morgan's regiment alone, Jordan "felt little fears as to the result, as my men had twice met him before and felt sure of victory." He watched the enemy through his glasses while they came over a bald hill about three-quarters of a mile away, and was quickly disillusioned. While he watched, two bodies of men, each more numerous than his force, deployed at the base of the hill. These groups were followed by the two pieces of artillery and then by two more large bodies of troops. Only then did Jordan realize that "my poor little command would have to fight four regiments and two pieces of artillery."[15]

Actually, the Confederates on the Union front were only two regiments. These were Morgan's own Kentucky regiment, deployed about 300 yards in front of the Union left, and Colonel A. A. Hunt's Fifth

[12] Duke, p. 183.
[13] *Ibid.*; O. R., Ser. 1, XVI, pt. 1, p. 771.
[14] Jordan, "Some Military Reminiscances," pp. 509–10; O. R., Ser. 1, XVI, pt. 1, p. 754.
[15] Jordan, "Some Military Reminiscances," p. 510.

Georgia regiment, opposite the Federal right. The artillery was placed in the center and soon began to fire upon the Union position.[16] Because it was too dangerous for the Pennsylvanians to leave the cover of the woods and escape the firing on the open road, Jordan decided to accept a few rounds of artillery fire and wait for the inevitable charge of the enemy cavalry, knowing that the artillery fire would cease when the Confederate charge came close enough to his lines that the shells would endanger the attacking Rebels. Colonel Hunt's Georgians charged, and the artillery firing stopped. The charge was repulsed. After the Confederates were thrown back, Jordan ordered his men to wheel and retreat. "This movement was done with the precision of a parade, my men remaining perfectly cool and obedient to my orders," he reported.[17]

Before reaching Tompkinsville, the retreating column ran into the squadron of Texas Rangers, who had been sent around to their rear. Jordan ordered a saber charge to open the way to retreat. The men attacked "in the most gallant manner, literally overturning the Rangers and driving them from the field." Jordan reported that he had no idea how many Rebels were killed and wounded during this charge.[18]

Among the several roads leading out of Tompkinsville, the most important was one leading northwest to Glasgow. Another ran east toward Burkesville. The Glasgow road had been blocked by the guerrilla force that Morgan had sent around early in the morning. With the most likely route of retreat cut off, Jordan ordered his men to ride toward Burkesville.[19] Somehow orders got fouled up coming down the chain of command, and Bugler Cornelius Baker received orders to blow for a retreat up the Glasgow road. Either he knew that the Glasgow road was blocked or his intuition told him that the order was wrong because he blew a command for the column to ride onto the Burkesville road. He said later that the men who followed him got away and those that went the other way were captured. Second Lieutenant William Campbell and seven men of Baker's company were captured, making his story credible.[20]

---

16 Duke, p. 184.
17 O. R., Ser. 1, XVI, pt. 1, p. 755.
18 *Ibid.*
19 *Ibid.*
20 The enlisted men captured were John Berrier, John M. Daugherty, James P.

The well-disciplined Union troopers, riding in orderly ranks, gained a two-mile head start while the poorly disciplined Rebels stopped to loot the Federal camp. However, firing was soon heard again at the rear of the column. Major Jordan "deemed it proper for me personally to look to my rear guard, that I had placed under the charge of Lieutenant [Aaron] Sullivan, of Company E." Jordan continued:

> For this purpose I rode to the rear of my column and found that the firing proceeded from beyond a turn in the road some 200 yards behind my rear guard. Fearing that some of my men might have become separated from my command and were being attacked, I rode back to the turn, so as to be able to see, when I discovered Lieutenant Sullivan in the act of being murdered by some 20 of the enemy, who surrounded him. I at once turned my horse for the purpose of rejoining my command, when I found two of the enemy already in the road before me and in a moment they were increased to six, thus cutting me off from my men. I determined to try to force my way through them, with my pistol answering their shotguns, but I soon found that resistance would be madness and surrendered myself a prisoner of war. After I had surrendered I was fired upon at a distance of but a few feet, the charge, happily for me, missing its mark, but blackening the side of my face with powder.[21]

Major Jordan was sent to Knoxville and then on to Castle Thunder prison in Richmond. He was exchanged in December and returned to the regiment.[22] The captured enlisted men were paroled; that is, they signed papers swearing that they would not fight again until properly exchanged. After signing these papers, these men were set free.[23] They also were exchanged a few months later and returned to the regiment.

The men who got away from Tompkinsville rode to Burkesville under the command of Captain William Harris of Company C. Harris reported losses of sixty to seventy-five in killed, wounded, and missing "with some of the missing probably hidden out in the woods."[24] Jordan's report, written after his return from prison, gave the losses as four killed, seven wounded, and nineteen prisoners. He said that he was informed that the Rebel loss was nineteen killed and twenty-eight

Campbell, Joseph A. Chestnut, John Coalhouse, Isaiah Holtzapple, and Jonathan Shaeffer (Bates, III, pp. 249–52).

[21] O. R., Ser. 1, XVI, pt. 1, p. 755.
[22] Jordan, "Some Military Reminiscances," pp. 516–21.
[23] Duke, p. 184.
[24] National Archives, Report of Capt. Harris, 9th Pa. Cav. (unbound records).

wounded.[25] Because he spent several days in the enemy camp before going to Knoxville, his information may have been accurate. However, Morgan reported that his only casualties were wounded, including Colonel Hunt who was mortally wounded during the initial charge. Morgan said the Union casualties were twenty-two killed and thirty to forty captured, including the wounded.[26] As with most casualty figures in the officers' reports, the reader has a wide choice of what to believe.

The day after the fight, Bugler Cornelius Baker was called into headquarters at Burkesville. Expecting a reprimand for disobedience, he was greatly pleased when his officers complimented him for his initiative.

General Jerry Boyle in Louisville panicked when word reached him that Morgan was loose in Kentucky again. First reports informed him that Morgan had captured all of Jordan's command. These reports also doubled the true size of Morgan's force. Morgan put his own operator on the telegraph line and sent fake reports directly to the Union army headquarters, thus adding to the confusion.[27] Boyle sent a series of telegrams pleading for troops to Governor Oliver P. Morton in Indianapolis, to General Buell in Nashville, and directly to Washington. Morton responded with some raw troops. General Buell refused to release cavalry to combat a raid because he was expecting to be attacked by the Confederate army and needed all his mounted men for scouting.[28] President Lincoln wired Major General Henry W. Halleck, the supreme commander of all Western departments, "They are having a stampede in Kentucky. Please look to it."[29]

Boyle did have reason for concern. Only mounted men could hope to catch Morgan, and the only cavalry available was Colonel Williams's six companies of the Ninth Pennsylvania at Madisonville, far to the west of Morgan's route to the Lexington area. They were ordered to hurry to the opposite end of the state.

On the night of July 12, William Thomas was on picket duty out-

25 O. R., Ser. 1, XVI, pt. 1, p. 755.
26 *Ibid.*, p. 767.
27 O. R., Ser. 1, XVI, pt. 1, pp. 774–81.
28 *Ibid.*, pp. 731–52.
29 O. R., Ser. 1, XVI, pt. 1, p. 738; Halleck later became general-in-chief of the U. S. Army and Lincoln's principal military adviser.

side of the Ninth's camp at Madisonville. He halted two couriers who were riding hard toward the camp. They carried dispatches for Colonel Williams. "in about a half an hour Afterwards all Bustle in camp and Geting ready for a march," recorded Thomas, "Magor Jordan was taken prisoner by Morgan and a great many of his men at Tomkinsville." That night, Colonel Williams's command began to march north toward Henderson on the Ohio River. They marched 27 miles that night and the next day and "camped at the 14 mile House kept by H. G. Jones." Although tired, Thomas could appreciate incongruous sights: "Seen an ox team Full of Niger wenches all dressed in white."

On July 14, the column reached Henderson and, the next day, marched through town to the Ohio River. Here they "Ferried our teams across the river to indiana." "we got on the steamboat in the afternoon," continued Thomas, "passed Evansville in the evening   3 steamers take us up the river   Horses on board also." He gave the names of the boats: "Gray Eagle Little Gray Eagle and Courrier." During the evening of the sixteenth, the boats docked at Portland, below the Falls of the Ohio, and the regiment mounted and rode into Louisville.

They didn't dally in Louisville. William Thomas described the activity of July 17, "Got up early and partook of breakfast at the Hospital and then marched to the depot and Our company received 17 new Maynard Carbines Before getting on the cars   put our horses in the Cars and we rode on top and found ourselves going to frankfort as fast as Steam could take us   arrived at frankfort at 3 o clock in the afternoon   1 or 2 regts of infantry arrived before us   camped in the court yard   fed our Horses and got ready for a march again   Started at 11. o.clock. P.M. Under Gen Smith   Marched all night   passed through verssailles at daybreak."

Brigadier General Green Clay Smith had assembled a motley brigade in Frankfort. In addition to the 430 men of the Ninth Pennsylvania Cavalry, he had 100 Cincinnati policemen, two companies of the Eighteenth Kentucky Infantry, and some home guards for a total of 1,320 men.[30] He sent the foot soldiers and policemen on the direct road to Paris, where Morgan was bivouacked. The cavalry, under Smith's personal command, took the longer route through Lexington. About

[30] O. R., Ser. 1, XVI, pt. 1, pp. 759–61.

this march William Thomas wrote, "Arrived at Lexinton in the forenoon   All very tired   found business all Suspended and the citizens
all under arms   Heard that Morgan whole force was at Paris about
1500 strong   we were Joined in the evening by a Squadron of Ky. Cav.
[Second Kentucky]   We then started in the afternoon and marched
all night."

On July 19, General Smith's cavalry rejoined the foot soldiers
and police near Paris. William Thomas described the skirmish that
followed:

> We met a Battallion at daybreak With 3 peices of arttilery and a large
> number of Home gaurds and 500 cincinatti police   Some of the Home
> gaurd pickets drove in when we arrived   we then took the advance and
> throwed Skirmishers out on the right and Left of the road   we then ad-
> vanced on paris   our skirmishers on the right came on a party of Morgan
> pickets   drove them in and took 6 of them prisoners   we were then
> Ordered to Charge into paris But Morgan Retreated out as quick as he
> saw us coming   Killed 17 and about 50 wounded and taken prisoners
> not a man hurted on our side.

Morgan reported that his losses were two pickets.[31] Thomas's figures
probably were nearer the truth because Morgan began to ride fast for
the safety of Tennessee. "We started in pursuit of Morgan early this
morning and marched to Winchester," Thomas wrote on July 20. "Here
we fed and took supper and captured a lot of horses   Started off again
and marched all night over a pleasant country   Heard that Morgan
was going to make a stand at richmond Ky   Hired teams to Haul the
infantry from paris to winchester."

Morgan did have ideas of fighting at Richmond but reported that
he continued the retreat when he heard that a strong Union cavalry
force was approaching the town to reinforce General Smith.[32] There
were no large forces of Yankee cavalry in the area, but Smith's column
was reinforced. The Third Battalion of the Ninth Pennsylvania arrived
from Tompkinsville and rejoined the regiment.[33] Thus, the men who
had been attacked by Morgan when he first came into Kentucky had
the satisfaction of helping to chase him out. With these reinforcements

[31] *Ibid.*, p. 770; General Smith stated Morgan's casualties as 29 killed, 30
wounded, and 18 captured (*Ibid.*, p. 761).
[32] *Ibid.*, p. 770; Duke, p. 204.
[33] Dyer, III, 1562.

of mounted men, the slow-moving infantry was left at Richmond. The cavalry merely "stopped to feed and rest awhile," and then "Started off again and marched all night."

They marched all the next day, too, stopping only long enough to feed their horses at noon. On they rode through Stanford and Waynesburg. At this last town "one of the Magazines of the cannon exploded and wounded 3 camped at Cuba in the night Camp Starvation." Here General Smith learned that Morgan had crossed the Cumberland River into Tennessee and the chase ended. The Ninth marched back to Danville on the following day and went into camp at midnight. Thomas reported, "our Horses are worn out and poor." On July 25, the regiment reached Lebanon and "Encamped at a place where Morgan Destroyed a Hospital and a large Quantity of arms."

Morgan returned to Livingston, Tennessee, and reported that the raid had been a great success. He had captured seventeen towns in which he had destroyed all Federal arms and supplies. He claimed that he had dispersed 1,500 home guards and that he had captured and paroled 1,200 Union soldiers. His principal disappointment had been in recruiting. He had expected that Kentuckians would rush to enlist upon his appearance in the state, but only about 400 did so and these barely offset his losses.[34]

The Union was the big gainer from Morgan's raid. The Federal high command finally realized that cavalry was needed to stop such raids, and they authorized more regiments to be raised. Seven new cavalry regiments were recruited in Kentucky alone, and over 7,000 Kentuckians enlisted in these.[35] Enlistments also became more numerous in Indiana and Ohio after Morgan's raid, and Colonel Rutherford B. Hayes, recruiting in Ohio, enthusiastically wrote, "Hurrah for Morgan!"[36]

The Ninth Pennsylvania was assigned to help the new Kentucky regiments obtain horses. William Thomas was one of forty men from the Ninth who went on an expedition, along with forty Kentucky re-

34 O. R., Ser. 1, XVI, pt. 1, p. 770.

35 The 6th through 12th Ky. regiments were recruited following Morgan's raid. The author's grandfather, John Rowell, enlisted Aug. 16, 1862, in Co. E, 12th Ky. Cav., and was saddler of the company.

36 Robert Emmett McDowell, *City of Conflict* (Louisville: Louisville Civil War Round Table, 1962), pp. 73–74; Hayes was elected President of the United States in 1876.

cruits. "Pressing in horses for Col. [Dennis J.] Halisey regt [Sixth Kentucky]," he wrote.

From the camp at Lebanon, the scout rode through Springfield and on to Bloomfield. "The town Seceded from the County," Thomas noted. Here the soldiers "Pressed in quite a large number [of horses] today from the secesh citizens but were treated kindly by them." When impressing horses, the Union officers gave receipts. People known to be Southern sympathizers sometimes had trouble collecting from the Federal paymasters, but taking the oath of allegiance was usually sufficient evidence of loyalty for payment.

Still at Bloomfield on the following day, Thomas wrote, "5 of us Staid back in town with Col Halisey and Lieut Gratz After the Colum Had left   Col Halisey made them put up a Union flag before We left." An expedition of this kind was good duty. William Thomas rode out of Bardstown toward Shepherdsville at 3 A.M. one day. "eat breakfast at a Secesh and took one of his horses," he wrote. "Made chase after 2 men who undertook to get away   got their horses but the Men made their escape   eat dinner at a Union man House along with 6 fine young ladies   Had a pleasant time."

This detachment returned to camp at Lebanon on August 15. Two days later Thomas was on less pleasant duty. "Started out on a scout 10 men out of each company under Magor Russell," he recorded, "marched to Greywich [Raywick]   marched through swamps and scoured the woods after guerillas all day and marched through the swamps all night." This party returned to camp on the evening of August 18 only to find that the regiment had left suddenly. The scouting party had to keep on riding until they caught up to the main body at Danville at three o'clock the following morning.

The men knew instinctively that the sudden move by the regiment meant that an exciting and important assignment lay ahead.

IX

Crisis in Kentucky

*we then went out on a scout towards
Mt Vernon   Co. B H & D and met
200 of the rebel cavalry   we then
charged on them and took one of their
Capt prisoner and wounded 1 man
they then fell back on the main body
of the rebels fortified on a High
mountain with their artilery planted
The rebels are the advance of Braggs
army into Ky*

The encounter of August 22 described by William Thomas in this quotation was the second meeting of the Ninth Pennsylvania Cavalry and the Rebel cavalry at the beginning of the Confederate invasion of Kentucky in 1862. Two days before, the Ninth had made a rapid march from Danville to Crab Orchard. "Here we were looking for a place to camp," wrote William Thomas, "When our advance came on a body of Scotts cavalry   we then charged on them and chased them for over 8 miles   we wounded 2 and took 2 prisoners."

Colonel John S. Scott's First Louisiana Cavalry was the advance unit of Major General E. Kirby Smith's wing of Braxton Bragg's Confederate Army of Tennessee. Twenty thousand strong, Smith's army was marching toward Lexington from Knoxville. Once in Lexington, they could threaten Louisville and Cincinnati. General Bragg would soon march with a larger army from Chattanooga toward Louisville. The plan called for the two armies to join for an attack on Louisville.[1]

Colonel Scott had been ordered to occupy Mount Vernon and Crab Orchard, Kentucky, but he wrote that the Federal cavalry had occupied the latter place a few hours before his arrival. He reported, "Finding

---

[1] E. Kirby Smith commanded the District of East Tennessee (William Frayne Amann, ed., *Personnel of the Civil War* [New York: Joseph Yoseloff, 1961] I, 345); Braxton Bragg commanded the Confederate Army of the Mississippi, Department No. 2, which included Alabama, Mississippi, Tennessee, and northern Georgia (Amann, I, 226).

the forces of Gen. [Green Clay] Smith too strong to be dispersed, I concluded to drive in his pickets and engage his attention until I could remove all the wagons along my route."[2] Being chased for eight miles probably engaged the Yankees' attention differently than Scott intended. He apparently overestimated the strength of General Green Clay Smith's force. The Ninth Pennsylvania appears to have been the only regiment at Crab Orchard.

Although the men of the Ninth Pennsylvania had "nothing to eat but green corn and our horses almost starving," they rode toward Mount Vernon at full gallop on August 23. They found "the rebels had left there   then we received a dispatch that the rebels were surrounding us   we then started back for Crab Orchard." That night, the Ninth retired to Lancaster; and on the following day, they moved to Hickman's bridge on the Kentucky River. "Here was the first time [August 25] our Horses were unsaddled since we left Leabonon [August 18]," wrote William Thomas. They saddled up again that evening and remained ready to mount all night.

While the Pennsylvanians were scouting the enemy advance, Major General William Nelson arrived in Kentucky from Buell's army to try to defend the state. As Buell did not send any soldiers along, Nelson had to try to do the job with the few troops then in Kentucky and those he could get from Indiana and Ohio. Major General Horatio G. Wright, headquartered in Cincinnati, had nominal command of the Kentucky theater; and Nelson's arrival resulted in telegrams to Washington to determine who was senior officer. Wright was told that he was; and he agreed that Nelson would have the field command, an arrangement agreeable to Nelson, who was more fighter than administrator.[3]

One of Nelson's first moves was to appoint Brigadier General James S. Jackson as Chief of Cavalry. Nelson's orders to Jackson read:

> You will proceed to Nicholasville and take command of [Colonel Richard T.] Jacob's Ninth Kentucky Cavalry and go thence to Hickman's Bridge and take command of the Ninth Pennsylvania Cavalry, commanded by Colonel Williams. You will then take position on the flanks of the enemy

[2] O. R., Ser. 1, XVI, pt. 1, p. 885.

[3] Maj. Gen. Wright was designated commander of the Department of the Ohio; Maj. Gen. Nelson, whose commission was dated one day earlier than Wright's, was named commander of the Army of Kentucky (McDowell, p. 78; Amann, II, 9).

and observe his movements. You will be very cautious. Colonel Jacob's regiment is just recruited, and you must not risk an engagement unless the chances are in your favor. You will from time to time send me such information as may be obtained.[4]

On August 26, Jackson's cavalry marched. William Thomas wrote, "We started off again in the morning   Gen Smith left us and Gen Jackson Took command of us   Jacobs Ky Cavalry Joined us   Marched back to Lancaster."

Jackson's little brigade continued on to Crab Orchard, and his scouts rode ahead to Mount Vernon and as far away as the Big Hill. William Thomas spent the night of August 27 as a picket on the Somerset road. From the positions occupied by scouts, all roads along which the enemy were moving were under observation. The situation was dangerous for such a small force. At the base camp in Crab Orchard, Jackson ordered the men to form a line-of-battle every morning at three o'clock. Soon the entire enemy army had moved past, leaving Jackson's cavalrymen behind. However, Jackson's men had observed well, and he reported the enemy numbers accurately. He reported later:

> I ascertained distinctly at 9 P.M. on Thursday, August 28, the actual force of the enemy, and dispatched the same to you [Nelson] at Richmond by a reliable courier. Knowing the force of the enemy as I did, you may be satisfied that I was astounded at receiving from you the following dispatch, dated Saturday, August 30, at 1:30 P.M.:
> 'They are fighting at Richmond. Proceed there at once.'[5]

General Jackson had good reason to be astounded. Brigadier General Mahlon D. Manson was in command of about 7,000 Union soldiers at Richmond. The troops were nearly all new regiments from Indiana and Ohio. Nelson had ordered Manson to avoid an engagement and to fall back on Lancaster at the approach of heavy enemy forces. Nelson planned to combine Manson's soldiers with other troops he was assembling and to take position along the Palisades of the Kentucky River. This deep gorge was a line that could be defended with a good chance of success by newly recruited soldiers. However, instead of avoiding an encounter with the enemy as he had been ordered, Manson actually marched his 7,000 inexperienced soldiers five miles south of

4 O. R., Ser. 1, XVI, pt. 1, p. 885.
5 *Ibid.*

Richmond to the vicinity of Mt. Zion Church to fight Kirby Smith's 20,000 veterans.[6]

The Federal force was quickly routed when the more numerous and experienced enemy flanked both ends of the line. General Nelson arrived on the field after the stampede began and was able to rally about 2,000 of the fleeing troops. These stood for about three rounds and then, assaulted from front and flank, they also broke and ran. Nelson was wounded but did manage to slip through the Confederate cavalry that had reached the rear to make his escape. The reported Union losses were 5,000, of whom more than 4,000 were prisoners.[7] The remainder of the force became fugitives, hiding in the woods or attempting to make their way back to Lexington. As usual with inexperienced soldiers in a rout, most of the fugitives threw their arms away.

Jackson's cavalry brigade began marching toward Richmond as soon as he received Nelson's order. When fourteen miles from Richmond, Jackson heard reports of the disaster. However, he continued on toward the town. When six miles away, he learned the full extent of the rout. General Jackson "determined to pass around the town and fall in with your [Nelson's] command on the road to Lexington."[8] The danger of such a march was fully appreciated. Six men of Company B, Ninth Pennsylvania, who had been arrested that morning for falling asleep while on picket duty, were released and had their arms returned.

It was dark when the cavalrymen began to ride around the town and battlefield. "passed through feilds and Hollows all night   passed within 3 miles of Richmond   we passed through the rebel pickets," wrote William Thomas. Probably the enemy pickets thought the column of horsemen coming from the south was Confederate cavalry and allowed them to pass unchallenged. William Thomas recorded the only casualty when he wrote, "Phillip Messner of our co was shot dead by Accident   a carbine in the Hands of Samuel Harper discharged and shot Him Through the Head   two of our men Left back to bury Phillip."[9]

General Jackson reported that the brigade reached the Lexington

6 *Ibid.*, pp. 908–17.
7 *Ibid.*; Cist, pp. 52–55.
8 O. R., Ser. 1, XVI, pt. 1, p. 910.
9 Phillip Messner is buried in the National Cemetery, Lexington, Ky., Circle 8, grave 84 (Bates, *Pennsylvania Volunteers*, III, 248).

road at 4:30 A.M. on August 31 and "halted at the farm of Major Gen. C. M. Clay."[10] At 7:30 A.M., General Jackson saw enemy cavalry, infantry, and artillery moving up roads on both sides of the Clay farm. He ordered his weary troopers to remount and take up their march once more. They crossed the Kentucky River at Jack's Ferry and then rode over to the Clay's Ferry road, coming into it ahead of the Confederate column.[11] On this march, William Thomas observed, "we found our men scattered through the woods." These were the fugitives from the battle. Many fell in behind the column of cavalrymen and, thus, made their way to Lexington.

On the road to Lexington, the Union force was strengthened. The cavalry met the Fifty-second Ohio Infantry, which had not been in the battle.[12] The infantrymen, the stragglers, and most of the cavalry continued on toward Lexington. However, part of the cavalry still had work to do. William Thomas reported, "we went out towards the Enemey to reconoiter   we came to their front at the Ky river when the rain Commenced to pour down in Torrents   we then turned Back toward Lexington   arrived there at night   Men and Horses had nothing to eat but green corn all day   Marched about 60 miles."

On September 1, Thomas wrote, "Laid in the yard of Henry Clays residence today   got rations and forage again. Co A had a small skirmish with the Louisanna tigers [First Louisiana Cavalry].[13]

With General Nelson wounded and out of action, Major General Wright rushed to Lexington from his headquarters in Cincinnati on August 31 to see what might be done to stop the Confederate army. There was little that he could do. The only organized military forces in Lexington were six regiments of infantry and two of cavalry. About these troops, General Wright commented, "all new except the Ninth Pennsylvania Cavalry and much demoralized by the reverse that had

---

[10] Cassius Marcellus Clay, at whose farm the cavalry force halted, was the leading abolitionist of Kentucky. He was a candidate for vice-president at the 1860 Republican Convention. A staunch Lincoln supporter, Lincoln named him minister to Russia. For more information see William H. Townsend, "The Rage of the Aged Lion," *American Heritage*, X, No. 4 (June 1960), pp. 34–37, 93–94.

[11] O. R., Ser. 1, XVI, pt. 1, p. 910.

[12] *Ibid.*

[13] Henry Clay's home, Ashland, and its 20-acre yard has been preserved along with most of its original furnishings, by the Henry Clay Memorial Foundation.

been sustained." In addition to these organized troops, Wright found some 800 or 900 stragglers from the battle. These men were so completely demoralized that he ordered them to entrain for Covington, across the Ohio River from Cincinnati.[14]

Next, General Wright made the only practical decision to fit the circumstances. He ordered the organized units to retreat to Louisville. The Ninth Pennsylvania Cavalry, his only experienced soldiers, became the rear guard. On September 1, William Thomas wrote, "our whole army left in the evening towards Louisville and the soldiers are burning their knapsacks and lots of comissary stores burned so the rebels can not get them   marched all night reached Versailles in the morning   the enemy still fowling us."

On September 2 he continued, "the enemy captured company K of our regt out on picket at a bridge." When the campaign in Kentucky was over the captured men were exchanged and returned to the regiment.

On the same day Thomas reported, "Started Early and marched to Frankfort   our soldiers are suffering very much For want of water along the road   a great many gave out with the heat   our regt are rear gaurd to Nelsons forces." The late summer and early fall of 1862 were exceptionally hot and dry, and the soldiers of both armies suffered in this and the subsequent campaigns. Neither Thomas nor the officers commented about what the rear guard was able to do for the men who passed out on the march. Probably all they could do was to leave them to the care of the enemy.

The Federal force evacuated Frankfort on the third, and the Confederate cavalry moved in. Colonel Scott exulted, "[We] moved to Frankfort and hoisted the battle flag of the First Louisiana Cavalry on the Capitol of the State, while the rear guard of the enemy were quiet spectators from the opposite hills."[15] With the infantry "moving as fast as they can go," the Union column marched nearly to Shelbyville that day. Along the way, the enemy sent in a flag of truce that "Capt Savage [Company B] Went out to receive." According to William Thomas, the Rebels wanted a prisoner exchange but "our gen refused."

14 O. R., Ser. 1, XVI, pt. 1, p. 907.
15 *Ibid.*, pp. 938–39.

On September 4, the most severe skirmish of the retreat took place. Colonel Scott reported that he attacked at sunrise and drove the Union rear guard through Shelbyville and then burned the bridges west of the town.[16] Other reports indicate that this fight was not as simple a matter as Colonel Scott claimed. These reports tell that the Ninth Pennsylvania whipped the First Louisiana here, and that 27 Rebels were killed and 44 captured.[17] These numbers represent more than Scott admitted for the whole campaign. Of the part of the action William Thomas saw, he reported, "Started early in the morning the rebels came on the right of us and fired four shells after us Some passed over us we turned back and made a charge through Shellbyville and drove them back Lieut Smith [George Smith, Co. D] took two prisoners."

At Shelbyville the Confederates gave up the pursuit of the Federal column because General Kirby Smith had been ordered to wait until Bragg's army arrived before moving on Louisville. On the fifth of September, the weary Union soldiers marched through Middletown and into Louisville. Thomas commented on the hardships of the march, "Our soldiers are suffering very much for want of water along the road and a great many gave out with the Heat." Duty improved for Thomas the next day. "went on gaurd at the private residence of Wm Thompson Was treated kindly by them great difficulty to keep the soldiers away from the fruit."

General Smith's Confederate army did not follow Scott's cavalry toward Louisville. Smith sent a part of his army toward Cincinnati as a diversion that did succeed in drawing some Federal troops from Louisville. Most of Smith's army remained in the bluegrass region for a few weeks, waiting for General Braxton Bragg's army to arrive in Kentucky.

This army, 28,000 strong, left Chattanooga on August 28.[18] Bragg's army threatened Nashville as well as Kentucky, and Union General Don Carlos Buell first pulled his army together to defend Nashville. He did not start marching toward Louisville until September 10, when

---

[16] *Ibid.*

[17] Capt. George W. Skinner, ed. and comp., *Pennsylvania at Chickamauga and Chattanooga: Ceremonies at the Dedication of the Monuments* (Harrisburg: Wm. Stanley Ray—State Printer, 1897), p. 339.

[18] McDowell, p. 80.

the Confederate army was definitely committed to the march into Kentucky. The Confederate advance had crossed the Kentucky line on September 5.[19]

General Bragg's principal forces reached Glasgow on September 14 but were delayed at Munfordville by 4,000 men commanded by Colonel John Wilder, who delayed surrendering until after Bragg had given him a tour of the Confederate lines.[20] On September 17, when Wilder surrendered, Buell's army was just entering Bowling Green, forty miles southwest. By pushing hard, Bragg could have reached Louisville before Buell was within striking distance.

After capturing Munfordville, the Confederate army began marching north on the Elizabethtown road. Two days after the Confederates had left Munfordville, the Union army began to pass through. They followed the same road out of town that the Confederates had taken.

As Bragg's army marched closer to Louisville, the tension in the city mounted. Louisville was a Union city, more Midwestern than Southern in commercial ties and sentiment. The people became even more pro-Union when word reached Louisville that the Confederates planned to burn the place to the ground. When the Federal command called on the citizens, they willingly enrolled in home guard companies, began to drill, and worked on new fortifications on the edge of town.[21]

At first, the citizens thought they would have to defend the city almost unaided. The only troops in town were those who had retreated from Lexington and some new regiments from Indiana. The first veterans to arrive from Grant's army were sent on to Cincinnati because Kirby Smith's army near Covington convinced General Wright that Cincinnati was endangered.[22]

Much of the responsibility for scouting and observing the roads south of Louisville logically fell onto the Ninth Pennsylvania. On September 8, they marched south on the Bardstown road and rode through Bardstown, Boston, and Lebanon Junction. At this latter place they met their own teams, wagons, and equipment coming from Lebanon. When they returned to Louisville, they noticed that the whole army, such as it

19 Cist, pp. 55–59; McDowell, p. 82.
20 Cist, pp. 57–59.
21 McDowell, pp. 85–89.
22 *Ibid.*, p. 82.

was, had changed position in order to guard against both Bragg's on-coming army and Smith's stationary one. A few more soldiers had come into town.

To improve the morale of the Louisville citizens, the Federal command decided to parade their strength on September 16. William Thomas wrote, "Struck tents and loaded our wagons for inspection and then marched out to Broadway in Louisville   We were inspected by Gen Nelson   Jackson   Terrill   We then paraded through the streets of Louisville And a great many soldiers gave out with the Heat and some died   Gen Jackson tried to drive Some of the poor boys into the ranks that gave out   I seen Him Strike one poor fellow with His sabre"[23]

On September 18, Thomas reported, "Great forse Gathering here." The next day he wrote, "a great many troops arrived by steamboat." Bragg was getting close when the Ninth rode south again on the twenty-second. This time they burned the bridges across Salt River and Floyds Fork between Louisville and Bardstown. The destruction of the Salt River bridge was reported as decisive in halting the Confederate army.[24]

On the next day, the Ninth returned to Louisville, and Thomas wrote, "when we came to Louisville it was All Excitement and Bustle and preperation for a Battle   all the women and children are gone across the Ohio river for safety   we are camped in a woods where the infantry are busy cutting trees across the road and Digging Entrench-ments   Bragg and His whole forse is advancing on Louisville"

The Confederate army had turned eastward before reaching Eliza-bethtown and marched to Bardstown. Here they stopped and General Bragg busied himself with political instead of military activities. He issued proclamations calling upon the states of the Northwest to drop out of the war. He threatened invasion of those states if they continued the war. He took steps to establish a Confederate government in Kentucky. Also, finding that the Kentuckians did not volunteer for the Confederate service, he instituted a draft.[25]

23 The generals were William Nelson, James S. Jackson, and William R. Terrill.
24 Guernsey and Alden, p. 311.
25 Hambleton Tapp, "The Road Back," a reprint from *The Civil War in Kentucky*, by the *Courier-Journal* (Louisville), Nov. 20, 1960; McDowell, pp. 88–89; Guernsey and Alden, p. 312.

When Bragg reached Bardstown, he was closer to Louisville than was Buell's army. Buell did not follow Bragg's army toward Bardstown. Instead, he marched through Elizabethtown and continued on the western route. By getting into Louisville before Bragg made a move, Buell could regain the initiative. Once his army was in Louisville, it would be Buell who could choose the time and place for the next move of the game. Thus, William Thomas's diary entry of September 24 has historical significance:

> We were routed out at 2 o clock in the morning and started out on a scout we marched out on the Elizabethville pike   we were ordered to draw sabers   Before we were outside the pickets another Officer orders us to return sabers and drag pistols and another officer Losses His Hat and another officer detains the whole column till He gets Sober   we heard the rebels were at Bardstown   we started at daylight and marched along the pike a few miles   we then stopped to feed where the 2d Mich Cav passed us the advance of Buehl army

Behind the Michigan cavalrymen came Major General Thomas L. Crittenden's corps and then the rest of the Union army. By September 28, the entire army had marched into Louisville. Buell's men had marched 68 miles during the final three days of the campaign while Bragg sat at Bardstown.[26] With the arrival of the big, veteran army, Louisville was saved. The women and children returned to their homes from their temporary refuges in Indiana, and the men of the town went back to their civilian pursuits.

26 McDowell, p. 89.

X

"This is a Part Left Out of the History of Perryville"

A cavalry Reconnossens with the 9th Pennsylvania Cavalry towards Perryville under comand of Liutenent Cornel James on the left of the Pike on the morning of the Battle in order to find out their Position   Met the enimy with a pies of artilry   they opened fire on uss with shells   the first shell went beyond uss and exploded   the second one busted over uss dooing some damage   our Captens horse was struck in the rump with one pies of shell   We were so near the artilry that we could have shot their guners with our Navy revolvers Cornel James in his cool way gave the comand buy fours right about weel march – – steady boys steady   We fell back under the fire of their artilry   this was the first shot fired from the artilry the day of the Battle of Perryville   then we went to our left and suported a batry of artilry til the infantry got up   w[h]en we were relieved the rebel line was coming in ful view against McKooks devition Cornelius Baker of Co C 9th Penn Cavalry was present to this

The usual story of the Battle of Perryville not only omits the incident mentioned by Cornelius Baker but ignores completely the very important actions of Captain Ebenezer Gay's little cavalry brigade both before and during the battle. This unit consisted of about 950 experienced troopers of the Ninth Pennsylvania and Second Michigan Regiments and 500 new soldiers of the Ninth Kentucky Cavalry.[1] In addition to drawing the first artillery fire, this force suffered the first casualties of the battle. Of more importance were three actions by Gay's cavalry that influenced the battle.

1 O. R., Ser. 1, XVI, pt. 1, p. 1037.

First, Gay's cavalrymen, who were skirmishing in the advance of the Federal corps marching eastward on the Springfield-Perryville road, exerted such pressure on the enemy rear guard on October 7 that the Confederates were forced to stand at Perryville instead of in the Harrodsburg area as Confederate General Braxton Bragg had planned.

Second, during the evening of October 7, the cavalry succeeded in crossing Doctors Fork, a small stream with some pools of water in its otherwise dry bed. By occupying this position, the cavalry assured a water supply for the men and animals behind them.

Third, during the morning of October 8, Gay's cavalrymen occupied the position that Confederate Major General William J. Hardee[2] called the key to the field. This was the knoll on which the Russell house stood.[3] The cavalry held this position until Major General Alexander McD. McCook's corps, marching southeast from Mackville, was able to form beside the part of the Federal army already in action along the Springfield road.

When Captain Gay was appointed chief of cavalry in Kentucky during late September 1862, he found that he had two regiments that "can be depended upon." These were the Ninth Pennsylvania, with about 600 men on duty, and the Second Michigan, with 350 effective men. Also under Captain Gay's command were the Sixth, Seventh, Ninth, and Eleventh Kentucky and the Fourth Indiana, but all were "perfectly raw." Gay was not even sure of the strength of these regiments, and when he asked for morning reports, found that "Some of the regiments do not know what a morning report is, never having heard of such a thing, or a roll call."[4] The Ninth Kentucky had received some on-the-job training when they accompanied the Ninth Pennsylvania during that regiment's scout of Kirby Smith's army and while they protected the column of untrained soldiers during the retreat to Louisville that followed the Union debacle at Richmond.

At the start of the Perryville campaign, the Pennsylvania troopers were so deficient in arms that, in William Thomas's words, they "got

---

[2] Hardee commanded the left wing of Bragg's Army of the Mississippi (Amann, I, p. 273).

[3] McDowell, p. 111, and other sources locate Loomis's battery at the Russell house.

[4] O. R., Ser. 1, XVI, pt. 2, p. 552.

loaned of the 9 Ky carbines." There is no record of how many carbines were borrowed. The Ninth Pennsylvania had only forty-one Sharps and thirteen Maynard carbines of their own at the time.[5] Even with the borrowed weapons, most of the men had only revolvers and sabers for the work ahead. The Second Michigan, by contrast, was well armed. They were equipped with five-shot Colt carbines, one of the first repeating rifles.[6]

During the Perryville campaign, the Ninth Pennsylvania was commanded by Lieutenant Colonel James. Colonel Williams had resigned just before the campaign because, according to his biographer, of "a question of rank."[7] Probably the colonel could not understand the distinction between Regular Army and volunteer rank that made it possible for a captain to be named brigade commander when colonels were available.

While Union General Don Carlos Buell was reorganizing his army to incorporate the new soldiers recently arrived in Louisville with his veterans, Confederate General Bragg left his army at Bardstown and went to Frankfort to supervise the installation of a Confederate state government and the inauguration of a Rebel governor. The inaugural ceremony on October 4 was interrupted by Federal shells landing in the town. These shells were fired by the advance of Brigadier General Joshua Sill's division. General Buell had sent Sill's column toward Frankfort as a diversion. This move fooled General Bragg so completely that he continued to look for the principal Union army to come through Frankfort during the time it was closing on Perryville far to the south.[8]

Some men of the Ninth Pennsylvania appear to have helped clear the road for the first part of Sill's march. On September 29, William Thomas wrote, "12 men out of our Company under Lieut [Owen B.] McKnight and 3 or 4 Ky cav regts along marched to midletown met the 2d Mich out on picket one of their men shot during the night we drove the rebels out of Middletown."

On October 1, while Sill was marching toward Frankfort, fifty-eight

---

[5] National Archives, Col. James to Gov. Curtin, Oct. 27, 1862, unbound papers in 9th Pa. Cav. records.
[6] O. R., Ser. 1, XX, pt. 1, p. 95; O. R., Ser. 1, XXIII, pt. 1, p. 181.
[7] *Commemorative Encyclopedia*, p. 244.
[8] McDowell, p. 109; Tapp, "The Road Back."

thousand Union soldiers began to march south from Louisville toward Bardstown. This army was divided into three corps marching on different roads. The routes followed would allow the entire army to converge on the Confederate army at Bardstown. Major General Alexander Mc-Cook's corps marched on the eastern Taylorsville road, Brigadier General Charles C. Gilbert's corps followed the western Shepherdsville road, and Major General Thomas L. Crittenden's corps went down the central Bardstown pike.[9]

William Thomas wrote that the cavalry rode through the fields beside the Taylorsville road because McCook's infantrymen filled the road. However, before the first day's march ended, the cavalry brigade was ahead of the infantry column.

On October 2, Gay's men led the advance toward Taylorsville and met the first enemy pickets near this town. After "skirmishing at every bend of the road" the Union troopers drove the Rebel force through Taylorsville. By the evening of October 3, three companies of the Ninth Pennsylvania and two companies of the Second Michigan had reached the outskirts of Bloomfield. Here the enemy made a stand. The Federals dismounted and fought until their ammunition was exhausted. Then they rode back to Taylorsville. William Thomas recorded that the expedition captured one man and killed a man and a horse at the cost of one horse killed.

Upon reaching Taylorsville at 9:00 P.M., the expeditionary force found the remainder of the cavalry brigade ready to march to Bloomfield. The returning troopers were given enough time to feed their horses and to cook their supper before riding back toward Bloomfield. When the Union cavalry charged into this town at daybreak, they found that the enemy had left. The cavalry brigade camped in Bloomfield for the rest of the day. They remained in this camp through October 5 and watched General McCook's corps march through town.

On October 5, William Thomas heard that "Bragg is drove out of Bardstown." Upon learning that the principal Union army was converging on him, Major General Leonidas Polk,[10] who had been left in

9 McDowell, pp. 107–108; Cist, pp. 61–62.

10 Polk commanded the right wing of Bragg's Army of the Mississippi (Amann, I, p. 330).

command of the Confederate army at Bardstown, requested permission and received a reluctant approval from Bragg to evacuate the position. Bragg, still being entertained by General Sill, thought the march toward Bardstown was a diversion. By October 4, most of the Confederate army had left Bardstown and was marching eastward on the macadam pike that ran through Springfield and Perryville.[11]

On October 6, Gay's cavalry marched over to this same road and joined Gilbert's Union corps at a place named Glennville. Soon Gay's cavalrymen were in the van of the column and were skirmishing with the enemy rear guard. William Thomas wrote, "Marched through Springfield in hot pursuit of the rebels   Had a skirmish in the evening and took some prisoners."

The three corps of Buell's Union army were now marching eastward on parallel roads. Gilbert's corps was following the Confederates along the Springfield pike. McCook's corps was marching on a road a few miles north that ran from Bloomfield to Mackville and Harrodsburg. Crittenden's corps was on a road to the south that passed through Lebanon and Perryville.[12] Only Gay's cavalry in the advance of Gilbert's corps was in contact with the enemy.

On October 7, William Thomas wrote, "had a small brush in the morning But the rebels Left   we then marched very slow and catious." By noon they had reached a point within three miles of Perryville. Here they encountered artillery fire. The Second Michigan was deployed as skirmishers, the Ninth Pennsylvania was sent into a gulley behind the Michiganders, and Captain Oscar Pinney's Fifth Wisconsin Battery was unlimbered behind the cavalry.[13] While shells passed overhead, the Pennsylvania troopers "dismounted and went to cracking walnuts." Soon Captain Pinney's artillery drove the enemy cavalry pickets from the crossing over Doctors Fork, and the Union cavalrymen occupied the stream bed. At this time, the advance regiments of Federal infantry were nearly three miles in the rear.

The pressure exerted on the Confederate rear during the afternoon by Gay's cavalry and the advanced position of the Union artillery

---

[11] Tapp, "The Road Back"; O. R., Ser. 1, XVI, pt. 1, p. 1120.
[12] Cist, pp. 61–62; O. R., Ser. 1, XVI, pt. 1, p. 1124.
[13] O. R., Ser. 1, XVI, pt. 1, pp. 1076–77.

caused General Hardee, commanding the Confederate rear guard, to realize that he could not get his slow-moving wagon train safely to Harrodsburg, encumbered as it was with plunder-filled wagons. Hardee determined to fight at Perryville and requested reinforcements from General Bragg.[14]

After the fighting died at dusk, one Bridgewater of Company B, Ninth Pennsylvania, volunteered to capture the battery that had been firing on the Union troopers.[15] He asked Captain Edward G. Savage for six men, but the captain refused him. However, a short while later Captain Ebenezer Gay sent a larger force to occupy the position. The men found that the enemy artillery had been withdrawn. This new cavalry position was within two miles of Perryville and east of Doctors Fork.[16]

Thus, Gay's men gave the Union army possession of the only water in the area. Because of this fact, the men and animals of Gilbert's corps were able to remain in the region and to fight a battle there the next day. During the night the Union commanders realized the importance of this advanced position and sent Colonel Daniel McCook's infantry brigade forward to make the water source secure. Captain Gay reported that the infantry reached his position at 3:00 A.M. McCook then advanced a skirmish line, and the cavalry pickets retired to the cavalry camp.[17]

At dawn on October 8, Gay's cavalrymen rode through McCook's skirmishers to resume the pursuit. They were greeted by a volley of gunfire from the left of the road when they were barely past the skirmish line. The Ninth Pennsylvania quickly formed into line on the left of the road, the Second Michigan went forward as dismounted skirmishers, and the Ninth Kentucky formed a reserve at the rear.[18]

The Second Michigan advanced into some woods, ran into a battle line of Confederate infantry, and were repulsed by a volley of musketry. Four Michigan men were killed, and two officers and eleven soldiers were wounded.[19] These were the first casualties of the battle. The Mich-

14 McDowell, pp. 109–10.
15 William Thomas made this reference to Bridgewater, who cannot be identified in company or regimental rolls.
16 O. R., Ser. 1, XVI, pt. 1, p. 1024.
17 *Ibid.*, pp. 1037–38.
18 *Ibid.*
19 *Ibid.*

igan troopers retreated a short distance and then gave the enemy, who charged after them, a demonstration of the superior fire power of the Colt carbines. "the rebels charged upon them 2 or 3 times," wrote William Thomas, "they broke their charge every time and the rebels were Obliged to fall back." The sector was then taken over by Brigadier General Phillip H. Sheridan's infantry division and became the scene of bitter fighting later in the day.

After this first skirmish, Captain Gay ordered the Ninth Pennsylvania to ride to the left through open fields in an effort to ascertain the position of the enemy batteries. After riding a quarter of a mile, they found the batteries in the manner related by Cornelius Baker in this chapter's opening quotation. Company C appears to have been in the van when the artillery first fired upon the troopers. Cornelius Baker said that the first shell landed behind him, while William Thomas wrote that it landed in front of him. Captain Gay immediately brought up his artillery, now Captain William Augustus Hotchkiss's Minnesota battery, and emplaced it opposite the enemy position. Hotchkiss's fire soon silenced the Rebel guns.

Seeing enemy batteries still farther to the left, Gay moved his small command to a more advanced position "near a fork of Chaplin Creek, placing my battery in position on a knoll near it and throwing out portions of the Ninth Pennsylvania and Second Michigan as skirmishers in advance." Hotchkiss's battery temporarily drove the enemy artillery and cavalry from a position opposite the knoll.[20]

The position occupied by the Federal cavalry and artillery was the most important ground on the field. The knoll on which the Russell house stood covered both the road from Mackville, down which General McCook's corps was marching toward Perryville, and the ford where this road crossed Doctors Fork. If the Union troopers had not occupied this position when they did, Confederate cavalry very likely would have; and with support from their infantry and artillery then enroute from Harrodsburg, the Confederates might have prevented the junction of the Union army.

Shortly after Hotchkiss's guns had driven the enemy from the opposite position, Gay observed great clouds of dust on the Harrodsburg

20 *Ibid.*

road and behind the enemy lines, which meant that heavy reinforcements would soon be threatening his small force. Also aware of McCook's approach, Gay sent a courier to Brigadier General Lovell Rousseau, commanding McCook's lead division, with a request for a regiment of infantry to help defend the artillery. Rousseau sent the Forty-second Indiana forward at double-quick time. He personally accompanied these reinforcements to Gay's position and found Hotchkiss dueling with three enemy batteries. Rousseau observed that Hotchkiss's brass guns were outranged by the enemy pieces and ordered two Parrott guns of Captain Cyrus O. Loomis's Michigan battery to hurry forward from his column. These heavy, rifled guns were emplaced near the Russell house and soon began to answer the Confederate artillery.[21]

This was a bad time for the cavalrymen on the skirmish line. "the shells and balls [were] flying over us like hail," wrote William Thomas. The Ninth Pennsylvania remained in their assigned position for three-quarters of an hour under the concentrated fire of three enemy batteries. For this unflinching stand, they were cited in General Buell's special orders issued after the battle.[22] Everyone did his duty. Even Chaplain McKinney received special mention in Captain Gay's report for serving throughout the battle as a voluntary aide.[23]

The cavalrymen got a respite when the remainder of Loomis's battery came up. The fire of these heavy guns drove the enemy infantry and artillery in disorder from their position. By noon, enough Union infantry had arrived on the field to relieve the troopers who had been in almost continuous action since dawn.[24] As Cornelius Baker mentioned, the cavalry witnessed the first Rebel assault wave advance against McCook's corps when they left the Russell house knoll.

This first Rebel charge struck the extreme left of General James J. Jackson's division that had formed on the left of Rousseau's division. Unfortunately, Jackson had placed Brigadier General William R. Terrill's brigade of new soldiers in an advanced position, with both flanks exposed, near the New Mackville road. Colonel John C. Starkweather's veteran brigade was placed in the rear as a reserve. The Confederates

21 O. R., Ser. 1, XVI, pt. 1, p. 1044.
22 Skinner, p. 339; Bates, *Pennsylvania Volunteers*, III, 235–36.
23 O. R., Ser. 1, XVI, pt. 1, p. 1038.
24 *Ibid.*, p. 1044.

ran over Terrill, breaking up his command and capturing six guns. Both
Jackson and Terrill were killed while trying to rally their men. Captain
Gay, seeing this disaster, sent a regiment of cavalry toward this position.
As he made no further reference to this force, Starkweather's veterans
probably had stopped the Rebel drive and stabilized the sector by the
time the troopers arrived. Following this first attack, William Thomas
observed that the Confederates "Are moving in line and getting Battries in Position on every Hill and the infantry in Every ravine."

The cavalry did not leave the field when relieved. Instead, they occupied the gap, about 400 yards wide, above the H. P. Bottom house
between Gilbert's and McCook's battle lines. From this position, Hotchkiss's guns continued to fire all afternoon at the attacking Rebels, and
the cavalrymen were called upon to repulse several attacks. General
Buell later admitted that the gap was too wide for the strength of the
holding force.[25]

During the afternoon, Thomas reported, "the conflict became feirse
the enemy charged our Battries several times but were repulsed every
Time   the fire grew Hotter and Hotter until rolls of musketry and
claps of thunder from every Hill resounds from the cannon and fill the
Air with Heat."

Late in the afternoon, the Confederates made their strongest attack
of the day. The assault struck the right of Rousseau's division, just to
the left of the cavalry, and very nearly broke the Union line. The Confederates drove Rousseau's men back beyond the Bottom house and off
the Russell house knoll to the ridge beyond the road. William Thomas
wrote, "At sunset the conflict became Firse and terible   the rebels
were routed on our right [along the Springfield road] but our left had
to fall back."

Seeing the danger next to him, Captain Gay moved his brigade
again. They rode to support the weakening Union line. However, before they reached the endangered position, infantry reinforcements
from Gilbert's corps arrived and stopped this final Rebel drive.[26] Before
the fighting ceased and darkness fell over the field, William Thomas ob-

25 *Ibid.*, pp. 1026, 1038.
26 *Ibid.*, p. 1038; McDowell, p. 115; Col. Michael Gooding with the 13th Brigade
were the reinforcements sent by General Gilbert.

served that "the Feilds and woods are strewn with dead Bodies Of Both parties." After dark, the cavalrymen retired a mile to camp and "On our road back we wittnessed the Suffering of the wounded and the dying and Doctors trying to do all they can for them   The ambulances are coming in all the time filled with wounded   we have to suffer considerable for want of water."

Neither side had fought the battle with their full strength. General Bragg had a large part of his army too far north of Harrodsburg, waiting for the Union army to come through Frankfort, to get them to Perryville in time to participate. Crittenden's corps of the Union army had marched several miles south of the Lebanon road to find water on the night before the battle and did not reach the field. A freak atmospheric condition had kept the sound of battle from Buell and his staff until late in the afternoon. Thus, the Union troops fought without a plan from the top.

Because the Confederates had been so near to success, the Union officers expected that the battle would be renewed the next day. However, Bragg decided otherwise, and his army withdrew during the night. Captain Gay's cavalry learned of this decision on the morning of the ninth. William Thomas wrote:

> we started out this morning to reconnoitre When we found that the rebels Had Left During the night   we came across the battrie on the left   6 guns   the rebels were unable to take it Along   we sent them back to the rear   we marched over the Battle feild   It was a Horible sight   For 4 miles the feilds are strewn with the dead of both parties   some are torn to pices and Some in the dying agonies of death   the Ambulance are unable to take all the Wounded   we marched on and came to a house w[h]ere the rebels had their wounded And seen their suffering   A large pile of Legs and arms are Laying around That the Rebel doctors cut off and ampupate their limbs   The rebels Stripped our dead bodies of all their boots and shoes during the night and Some of their Clothes   we captured in the fight about 3000 stand of arms   The arms Have the English Stamp Upon them and we found a great many Catridges from Birminham England   The arms the rebels could not take along gathered in the feild.

The Union army did not begin to pursue the retreating Confederates promptly, and this was one reason why General Buell was removed from his command at the end of the campaign. However, on October 11 Gay's cavalrymen rode to Harrodsburg, capturing 873 stragglers along the way. They found that "Every house we passed on the road is turned into a hospital and full of wounded rebels   in Harrodsburg Here there are about 2000 wounded Rebels." The troopers pursued as far as Crab Orchard, having a few skirmishes with the rear guard and continuing to pick up stragglers. They were unable to go farther. General W. S. "Sooey" Smith, in the advance of Buell's infantry column, reported the location of Kirby Smith's camp on October 17 and observed, "If Gay could have crossed over this morning into that road, he might have intercepted stragglers, etc. but his horses were suffering to an extent that would not permit such movement, and there is no forage in that direction."[27]

The Confederate army marched out of Kentucky, never to return. The major effort to add this state to the Confederacy ended in failure. General Bragg complained bitterly of the few enlistments obtained during his army's occupation. The ten thousand stands of arms he had hauled from Tennessee to arm anticipated recruits had to be carried south again.

During the retreat, many Rebels deserted. While encamped at Crab Orchard, William Thomas wrote, "met a great many prisoners of Bragg's army going to Lancaster."

On October 19, the troopers were routed out of camp and began riding hard toward the west. John Hunt Morgan was raiding the L & N Railroad again, it was rumored. The cavalry passed through Perryville and across the battlefield during the night. "Stenching smell," reported William Thomas. At Perryville the Fourth Michigan and First Ohio Cavalry Regiments joined the column and all rode hard to New Market. Here they learned that the reported raid was just a false alarm.

The Ninth Pennsylvania was split temporarily. Four companies were sent to Somerset to protect the citizens on election day. Six companies were assigned to escort Major General George H. Thomas to Cave City. During the march, William Thomas wrote, "We passed a lot of Sutlers today   Some of their teams Broke down   Halted awhile to help releive Them of part of their load." General Thomas was delivered safely to Cave City, and the cavalry campaign ended.[28]

[27] O. R., Ser. 1, XVI, pt. 1, p. 1140.
[28] Gen. Thomas was second in command of the Army of the Ohio. He had been offered full command before the Battle of Perryville, but he had recommended that Buell be retained.

The Ninth was encamped at New Haven, Kentucky, by the middle of November. The men must have thought that they had earned a chance to relax because William Thomas reported:

> the officers had a dance at Head Quarter   Capt Gays tent   dancing and Hollering all Night   all drunk as fools   jumping about and Hollering i am a Rooster i am a turkey   Hoffman came in the tent about 2 o.clock in the morning from town and commenced jumping about the tent and Hollering i am a rooster too.

XI

First Yankee Cavalry Raid

The daring operations and brilliant achievements of General Carter and his command are without a parallel in the history of the war and deserve the thanks of the country. This expedition has proved the capacity of our cavalry for bold and dashing movements which I doubt not will be imitated by others.[1]

The complimentary telegram from General in Chief Henry W. Halleck was dispatched to Major General Horatio Wright on January 9, 1863, when news of the successful conclusion of a cavalry expedition known as Carter's Raid arrived in Washington. This expedition into East Tennessee by a small force of Pennsylvania, Michigan, and Ohio troopers was the first raid by Federal cavalry into Confederate territory.

During 1862, the initiative in making rapid and daring raids behind the opposing armies in the West remained with John Hunt Morgan, Nathan Bedford Forrest, Joseph Wheeler, and other Confederate cavalry leaders. In general, the Union cavalry was improperly used. Too often the cavalry regiments had been split into small units acting as scouts for infantry, as garrison troops, and as guards at railroad bridges. Carter's Raid demonstrated a better use of mounted troops, and as General Halleck suggested, the idea was imitated and increasingly devastating cavalry raids behind Confederate lines were made as the war progressed.

Major General Gordon Granger,[2] who had direct responsibility for planning and organizing the raid, characterized it as one of the most

[1] O. R., Ser. 1, XX, pt. 1, p. 89.
[2] Then in command of the Army of Kentucky, Granger formerly had been captain of the Third U. S. Cavalry and colonel of the Second Michigan Cavalry. Amann, II, 30.

hazardous and daring raids of the war and gave the almost impractical nature of the country, the length of the route, and inclement season as the reasons. Success was achieved only because of surprise, rapidity of movement, endurance, and luck. Cornelius Baker and William Thomas were among the 430 men of the Ninth Pennsylvania who made the raid. They were accompanied by the Second Michigan, with 320 men, and the Seventh Ohio, with 230 men.[3]

Field leadership of the small cavalry force was assigned to Brigadier General Samuel Powhatan Carter of East Tennessee. Carter was a lieutenant in the Navy who had turned soldier for the duration.[4]

President Lincoln had profound sympathy for the loyal people of East Tennessee, which was a salient of pro-Union sentiment thrust into the heart of the Confederacy. An army of occupation and martial law was required to prevent the area from seceding from the secessionist government.[5] Lincoln had frequently expressed a wish that a Union army occupy the region. However, events in Kentucky and Middle Tennessee and the logistic difficulty of marching and supplying an army through the wilderness of eastern Kentucky had prevented serious consideration of such a move in 1862.[6] Possibly, a part of the reason for Carter's Raid was to let the President know that his desires were being considered by the generals.

The region was of great military importance. The East Tennessee and Virginia Railroad ran through it; and this line, connecting Richmond with Knoxville and Chattanooga, was the cord that tied together the Confederate armies in the east and west. It was the only convenient route by which equipment from the arsenals of Virginia could move to the Army of Tennessee and by which food from the Southwest could reach the Army of Northern Virginia. At the time the raid was made, a break in the line might influence the outcome of the battle that was impending in Middle Tennessee between Major General William S. Rosecrans's Union Army of the Cumberland and General Braxton Bragg's

3 O. R., Ser. 1, XX, pt. 1, pp. 88–89.

4 Campbell H. Brown, "Carter's East Tennessee Raid," *Tennessee Historical Quarterly*, XXII, No. 1 (Mar. 1963), p. 66.

5 Digby Gordon Seymour, *Divided Loyalties* (Knoxville: The University of Tennessee Press, 1963), pp. 24–37; O. R., Ser. 1, X, pt. 2, pp. 424, 448.

6 Seymour, pp. 10, 18; Brown, p. 81.

Confederate Army of Tennessee.[7] The Battle of Stones River did, in fact, begin the day after Carter's men succeeded in breaking the rail line. General Carter had hoped to get his expedition on the way by November 27.[8] However, both the Ninth Pennsylvania and Second Michigan Regiments were held in camp at Lebanon, Kentucky, because of rumors that Morgan was about to make another raid into that state.[9] The rumors were quite believable and, on this same date, William Thomas wrote, "the assembly Blowed during the night and our regt Left and the 2d Mich Towards Campellsville   Expecting Morgan again." Morgan didn't come but the cavalrymen were held at Lebanon until December 6.

While waiting, both regiments received a howitzer. Thomas spent a day as a military policeman. "Had my Horse sadled all day to catch soldiers that were shooting around camp," he wrote. During a heavy snow on December 5, "a fatal accident happened in Co D   A tree fell down on one of the tents and killed one Man and wounded another."

The next morning, the Ninth Pennsylvania and Second Michigan left Lebanon in the bitter cold that followed the snow. That day they marched thirty-three miles to Harrodsburg, passing over the Perryville Battlefield once again. On December 7 they "passed through a splendid Shaker town [Pleasant Hill] much larger than the other we passed."[10]

East of Pleasant Hill, the soldiers "forded the Ky river at Brooklyn [Brooklin]   Ferried the teams across on a flat   High Hills [Palisades] at the Ky river and Beautiful Senery   good pike road all the way." That evening they reached Nicholasville and "fixed a great camp." Nicholasville was the headquarters of General Granger, and several infantry regiments also were encamped there. This town, on the rail line running southwest from Lexington, was a logical supply point for marches toward the southeast.

Now a raid by Nathan Bedford Forrest delayed the expedition a few

---

[7] General Rosecrans succeeded Buell in command of the army in Middle Kentucky and Tennessee. The army was reorganized and renamed the Army of the Cumberland.

[8] O. R., Ser. 1, XX, pt. 1, pp. 89–92.

[9] *Ibid.*, pt. 2, pp. 126–27.

[10] The Pleasant Hill Shakertown, composed of 21 buildings, is owned, preserved, and maintained by Shakertown at Pleasant Hill, Kentucky, Inc. During the past few years, buildings have been restored to create a historic tourist attraction.

more days.[11] The delay gave the troopers a chance to enjoy life in their new camp. "Fine country all around Here," reported William Thomas. "after Squirells the trees are running full and the boys are after them." They also had "a regular wash day" and, after dress parade on Sunday, "we formed a Hollow Square and Had preaching once Again from our worthy Chaplain."

The raid began officially on December 20 when the troopers of the Ninth Pennsylvania and Second Michigan left Nicholasville. Because they were marching under sealed orders, the men had no idea of the destination or purpose of the march. They knew it would be a long, hard march because they had been ordered to carry eleven days rations and 100 rounds of ammunition. Even more indicative that this would be a tough campaign was an order to strike tents and leave them behind,[12] which meant sleeping in the open during winter weather. A few wagons were brought along to carry rations. They also hauled their howitzers along over "rough roads and rough country" to their first night's camp at Kirksville. The next day they marched to the foot of Big Hill, which divides mountainous southeastern Kentucky from the bluegrass region. At Big Hill the troopers could deduce that their march would be through the mountains. They met forage wagons and a long train of pack mules.

William Thomas said that he had to walk up the Big Hill the next morning, indicating that the soldiers led their horses up this long, steep hill. The column reached McKee on December 22. William Thomas described the town: "it is right in the mountains county seat there is a court House and jail and tavern and one or two Houses." Here they "Met a company of Tennessee Refugees Going to richmond Ky to get armed." General Carter and his staff, headed by a Colonel C. J. Walker, also joined the column here.[13] From the Tennessee fugitives, Carter received information about Confederate troop dispositions in his target area.[14]

McKee was as far as the wagons could go at this late season, and the troopers spent December 23 transferring supplies and provisions from

---

[11] O. R., Ser. 1, XX, pt. 2, pp. 126–27.
[12] *Ibid.*, pt. 1, pp. 89–92.
[13] Brown, p. 68.
[14] O. R., Ser. 1, XX, pt. 1, pp. 89–92.

them to the pack mules. The wagons and the howitzers, that had been hauled this far at considerable effort, were sent back to Nicholasville. Here, too, the cold weather of the past several days changed. For the next few days the expedition had to march and camp in heavy rains. On December 24, they marched toward Manchester, crossed "wite Oak Hill," and camped on a hill ten miles north of that town.

Christmas was not a holiday. The column "marched through mountains and hollows all day." In the evening, they halted for a while at Goose Creek where the battalion of the Seventh Ohio joined them. The total of 980 men was a disappointment to General Carter. He had hoped for a force large enough to divide so he could strike the railroad at two points 100 miles apart and destroy the entire railroad in between by having the two sections march toward each other.[15] He now planned to accomplish what he could with one small force. After the pause at Goose Creek, the column marched on to the Red Bird River where they camped for the night.

On December 26, the column marched up the Red Bird valley, which was then and remains today one of the poorest and most desolate areas in the country. In the 1860's there were very few people in the valley and they lived in remote, widely scattered cabins. The soldiers marched on a trail along the riverbank, crossing the stream forty-seven times on the twenty-sixth. They stopped in the evening to feed their horses and then continued on to a place called Ascher's where they camped in the woods beside the river. Most of the next day was used reaching the head of the valley. In the evening, the column crossed Pine Mountain, marching single file along an old Indian trail, and went down into the river valley a short distance east of the present town of Pineville. They camped at midnight on Poor Fork of the Cumberland.

During the night, the rain that had been their constant companion from McKee ended, and the weather again turned cold. On December 28, the column struggled up Poor Fork. Again, there was only a trail to follow. Late in the afternoon, they reached the foot of Cumberland Mountain below Crank's Gap, about twelve miles southwest of Harlan. Here the horses were given a full feed, and the men had their last hot meal for several days. Ammunition and three days' food rations were

15 *Ibid.*

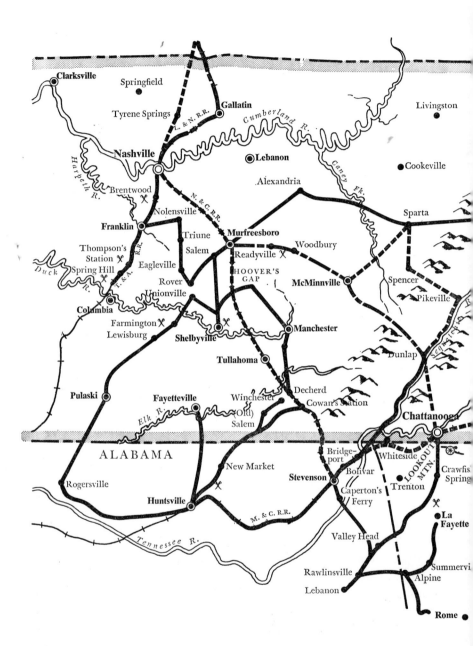

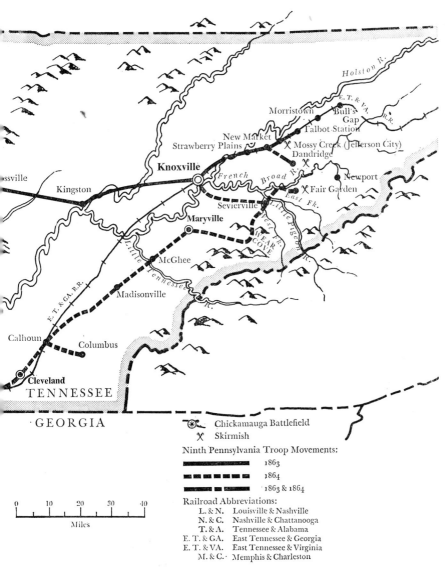

Holston R.

Morristown
Bull's
Gap
E. T. & VA.
R.R.
Talbot Station
New Market
Strawberry Plains
Mossy Creek (Jefferson City)
Dandridge
Knoxville
French Broad R.
Newport
ssville
Kingston
East Fk.
Fair Garden
Sevierville
Little Pigeon R.
Maryville
West Fk.
CADE'S
COVE
McGhee
Little Tennessee R.
Madisonville
E. T. & GA. R.R.
Calhoun
Columbus
Cleveland
TENNESSEE
GEORGIA

⊕ Chickamauga Battlefield
X Skirmish
Ninth Pennsylvania Troop Movements:
▬▬▬▬ 1863
▬ ▬ ▬ ▬ 1864
▬ ▬ ▬ ▬ 1863 & 1864
Railroad Abbreviations:
L. & N.   Louisville & Nashville
N. & C.   Nashville & Chattanooga
T. & A.   Tennessee & Alabama
E. T. & GA.   East Tennessee & Georgia
E. T. & VA.   East Tennessee & Virginia
M. & C.   Memphis & Charleston

0   10   20   30   40
Miles

FIGHTING IN TENNESSEE

transferred from the mules to the cavalrymen's saddlebags. The men were ordered to live on half rations for the next six days. A day's grain ration, nine pounds of corn and oats for the horses[16] or "two feeds" as the soldiers expressed it, was also loaded on the cavalry horses. The mule train was sent back to civilization with the detachment of Kentucky home guards that had accompanied the expedition to this point.

In the afternoon, the troopers began to ride single file up the mountain. The head of the column reached the summit at sunset. Another four hours was required to make the treacherous descent, but by ten o'clock the entire force had reached the foot of the mountain. Now they began to move faster, even risking travel at full gallop in the darkness. They skirted Jonesville, Virginia, at the foot of the mountain, because Carter had been told that there were 400 enemy troops in the town. Neither did he want his column to be seen. Therefore, they rode down Cove Creek and passed through Powell Valley five miles east of Jonesville. By daylight, the raiders were encamped on Wallen Ridge near Stickleyville, twenty-two miles from the foot of Cumberland Mountain.[17]

Carter did not want his men to go into Stickleyville but did not issue orders to prevent their going. He thought that the men would be too tired for sightseeing after an all-day and all-night march. However, there were some who were curious to see what a Rebel town looked like, and they walked into the town. These soldiers were observed from a distance by a group of partisan rangers. This Rebel party of twenty-four men, also curious, followed the Federals back to camp. The rangers were promptly arrested but where released as soon as they had signed parole papers.[18]

After the two hours delay that was necessary to feed the horses, Carter's column moved on once more. Carter wrote that they had been seen but that the Rebels did not credit the reports of the observers. Consequently, the raiders were not molested while they rode across Powell Mountain. They reached Pattonsville at 1:30 P.M. and continued their march along the Clinch River during the afternoon. After

16 Brown, p. 68.
17 O. R., Ser. 1, XX, pt. 1, pp. 89–92.
18 *Ibid.*

fording the river in the evening, they stopped once more to feed the horses the last of the grain they had brought along. The march was then resumed, and the column reached Estillville (now Gate City) after dark.[19]

When passing through Pattonsville, they had been observed by a captain of partisan rangers who immediately telegraphed Brigadier General Humphrey Marshall at Abingdon, Virginia.[20] For some reason, his telegram was sent to Morristown, Tennessee, far to the south. The alarm did not reach Abingdon for eight hours. By the time General Marshall had this first warning of the raid, Carter's men were moving into Big Moccasin Gap, north of Kingsport. A Union sympathizer told Carter that Confederate soldiers were posted in the gap. Carter decided to fight his way through and dismounted the Second Michigan to serve as skirmishers.[21]

Because the Confederate detachment in the gap had already marched back to Kingsport, the skirmishers did not meet the resistance expected. The only defense of the pass came from a few bushwhackers. They killed one soldier of the Second Michigan. After clearing the gap, the raiders marched east of Kingsport and struck the Kingsport-Blountville road on Eden's Ridge in the vicinity of the present town of Indian Springs.[22]

A light rain began to fall while Carter's column rode along Eden's Ridge toward Blountville. They entered this town at daylight on the thirtieth. Here they captured thirty sick Confederates in the hospital. A flying column of the Second Michigan was started toward Union (now Bluff City) on the railroad twelve miles from Blountville. The main body followed after a short rest.[23]

The advance party found two companies of North Carolina infantry at Union, but these men surrendered without resistance. Then the advance column began to destroy the railroad bridge which, because it was wet with rain and was built mostly of green wood, did not burn

---

19 *Ibid.*

20 Humphrey Marshall was in command of the Confederate District of Abingdon, Va. (Amann, I, p. 312).

21 Brown, pp. 69–70.

22 *Ibid.*, pp. 70–71.

23 *Ibid.*, p. 73.

readily. However, when the main body came up, enough kindling was brought in to start a hot fire in the covered bridge. The raiders also tore down the vehicular bridge, burned the depot, and destroyed a car, three wagon loads of salt, and a large number of arms. Once more, the prisoners were paroled and were started on their way across the mountains to North Carolina. Carter wrote that the prisoners seemed genuinely pleased that the war was over for them. They told him that the Confederates would not succeed in drafting them again.[24]

Once the destruction at Union was well under way, the Ninth Pennsylvania was sent toward Carter's Station on the Watauga River. Along the way they captured a locomotive that the skirmishers used as a shield when they advanced into the town. At Carter's Station, the 200-man garrison of North Carolinians formed a line to defend the town and the bridge. A brief fire fight ensued; but at dusk, two companies of the Ninth Pennsylvania remounted and, led by Captain Jones, charged into the town, captured it, and drove the enemy away. William Thomas recorded that a man of the Seventh Ohio was killed and two men of Company A of the Ninth were wounded in this action. Twelve or sixteen of the enemy were killed and thirteen badly wounded in this action. The other Rebels disappeared into the woods.[25]

"We then burned the bridge at the station," recorded William Thomas, "and laid there until midnight Expecting another train   our command all came in at dusk   Before we left we run the Engine into the river   We captured a lot of corn in the depot   laid down to rest a little while   Started of[f] again at midnight and so dark you could not see the next man to you   We Had to lay over till daylight   We Had orders to dismount and build fires   One of the officer mistook the order and ordered his men to dismount and prepare to fire   The bridges were burned on the East Tennessee Virginia railroad   the depot was not burned at the 2d Bridge   we took some flour along with us from the depot to make our rations hold out as our hard bread is Run out." The destruction of the locomotive was the spectacular event of the campaign. When the bridge was blazing and nearing collapse, the engine was run onto the bridge. After passing the first pier, the

24 *Ibid.*
25 O. R., Ser. 1, XX, pt. 1, pp. 89–92.

locomotive crashed through the weakened structure and fell, along with the blazing bridge, into the river.[26]

While all this was going on, the Confederates were having trouble getting a pursuit under way. Although they had 8,000 men in the area, the command was divided between southwest Virginia and eastern Tennessee. Of course, Carter's men had cut the telegraph line between the two commands and thereby had eliminated a coordinated pursuit by the enemy.

Before the line had been cut, General Marshall in Abingdon sent a telegram to Major General E. Kirby Smith in Knoxville.[27] However, the telegraph operator in Bristol, a J. C. Duncan, refused to relay the message. On investigation, Marshall found that Duncan was a strong Union man and sent men to arrest him. They found that he had disappeared and could not find him or his telegraph key for two days. The sequel was that he later was arrested, but General Smith ordered his release from jail because Marshall did not have authority to make arrests in Tennessee.[28]

About noon on December 30, Marshall learned that Carter was marching toward Union. He decided to send a regiment of infantry from Abingdon to Bristol to begin the pursuit in force. He also knew that the people in Bristol had sent government stores to Abingdon for safety on a train the night before. He had his regiment march to the depot to take the train back to Bristol. When they reached the depot they found that the train had returned empty to Bristol earlier in the morning. Immediately, Marshall had the operator at Abingdon wire Bristol to send the cars back. After an hour and a half delay, a query came back from Bristol asking the general how many soldiers he wished to move. The next exchange of telegrams informed the general that, if he wanted to move trains, he should get clearance from the superintendent in Lynchburg, Virginia. The superintendent arranged for the trains but cautioned the general about the danger of ordering train movements without contacting the general office. "Otherwise," he wired, "collisions might occur." The exchange of telegrams had delayed

---

[26] Brown, p. 74.

[27] E. Kirby Smith commanded the Confederate Department of East Tennessee. (Amann, I, 345).

[28] O. R., Ser. I, XX, pt. 1, pp. 99, 103.

the troop movement by eight hours.[29] A later investigation produced evidence that the railroad agent at Bristol, like the telegraph operator, was a strong Union man.[30]

Marshall did succeed in getting one cavalry regiment into position. This unit was stationed at Saltville and, after an all-night ride, reached Abingdon at 5:30 A.M. on December 31. Here they paused to pick up rations and ammunition and were in Bristol by 2:00 P.M. Shortly afterward, this cavalry regiment was on the road to Blountville.[31]

After their brief layover at Carter's Station, the Yankee cavalrymen started for home, marching on the most direct road to Kingsport. Army routine seems to have continued as usual. William Thomas reported, "Got mustered in for pay in the morning." He also told about the day's hard march:

> Started off again and marched through mountains and Hollows all day Our Horses are giving out very fast   the boys are pressing in horses at every farm house   Arrived at dusk at Kingsport   a bushwhacker was firing at our ranks across the river   We then forded the river and camped   Firing all night with Bushwhackers And part of our men   Daniel Hoober Horse fell in the river   Dan fell in and got all wet   Marching through Tennessee today   So ended the year 1862.

The raiders encamped that night west of Kingsport near the confluence of the two forks of the Holston River. Carter had decided to march south and west rather than to try to pass through Big Moccasin Gap.[32] It is well that he made this decision because the Confederate cavalry from Blountville reached the gap during the night. There is evidence also that Thomas's bushwhackers were actually a force of partisan rangers who had picked up the column on the thirty-first and stayed on their tail for the next two days. At times this party became so troublesome that the Federals were forced to form a skirmish line.[33]

Before daylight on January 1, the Yankees were on the march again. They followed the road toward Rogersville. Again they pressed horses all along the way. They did this so effectively that Captain William W.

[29] Brown, pp. 74–75.
[30] O. R., Ser. 1, XX, pt. 1, p. 98.
[31] Brown, p. 75.
[32] O. R., Ser. 1, XX, pt. 1, pp. 89–92.
[33] *Ibid.*; Brown, pp. 76–78.

Baldwin, the leader of the partisan rangers who were in pursuit, complained, "almost every serviceable horse on the route has been taken off by these robbers."[34]

Before reaching Rogersville, the Union column turned north on the road through Looney's Gap.[35] At midnight the men encamped about four miles south of Kyle's Ford. Thomas reported that they had no hard bread and baked "slapjacks." A short while after Carter's force encamped, scouts told Marshall where the raiders were. Instead of getting his men on the move to cut the raiders off, Marshall let his troops enjoy a full night's sleep.[36]

Carter's men were marching again at daylight. They crossed the Clinch River at Kyle's Ford and continued north toward Jonesville. "The citizens were Bushwhacking us all a long the road," wrote William Thomas. Once more Captain Baldwin's partisan rangers were the troublemakers. Two companies of these rangers managed to get around the Federal column and into position ahead of the Yankees at Hunter's Gap, two miles from Jonesville.[37]

Here the troopers had to dismount and form a skirmish line to drive the rangers from the gap. The firing became so heavy that the advance of the Confederate column, then seven or eight miles east of Jonesville, thought that they heard artillery, which neither the raiders nor the rangers possessed.[38]

Marshall now speeded up his march. One battalion of infantry was relatively fresh and able to move fairly rapidly. However, the cavalry that had ridden over 100 miles in less than three days began to fall behind and get strung out. By the time the advance guard of 250 infantrymen got close to Jonesville, they found that Carter's men had beaten through the resistance at Hunter's Gap and were already in the town.

These Confederate soldiers formed a line and charged toward the town, but were quickly beaten off by the Federal rear guard. The Yan-

---

[34] O. R., Ser. 1, XX, pt. 1, p. 123.

[35] The road followed by the Union cavalry is now called "The Trail of the Lonesome Pine," a scenic route from Rogersville, Tenn. to Jonesville, Va.

[36] O. R., Ser. 1, XX, pt. 1, pp. 89–92; Brown, p. 78.

[37] O. R., Ser. 1, XX, pt. 1, pp. 89–92.

[38] Brown, p. 79.

kees captured twenty of the assailants. The rest of the Rebels retired to a line in some woods 300 yards east of town to await reinforcements. Soon, the cavalry regiment came up. While they were preparing to charge into the town, they heard a Federal bugle sound boots and saddles. When the Rebel force swept into Jonesville, there was not a Union trooper remaining.[39] It may have been Bugler Cornelius Baker who sounded the retreat at Jonesville.

The Union column was not yet completely out of danger. It was still daylight and they had several miles to march before reaching Cumberland Mountain. "We had a Strong rear gaurd Behind Skirmishing till the foot of the mt," wrote William Thomas. When the Yankees began to ascend the mountain toward Crank's Gap, Marshall gave up the chase. He feared an ambush in the dark among the slopes and ridges and blackjack undergrowth.[40]

Thomas described the march over the mountain: "A great many horses gave out climbing Up the Mt   Crossed the mt and camped at the foot about midnight   all tired   Pressed in all the horses we could find   Passed back over the mountain through Kranks Gap   we brought the prisoners across the mountain with us   camped again in Ky to night   all tired and glad to get An oppertunity to rest for a few Hours."

On January 3, the column straggled back down the narrow trail and camped on the bank of Poor Fork of the Cumberland River. A large number of horses gave out, and the dismounted men had to walk because "Pressing is stoped As the people this side of the mt are all Union." Thomas also observed the condition of the mountaineers: "Here and there you see a small Hut of the Backwoodsman of Ky.   the people through the mountains are all poor."

January 4 was another hard march. Thomas reported, "Rainy day Started of[f] early again this morning and crossed pine mountain this morning   Hard storm when we crossed the mountain The trees fell and cracking all over the mountain   Marched along red bird fork to day again   Great many of our Horses gave out to day   Again i walked all day for france [Feindt]   His old mule gave out   Camped

39 Brown, pp. 79–80.
40 O. R., Ser. 1, XX, pt. 1, pp. 95, 102.

in the evening at aschers   Marched along a Foot path all day and up
to our knees in mud   reached camp late in the evening   Found France
Had Supper waiting for me Slapjacks coffee and pork."

The following day was much the same. Marching down Red Bird
River and Flat Creek, many more horses broke down. Because they had
no way to carry the saddles, the men threw them away. Thomas observed an old salt mine that had been destroyed several months before.
The evening meal in Manchester was one corn dodger that the quartermaster issued. On January 6, the column lay over in Manchester. Rations were a corn dodger and a pound of meat.

The column reached the foot of the Big Hill during the afternoon
of January 8 after marching all day on both the seventh and the eighth.
Here the soldiers were met by a train of wagons carrying rations. "It
was a welcome sight to the boys as some of them were nearly starved
with hunger," wrote William Thomas. On January 9, many of the unmounted men rode in the wagons to Richmond. The lucky mounted
men rode their tired horses and the plucky dismounted men hiked to
the same destination. At Richmond, General Carter and the squadron
of the Seventh Ohio left the expedition.

On January 10, the Pennsylvania troopers marched through torrential rains to Nicholasville. Here they found Major Jordan in command of the regiment. He had returned to the regiment after being
exchanged. The change of command was permanent because Colonel
James had died unexpectedly on January 1 while visiting his home in
Philadelphia.

During Carter's Raid, the men had ridden, or walked, 470 miles,
including 150 miles in enemy country. They had captured 400 of the
enemy. They had destroyed 2 important railroad bridges, a locomotive,
10 miles of track, over 600 stands of arms, and a large quantity of military supplies.[41] The small force had accomplished a successful mission
in a winter that otherwise was marked with failure for Federal arms.
As General Halleck hoped they would, other commanders followed this
example and, as the war progressed, larger and larger bodies of Union
cavalry made increasingly devastating raids.

The hardships of this march through a wilderness in wintertime are

[41] O. R., Ser. 1, XX, pt. 1, p. 92.

difficult to imagine. However, some idea can be gained from William Thomas's horse statistics. He wrote, "We [Company B] Have 27 Horses yet 26 of them captured all the rest gave out we only brought one Horse Into camp that we took out out of 60 horses i had 2 Horses on the raid."

XII

The Battle of Thompson's Station

My advance guard surprised and captured Surgeon —— of Colonel Wheeler's Cavalry, just as he was in the act of taking a parting kiss from a most beautiful girl, who had by her surpassing charm inveigled him from the safety of his camp.[1]

The capture of the surgeon, as reported by Colonel Jordan, was the first contact with the enemy during the Ninth Pennsylvania's first scout south of Franklin, Tennessee, on February 21, 1863. A few days before, the regiment had driven detachments of Confederate cavalry out of Franklin and had occupied the town that stands on the south bank of the Harpeth River, twenty miles south of Nashville. A division of Union infantry and artillery had occupied and fortified the north bank of the river opposite Franklin. This position was the right flank of the Army of the Cumberland.

Following the indecisive Battle of Stones River at the turn of the year, Confederate General Braxton Bragg had retreated to a strong position centered at Tullahoma. Strong posts on the flanks formed an arc stretching from Sparta in the north, through Tullahoma, to Shelbyville and Columbia in the west. General Rosecrans's Army of the Cumberland was spread in a parallel crescent reaching from Lebanon to Franklin and centered at Murfreesboro.

Between the two armies lay an area of unoccupied land twenty to thirty miles in width. Moreover, both small and large bodies from both armies frequently moved through the area on scouting, foraging, and

[1] O. R., Ser. 1, XXIII, pt. 1, pp. 59, 60; the reference is to Maj. Gen. Joseph Wheeler, then commanding all Confederate cavalry in Middle Tennessee (Amann, I, 367).

raiding expeditions. These movements, principally by the cavalry of the two armies, led to frequent collisions.

The Ninth Pennsylvania Cavalry was at Nicholasville, Kentucky, in early January 1863. Near the end of the month, orders came for a march to Louisville. Although more than half of the men were without horses as a result of the attrition during Carter's Raid, morale was high and William Thomas reported, "Boys are all Jolly." Perhaps payday helped. "received our pay this morning for 2 months ammounting to $26.00   received six as 20 goes Home on the allotment roll," he continued.

The regiment rode and walked to Versailles on January 26 and on to Frankfort on the twenty-seventh and twenty-eighth. Marching was slow because the dismounted men had to slog through heavy rain and snow. The column reached Frankfort about noon on January 28, and the mounted men continued toward Louisville. The dismounted troopers stayed in Frankfort waiting for rail transportation. Cornelius Baker was one of these men. During the layover, he was given a Testament by the Bible Society, and he carried it for the remainder of the war.[2]

The mounted column rode into Louisville the next day and went into camp at Oakland. They were joined in the evening by the dismounted group, who had entrained about noon, and by the Second Michigan. These men were business prospects for the local citizens. Thomas wrote, "the Camp is thronged with women Selling cakes and Rabbits." During the next few days, the regiment was re-equipped. They were issued new clothing. The dismounted men received fresh horses and new saddles to replace those they had discarded in the mountains.

"Heavy snow during the night   about a foot of snow on the ground," reported William Thomas on February 5, "The boys Had a Battle with Snow balls." A few days later, they "Caught a Boy in camp trying to steal a pistol   tied him to a post for punishment."

The men began to entrain for Nashville on February 4. The Second Michigan went first, and by the eighth the last of the Ninth Pennsylva-

2 Elizabeth Eisenhart, librarian, American Bible Society, to author, Jan. 14, 1964, advised that 5,297,831 Bibles, Testaments, and portions were issued by the Society to soldiers and sailors during the war.

Baker homestead, Blain, Pennsylvania.

Upper left: Farrier Samuel Duncan, Company C. *Upper right*: Private Jacob Epler, Company C. *Lower left*: Private James A. Anderson, Company C. *Lower right*: Private Isaiah Holtzapple, Company C.

Center Family House, Shaker Village, South Union, Kentucky, built in 1824.

White Hall, home of Cassius Marcellus Clay, Kentucky's most outspoken abolitionist, Richmond, Kentucky.

Capitol of Tennessee during the Civil War. The grounds were fortified and served as a Union camp. *U.S. War Department General Staff photograph, National Archives.*

Upper: General Edward C. Williams, who
recruited the Ninth Pennsylvania Cavalry
and became the regiment's first colonel.
Lower: General Thomas Jefferson Jordan,
who served as colonel of the Ninth Pennsylvania Cavalry during 1863 and 1864.
Courtesy of the Library of Congress.

Ninth Pennsylvania Cavalry Monument, Chickamauga Battlefield.

Corporal William Thomas, Company B, Ninth Pennsylvania Cavalry.
Courtesy of Leroy R. Matter.

nia had shipped. Thomas was among the last to leave. "Struck our tents
In the evening and put them on the train and our Horses on the Nashville train   Started from Louisville at 8 p.m.   rode in the cars all night
passed through Elizabethtown and Mumfordsville During the night
4 companies of us on the train   the last of our regt   Rode in the
freight cars." During the next day, Thomas observed a large concentration of troops around Gallatin, Tennessee, and also noted that there
was no snow on the ground south of Franklin, Kentucky. He reached
Nashville at dusk on the ninth and encamped at Edgefield.

Most of the regiment moved on to Franklin, but William Thomas
and Company B were assigned as an escort for the brigade commander,
Brigadier General Green Clay Smith. They missed the actions described
in this chapter. However, there were compensations to being left in
Nashville. "was out this morning at a planters House Looking arround
His premises," Thomas wrote on February 17, "went through the Hot
beds in the glass house   was up On top of the tower   walked around
the yard Looking at the Statues   Splendid yard." On Washington's
birthday, some of the boys went to town with General Smith to celebrate.

Meanwhile, Colonel Jordan had led the rest of the regiment across
the Harpeth River and into the town of Franklin. They were the only
force of Union soldiers south of the river, but were backed up by Brigadier General Charles Gilbert's division of the Army of Kentucky on
the north bank of the river.[3] Jordan immediately attempted to find out
who might be in front of his position and began the scout that resulted
in the capture of Colonel Wheeler's surgeon. Jordan, with seventy-three
men, rode down the Columbia pike. Major Griffith Jones led sixty-
five men down the Lewisburg road to the east, and Captain Michael
O'Reilly marched with sixty-two men on the Carter Creek road, which
parallels the Columbia road a few miles to the west.

Jordan had told the other two officers to march six or seven miles
and then cross to the Columbia road and meet him at a brick church
seven miles south of Franklin. Jordan reached the church first, and
Major Jones with his party appeared about half an hour later. Hearing
nothing from O'Reilly after waiting for a reasonable period, the colo-

---

3 Jordan, "The Battle of Thompson's Station," p. 302.

nel marched two miles farther south and then turned back toward Franklin.

Captain O'Reilly had found two Confederate soldiers. The first he captured and paroled. The second was sick in a house near the road. O'Reilly ordered his command to move on while he entered the house to make out the parole papers for the sick man. This was the last his men saw of the captain. A short while later, Lieutenant George Smith observed a body of Confederate cavalry, which he estimated as 500 men, go to the same house. Soon afterward, Captain O'Reilly's horse joined the column "with bridle reins hanging about his feet." This column rejoined Colonel Jordan near Franklin. O'Reilly had been captured.[4]

This and other scouting parties which Colonel Jordan sent out during the next few days determined that the Ninth Pennsylvania and three companies of the Second Michigan, all under Jordan's command, were facing the combined brigades of Generals Joseph Wheeler and Nathan Bedford Forrest.[5] On March 3, scouts learned that this force had been joined by Major General Earl Van Dorn's infantry division.[6]

The next morning, Colonel John Coburn led a Union infantry brigade and eighty forage wagons across the Harpeth into Franklin. This expedition was to forage in the rich country toward Spring Hill and determine more precisely the strength of the opposing force. Coburn's orders directed him to take along Jordan and his command. Colonel Coburn's force then totaled 1,800 infantry and 600 cavalry. The infantry regiments were the Thirty-third and Eighty-fifth Indiana, the Nineteenth Michigan, and the Twenty-second Wisconsin. Jordan's cavalry included most of the Ninth Pennsylvania and detachments of the Second Michigan and Fourth Kentucky.[7]

Jordan suggested to Coburn that they ought to take a battery of artillery with them. At first, Coburn disagreed and remarked, "We won't need any [artillery]; Wheeler and Forrest will not dare to attack

---

[4] O. R., Ser. 1, XXIII, pt. 1, pp. 59–60.

[5] Jordan, "The Battle of Thompson's Station," p. 303; Forrest, a brigadier general at this time, commanded the 2d Corps Cavalry of Bragg's Army of the Mississippi (Amann, I, 261).

[6] Van Dorn, who previously held independent commands, commanded the 1st Corps, Army of the Mississippi (Amann, I, 361).

[7] Cist, p. 141.

me." Jordan then informed him that Van Dorn's division had joined the opposing force, and with three or four times the strength of Coburn's column, they most certainly would attack him. Coburn agreed reluctantly, and Jordan galloped across the river to General Gilbert's headquarters to obtain a battery. Captain Charles C. Aleshire's Eighteenth Ohio Battery of six rifled Rodman guns was assigned to the expedition.[8]

While the Union expedition was thus being organized, Van Dorn's Confederate division, led by Forrest's cavalry, was marching north from Columbia. Van Dorn, believing that Jordan's cavalry alone was south of the Harpeth River, planned to drive them away and fortify a position near Franklin from which he could threaten the right flank of the Union army. This led to a head-on collision of Forrest's and Jordan's cavalry forces on March 4 and to the larger Battle of Thompson's Station on the following day.

After the return of Colonel Jordan with the battery, the Union column marched out of Franklin with the cavalry in the van followed by the artillery, the infantry, and the wagons. About four miles south of Franklin, the advance cavalry scouts, upon reaching the crest of one of the several high ridges over which the road passed, observed a long enemy column approaching. Jordan immediately brought his troopers into line, had them trot to the crest of the ridge, and positioned the artillery. Captain Aleshire fired the first shot of the skirmish at 10:40 A.M., surprising the enemy who had expected to meet nothing more than a screen of cavalry. However, as the visible Yankee force was much smaller than their own, they decided to attack, answering Aleshire's guns with their own artillery.[9]

Here, the Federals had the advantage. Jordan wrote, "Before they could dismount, break down the walls, and get into line of battle, they were very severely punished, as every shot from our six guns told upon their column, and many a poor fellow bit the dust before he could get

[8] Col. Coburn's force had been temporarily assigned to Gilbert. It was officially a part of Brig. Gen. Absalom Baird's Third Division, Army of Kentucky (O. R., Ser. 1, XXIII, pt. 1, pp. 80, 83, 84).

[9] Jordan, "The Battle of Thompson's Station," p. 303; various Union officers estimated the Confederate force engaged in the skirmish at from 1,000 to 4,000 men (O. R., Ser. 1, XXIII, pt. 1, pp. 79, 80).

from under our fire."[10] Cavalry skirmishers also met some of the enemy in the hills and ravines on the left of the road and drove these men from the position. Then the Rebel force retreated. They left fifteen dead on the field, and Jordan observed that they carried off a large number of wounded. The only Union casualties were two troopers with slight wounds.

This action had just ended when Colonel Coburn was informed that another body of enemy cavalry was riding up the Lewisburg road toward Franklin. He ordered Jordan to protect this flank, and Jordan led his detachment of the Second Michigan to meet the threat. They got on the flank of the enemy and forced them to retire. That evening, while the remainder of the Union cavalry encamped on the ridge where they had fought, the Michigan men picketed the Lewisburg road.[11]

Coburn advised General Gilbert that Negroes had told him that a large force of enemy infantry, cavalry, and artillery lay on the road ahead. He also sent thirty-nine filled forage wagons back to Franklin.[12]

By a fortunate coincidence, Jordan heard that the carbines he had requested had arrived in Franklin that same day. He had them brought up and distributed to the men during the night. The weapons were Burnside carbines,[13] which were breechloaders using brass cartridges. Jordan's men would test their new arms under trying circumstances during the next day's actions.

Shortly after daylight on March 5, Colonel Coburn's column began to march. Ahead of and flanking the marching column, the Ninth Pennsylvania and the detachment of the Second Michigan were deployed as skirmishers. Jordan sent a small detachment of the Fourth Kentucky to observe the Carter Creek and Lewisburg roads in the event the enemy should attempt to flank the column from them.[14]

About a mile from camp, five miles south of Franklin, the cavalry skirmishers met Rebel pickets who fired a few rounds. Then they retired, according to Colonel Jordan, "but so slowly as to keep up a con-

10 Jordan, "The Battle of Thompson's Station," p. 303.

11 O. R., Ser. 1, XXIII, pt. 1, pp. 79–80; Jordan, "The Battle of Thompson's Station," p. 303.

12 O. R., Ser. 1, XXIII, pt. 1, p. 80.

13 Jordan, "The Battle of Thompson's Station," pp. 303–304; O. R., Ser. 1, XXIII, pt. 1, p. 181; Lustyck, p. 22.

14 O. R., Ser. 1, XXIII, pt. 1, pp. 80–81.

tinual skirmish till the battle opened." He continued, "At the range of hills overlooking Thompson's Station, about nine miles from Franklin, the skirmishers of the enemy made a very determined resistance, but we charged them, and they retired over the intervening valley and to the opposite hills."[15]

From the top of the hills, more properly ridge, that they had occupied, the Union troopers overlooked the strong defensive position the Confederates had selected for the battle. From the ridge, the road ran straight south across the valley and into the hills beyond the station. The railroad paralleled the road about half a mile to the west.[16] The station on the railroad was about three-quarters of a mile from the ridge occupied by the Union troopers. Except where the road and railroad passed, stone walls extended east and west in front of the station to the base of low hills about three-quarters of a mile away in both directions. These hills, trending south, formed a horseshoe around the area of the station. Between the ridge and the stone walls were open fields, providing a clear field of fire for the Confederates posted behind the walls against any assault from the north.

Shortly after the cavalry occupied the ridge, the Union infantry came up. When the head of the column moved into the gap at the top of the ridge, they were greeted by a shell from an eighteen-pounder. The shell passed over the advance units and landed 150 yards to the rear in a ditch beside the road that now was jammed with Union soldiers. The explosion plowed up dirt and stones, but in Colonel Jordan's words, "by some wonderful interposition of Providence, without killing or wounding any one."[17]

Other shells, mostly from six-pounders, followed, and the Union infantry was deployed to the right and left of the road behind the brow of the ridge. Captain Aleshire's guns were emplaced on both sides of the road and began replying to the Confederate guns. They had just begun to fire when shells began to come in from the left, placing the

---

[15] *Ibid.*

[16] Jordan, "The Battle of Thompson's Station," p. 304, said the road turned west, following the railroad. However, Coburn (O. R., Ser. 1, XXIII, pt. 1, p. 86), said the railroad turned away from the turnpike and the station was 300 yards west. This is the same relation of the station and U. S. highway 31 today.

[17] O. R., Ser. 1, XXIII, pt. 1, pp. 80–81.

Ohio gunners under a cross fire. Coburn asked Jordan to see if he could spot the flanking battery.

The colonel rode to the left and examined the hills beyond through his glasses. Suddenly, he saw a wreath of smoke and "in an instant saw the shell. It came as straight for me as though it had been aimed and intended for my special benefit. I had no time to move my horse, but took the precaution to lean over on my left side as far as possible, and my horse, from fright, stooped till his belly almost touched the ground; the shell passed me and struck the ground within fifty yards to my rear and among the roots of a large whiteoak-tree, and from some cause was thrown more than a hundred feet in the air, where it exploded and the butt of the shell fell within a few feet of me."[18] Jordan picked up the butt and kept it for many years as a memento of the war.

When Jordan reported the position of the battery to Coburn, the latter decided to ignore it and attempt to capture a battery on the Union right that had just then opened fire. He hoped to turn the enemy position at that end of the line. For this maneuver he ordered the Thirty-third and Eighty-fifth Indiana to attack across the level valley. As they marched forward, all the enemy artillery concentrated on them. Many of the men fell, but those remaining closed ranks and continued to advance.[19]

When the infantrymen were about two hundred yards from the stone walls, they were ordered to charge. As they approached, riflemen posted by Forrest behind the walls rose and fired two volleys that broke the charge. Jordan was impressed by the bravery of the Indiana soldiers, who advanced through severe artillery fire and then charged into this overwhelming fire of small arms.[20]

As soon as the Indiana soldiers began to fall back, masses of Confederate infantry appeared on the hill to the east of the station, charged down the slopes, and began to force the Union troops toward the west and away from the Franklin road. After asking Jordan to hold the road

[18] Jordan, "The Battle of Thompson's Station," pp. 304–305.
[19] The records are not clear about point of origin and direction of the attack by the Union regiments. However, to attack the Confederate left, the attack was probably made along or west of the railroad.
[20] O. R., Ser. 1, XXIII, pt. 1, pp. 80, 88; Jordan, "The Battle of Thompson's Station," pp. 305–306.

open for a retreat, Coburn led his two remaining infantry regiments into the valley in an attempt to extricate the two that were now in a desperate situation. The fresh regiments were inadequate to stem the drive of so numerous an enemy, and they also were caught in the tide and driven toward the west, beyond the railroad and away from the road that was being guarded by the cavalry.[21]

About the same time that he lost contact with the infantry regiments, Colonel Jordan observed enemy cavalry sweeping around his own left with the obvious intent of cutting his retreat route. He ordered most of his troopers to dismount, and by taking advantage of the stone walls, fences, and any irregularities of the ground, hold off the enemy until he could remove the battery. The artillery could no longer fire at the Confederates who were driving the Union infantry because of the danger of hitting their own men. The order to pull out came just in time for the artillery. A "swarm of enemy infantry" was about to enclose the guns on the left, and the enemy line was already within sixty yards of the totally unsupported guns on the right. The guns were successfully removed and started toward Franklin with a small cavalry escort while the remainder of the troopers continued to hold off the Rebels.[22]

By this time, the firing in front of the station had stopped, and Jordan knew that Coburn had surrendered. Now his responsibility was to save his own men if he could. He was about to order a general retreat when Lieutenant Colonel Edward Bloodgood of the Wisconsin regiment came out of the woods with about 200 of his men and 60 prisoners. Jordan let these men get a start on the road to Franklin before beginning his own retreat. Then the cavalrymen began to retire, dismounting behind walls or fences long enough to fire a volley to check the enemy advance and then mounting and retreating to the next strong position, where the maneuver was repeated. In this manner, they retreated slowly to the West Harpeth River.[23]

North of this river, a high ridge seemed a good defensive position, and it was here that Jordan had asked Aleshire to stop and cover his own crossing of the stream, which Aleshire did. There was a pleasant

---

21 Jordan, "The Battle of Thompson's Station," pp. 305–306.
22 O. R., Ser. 1, XXIII, pt. 1, p. 82.
23 *Ibid.*; Jordan, "The Battle of Thompson's Station," p. 306.

surprise in store for Jordan when he reached the position. In addition to the artillery, he found a fresh infantry regiment, the One Hundred and Twenty-fourth Ohio, in line-of-battle. This regiment had been a part of Coburn's command but had been left behind and Coburn had not mentioned its existence to Jordan.[24]

Jordan was no more surprised than the enemy when they suddenly found that the small band of cavalry they had been pursuing now had artillery and infantry support. Upon making this discovery, the Rebels began to file off to the right to flank the position. Jordan countered by retreating to the ridge on which the previous day's fight had taken place.[25]

Captain Benjamin G. Heistand and sixty men of Company G were posted in a graveyard at the foot of the ridge and some distance in front of the main battle line. The cemetery was at the intersection of two roads and, from their position behind the wall, Heistand's men could cover both roads. They did drive the first group of the enemy back with a volley but soon became involved in a continuous fire fight with Rebel skirmishers.[26]

At about dusk, Colonel Jordan received orders to retreat to Franklin. The orders informed him that General Gilbert's entire division was on the first ridge south of Franklin. Before retiring, Jordan wanted to bring Heistand and his company in from their dangerous position. To accomplish this feat, the entire cavalry force charged down the slope and drove the enemy skirmishers back. In the charge, one man was killed and two were wounded, but the beleaguered company was rescued. The entire command then marched back to Franklin without additional incidents.[27]

In the battle, Coburn's losses totaled 1,446 men, of whom 1,151 were captured. The Ninth Pennsylvania had 2 killed, 5 wounded, and 6 missing.[28]

As with most Federal disasters, a court of inquiry was conducted

24 O. R., Ser. 1, XXIII, pt. 1, p. 82; Jordan, "The Battle of Thompson's Station," p. 306.
25 O. R., Ser. 1, XXIII, pt. 1, p. 82.
26 Jordan, "The Battle of Thompson's Station," p. 307.
27 *Ibid.*
28 O. R., Ser. 1, XXIII, pt. 1, p. 75.

afterwards. General Gilbert was removed from his command as a result. The consensus of the court was that Gilbert should have marched his entire division to the scene. The sounds of the battle were clearly audible at his headquarters in Franklin.[29] Both Generals Rosecrans and Sheridan considered the attack that Coburn made to have been very rash when the size of the attacking force and the strength of the position were considered.[30]

The cavalry force was complimented for their part in the action in general orders issued by Major General Gordon Granger, who commanded the Army of Kentucky.[31] Captain Aleshire reported, "The conduct of the cavalry, under command of Colonel Jordan, during the whole time, and particularly during the retreat was unexceptionable. Had it not been for their repeated efforts to drive back the enemy, neither my battery nor the wagon train could possibly have been saved."[32]

Colonel Jordan gave much credit for the successful withdrawal to Chaplain Edmund McKinney: "During the retreat he remained with the rear guard, and by his coolness and bravery during a most critical moment, when hundreds of the enemy were thrown on a handful, contributed largely to the safety of my command."[33] Company C was in the hottest part of the field. Samuel Snyder of Blain was killed, and Sergeant George A. Shuman later found eleven bullet holes in his clothing. Another ball had clipped his beard. Shuman was commissioned a second lieutenant because of his conduct in this battle.[34]

This action demonstrated that the Union cavalry was becoming as proficient as the enemy. They had conducted an orderly withdrawal in the face of superior numbers of Rebel cavalry commanded by Nathan Bedford Forrest, considered by many military authorities to have been the best soldier developed in the Confederacy.

[29] Subsequently, Gilbert's appointment as brigadier general was not confirmed by Congress (Jordan, "The Battle of Thompson's Station," p. 307).

[30] Jordan, "The Battle of Thompson's Station," p. 308; O. R., Ser. 1, XXIII, pt. 1, p. 74.

[31] National Archives, "9th Cav. Order Book," General Order No. 23 from Gordon Granger. Granger moved the headquarters of the Army of Kentucky to Franklin (O. R., Ser. 1, XXIII, pt. 1, p. 113).

[32] O. R., Ser. 1, XXIII, pt. 1, p. 85.

[33] *Ibid.*, p. 83.

[34] Hain, p. 544.

XIII

Skirmishes, A Husband Wronged, and Spies

Pleasant day   went out this morning
To reconoitere   the rebels were in
line of Battle   We fought till noon
When the Rebels Cleared out   At
noon the 4 regulars and the 7th Pa
Cav And the 4 Mich came in at
Thompson On another road   the
rebels fell back for fear of being sur-
rounded   we Followed them through
Spring Hill   Halted in a woods rain
pouring down In torrents all night
the infantry Caught up tonight under
comand of Gen Granger with some 4
or 5 Battries   We Had some men
killed and wounded to day

William Thomas's diary entry of March 9, 1863, reflects a change of tactics in the use of Federal cavalry. Now the cavalry marched and fought as brigades and divisions. Gone were the days when single regiments and detachments were sent on missions that required larger numbers of men.

Immediately after the Battle of Thompson's Station, the Ninth Pennsylvania was a part of Brigadier General Green Clay Smith's Fourth Brigade, Army of the Cumberland. In addition to the Ninth, Smith's brigade included the Second Michigan, and the Fourth, Sixth, and Seventh Kentucky Regiments.[1]

Major General Gordon Granger's march to the south, mentioned in the quotation, was intended to frustrate Confederate General Earl Van Dorn's attempt to fortify a position close to Franklin. Also, the brief campaign was a punitive expedition to even the score for Thompson's Station, if the Federals could bring on a fight. Colonel Robert H. G. Minty's cavalry brigade and Major General Phil Sheridan's division moved in from the east to lend a hand. It was Minty's cavalry that forced the Rebels out of Thompson's Station.[2]

General Green Clay Smith's cavalry marched out of Franklin on

1 O. R., Ser. 1, XXIII, pt. 1, p. 180.
2 Jordan, "The Battle of Thompson's Station," p. 308.

March 8 in advance of Granger's division. The Ninth Pennsylvania, Second Michigan, and Seventh Kentucky led the way down the Columbia pike while the Fourth and Sixth Kentucky moved down the Lewisburg road. Both groups met enemy pickets about three miles from Franklin and drove them back slowly for the remainder of the day. At dark, Smith's troopers camped seven miles south of Franklin.[3]

The next morning, both columns of Smith's cavalry pushed ahead against the enemy pickets until they came up against strong positions and artillery. The column on the Columbia road encountered a force of 1,000 enemy cavalry and three pieces of artillery a mile north of Thompson's Station. Smith reported, "A heavy and spirited skirmish took place, in which the Second Michigan and Ninth Pennsylvania acted with great coolness, bravery, and promptness." A move by the Rebels around the right flank of the Union skirmish line required a change of position by a large part of the brigade, but the change was made quickly enough to repulse the enemy charge that followed. After this one effort, Confederate resistance suddenly collapsed. The reason was the approach of Minty's force from the east. The rebels were no more surprised by his approach than was General Smith, who regretted that there had been no chance to coordinate an attack because of a lack of communications.

General Smith's command proceeded next to Spring Hill, where they met a few Confederates and drove them out of town toward Columbia. Van Dorn and Forrest had retreated from Spring Hill about three hours before the Federal troopers arrived. The aggressiveness of the Union cavalry may have fooled these officers. General Granger wrote, "Van Dorn greatly overestimates the strength of my force."[4]

The action continued on March 10, and William Thomas summarized it in his diary:

> Rainy Day   Marched on again this morning   the rebels fell Back across the rutherford Creeck and destroyed the bridge   We lay on the bank of the creek Reconnoitering their position in the Hills   fell back in the evening and Camped at a Union man House   Gen Smith Had His Head Quarters in the House   the man was Home for the First time to see His family for Six months

3 O. R., Ser. 1, XXIII, pt. 1, p. 142.
4 *Ibid.*, pp. 142–43.

General Smith's report added that Rutherford Creek was "high, rapid and swelling," while Granger wrote, "The ground is so miry it is impossible to move artillery, except on the pike."[5] Along the creek, the Pennsylvania and Michigan troopers maintained a lively skirmish with Rebel sharpshooters on the opposite side of the stream.

Thomas also wrote of the action on the eleventh:

> pleasant Day   we started out early and commenced Skirmishing Early in the Morning   we shelled the rebels out from behind A barn   they fell back   We crossed the creek at Jamison Ford   we Had a Brisk fight after we were across the creek   We drove the rebels across duck river and then fell Back on the other side of the creek   crossed at the Lower ford   a Swift current 3 of our men got drowned crossing.

This brief entry agrees substantially with the reports of the officers, except that General Smith wrote that the enemy sharpshooters were shelled out of a house and a cotton gin. The artillery belonged to Minty's brigade, and General Smith wrote that he could do a much more effective job in the future if he could have a battery added to his command. Once across Rutherford Creek, the Yankee cavalry formed a line-of-battle, but the enemy retreated across the Duck River and into Columbia.[6] Thomas wrote that he camped at the same house as on the previous night. The next day the entire force marched back to Franklin.

On March 19, Colonel Jordan, with 330 men, marched once again toward Spring Hill. In a parallel move, Colonel Louis D. Watkins, with a detachment of the Sixth Kentucky, marched down the Carter Creek road. Four miles south of Franklin, Jordan's men captured two prisoners who told him that a Confederate division had moved into Spring Hill.[7] Jordan moved cautiously on to Thompson's Station and then, with nearly all his command deployed as flankers and skirmishers, proceeded toward Spring Hill.

As soon as the small force passed through Spring Hill, they ran into 800 or 900 of the enemy posted in some woods on a hill to the right of the road. This group poured "a most galling fire" into Company A of the Ninth, killing one man and seriously wounding another. Jordan

[5] *Ibid.*
[6] *Ibid.*, pp. 143–44.
[7] *Ibid.*, p. 150.

immediately ordered the rest of the command to dismount and advance carefully "taking advantage of the fences and irregularities of the ground to shelter them and, if possible, drive the enemy from their position."[8] After a sharp fight, the enemy retired. Jordan followed for about one mile and then halted to await Colonel Watkins's force. The combined force then drove the enemy across Rutherford Creek, but began a march back to Franklin at the approach of night.

On March 25 an especially large and fierce skirmish took place at Brentwood, between Nashville and Franklin. On this day, two major Confederate cavalry forces swept through the area north of Franklin while a third force kept the Federals entertained south of the town.

General Granger had anticipated trouble and, during the previous evening, had ordered the cavalry to be saddled and ready to ride at dawn. At daybreak the Union pickets on the Lewisburg, Columbia, and Carter Creek roads south of Franklin were vigorously attacked, and Granger sent 300 of his cavalry in that direction. Before he committed others, however, a courier arrived from the post at Triune advising him that nearly 1,000 enemy cavalry had passed that post and were apparently headed for Brentwood. Almost immediately, a loyal citizen came in from the opposite direction with advice that Forrest and Brigadier General John A. Wharton[9] had crossed the Harpeth north of Franklin and also appeared to be marching toward Brentwood.

Granger interpreted the raid as an attempt to capture Brentwood, the stockade at the railroad bridge, and the morning train from Nashville. To thwart the move, he sent Green Clay Smith and the 600 cavalrymen still in camp toward Brentwood with orders "To save Brentwood, guards, and train, cost what it will."[10]

The town of Brentwood was defended by 400 infantry under Lieutenant Colonel Edward Bloodgood, the same officer who had led a force out of the encirclement at Thompson's Station. Another detachment defended the strong stockade at the railroad bridge, one and one-half

---

[8] *Ibid.*, pp. 150–51.
[9] Wharton commanded the 2d Brigade, II Corps, Army of the Mississippi.
[10] O. R., Ser. 1, XXIII, pt. 1, p. 178.

miles from town. The Rebels came in so suddenly that Bloodgood was surrounded before reaching the area of the stockade. These men appear to have surrendered without a fight, which led Granger to call them "our milk and water soldiers." The stockade was then surrendered; and Granger, afterward failing to find the mark of a bullet on it, concluded that it had been surrendered too quickly.[11]

Thus, when the cavalry force arrived, they found the bridge burned and the railroad torn up. They learned that the enemy were riding westward with the captured men, guns, and wagons. William Thomas described the ensuing action:

> we Charged after them for 4 miles when they made a stand and We Had a brisk fight for a while   When another large body came on the Right and made a charge on us the 2d Miche poured into them heavy and checked them   [Then] we Had to Fall Back to brentwood Station where we met Gen [James D.] Morgan coming from Nashville   We recaptured 5 of our teams back But had to Leave them in the hands of the Rebes again   We took 40 prisoners   killed Unknown

General Smith wrote that as soon as he reached Brentwood he began a pursuit of the retreating enemy. After riding for three and a half miles, Smith's men came upon the enemy, and a running fight was kept up for the next two and a half miles. During this part of the action, Smith reported, "We recaptured all the wagons and mules, about four hundred stand of arms, a large number of knapsacks, and two loads of ammunition, with one hundred stand of arms dropped by the fleeing rebels."

Upon reaching the Granny White pike, Colonel J. W. Starnes, who commanded the Rebel band, made a stand. His force was promptly driven past the crossroads to the ford over the Little Harpeth River. After fighting for an hour and a half, victory seemed near for the Union troopers, and Smith said that they became exhilarated with the prospect. However, Wharton's Confederate cavalry, 1,500 strong, suddenly appeared on the right; and Forrest, with an even larger force, appeared on the left. The reinforcements made three charges, each with heavy losses, that were repulsed by the combined forces of the Second Michigan, the Sixth Kentucky, and two companies of the Ninth Pennsyl-

11 *Ibid.*, p. 179.

vania. During these fights, the remainder of the Ninth was held as a reserve on the road, and detachments were quickly sent to points that appeared to be weakening.

General Smith ordered a retreat when it appeared that the enemy might surround his force. The Second Michigan and the Ninth Pennsylvania dismounted and fought from behind a stone wall while the rest of the force began their retreat. Then they too "fell back slowly from tree to tree and rock to rock." Captain David Kimmel of the Ninth came across fifteen or twenty loaded guns which he calmly fired, one at a time, at the advancing enemy and then broke each of the rifles over a tree. Fighting a rear-guard action, the column made its way back to Brentwood. The enemy then withdrew because of the approach of General Morgan's strong infantry column.

Smith gave his casualties as four killed, nineteen wounded, and four missing. He observed, "The loss of the enemy was not less, in the judgement of my officers and myself, than from 400 to 500 killed, wounded, and prisoners. Forty-six prisoners were brought in, and from the number of men seen lying on the field, and the number of empty saddles observed, and the busy squads packing the dead and disabled to the rear, makes the above estimate very reasonable." For these heavy enemy losses he credited the five-shooters of the Second Michigan and the speed with which the Burnside carbines, used by the Ninth Pennsylvania, could be loaded and fired.

Smith continued, "It may well be the boast of that small force of 600 men that they drove more than twice their number, with two pieces of artillery, over six miles, perfectly dismayed and whipped, and fought, for over two hours, almost ten times their strength, and successfully resisted their charges for two miles, when we came to a halt, and the enemy thought proper to desist."[12]

General Rosecrans, on learning of this action, sent a complimentary order thanking General Smith, his officers, and men "for the spirit and gallantry of their behavior" and congratulating them "as well as himself [Rosecrans] and the country, that our cavalry thus show themselves worthy of the cause in which they combat."[13] Many small skirmishes

12 *Ibid.*, pp. 179, 181.
13 *Ibid.*, p. 178.

took place during the next month, some so insignificant that they went unrecorded in the *Official Records*. William Thomas noted the following actions:

March 31:

> Our regt went out   came in the evening   Captured 12 prisoners.

April 5:

> Co. H. of our regt drove in from picket this Morning   2 men wounded 4 missing   Had our Horses Saddled up all day.

April 10:

> Gen Stanley arrived with His Cavalry this morning   the rebels drove our pickets in and made a dash into Franklin But were repulsed with a Heavy Loss   We captured 30 prisoners and Cut up 6 pices of artillery for them and a great many Killed   Our Brig went out in the afternoon and came out on the pike to Brentwood   arrived in camp in the evening without seeing anything of the rebs.

April 20:

> Turned over our old tents and drawed new ones   Shelter tents or dog tents   1 for each 2 men.

April 27:

> Our Brig went out on a Scout last night and took a rebel camp by Surprise   They took 128 prisoners and Brought them in this morning   Killd unknown.

May 1:

> our brigade went out Last Night to surprise a rebel camp but The rebels were in line of battle when we came   We Had a brisk fight for a little While   We Killed 8 and took 12 prisoners.

The arrival of Major General David S. Stanley, chief of cavalry, Army of the Cumberland, as recorded by William Thomas on April 10, signaled a change in the organization of the cavalry; and the Ninth Pennsylvania became a part of the First Brigade of the First Division, Army of the Cumberland Cavalry. The brigade included the same regiments as the previous organization—Ninth Pennsylvania, Second Michigan, Fourth and Sixth Kentucky—but General Smith went home, and Colonel Archibald Campbell of the Second Michigan became brigade commander.

The skirmishing became less frequent for a while after May 1, and events outside of camp were noted by the soldiers. On May 11, Thomas wrote, "Rumors that Van Dorn was Shot by a citizen at Spring Hill." The rumors were correct.

After the fight at Rutherford Creek and the withdrawal of the Union force from the immediate area, General Van Dorn moved his headquarters to Spring Hill. He took up residence in the home of a Dr. Peters about a mile south of the town. Dr. Peters was a highly respected physician and had a fine farm and a spacious house. He had invited Van Dorn to be his guest. Mrs. Peters was a charming young woman and a patriotic Confederate. The good doctor was away from home for extended periods caring for the sick, and while he was away, the general and the lady had an affair. At least, the doctor believed they had.

On May 10, Dr. Peters went to Van Dorn's headquarters and, being well known, walked past the guard and various officers and entered the general's office. He then blew Van Dorn's brains out with a pistol. He left the office, mounted his horse, and galloped away to the north before the men around the post realized what had happened. By the time cavalry went after him, he was too far ahead and reached the Federal cavalry pickets at Franklin before he could be apprehended. He asked for protection after telling the Union officers what he had done. General Granger sent him on to Nashville where he remained for the duration.

Colonel Jordan told the story and ended with a strong opinion of the victim. He wrote, "Thus perished General Earl Van Dorn, a graduate of West Point, before the war a major in the old Second Cavalry, who deserted his regiment, took office in the Confederate army, and died the death due to a rebel to the flag of the country that had educated him and given him position, a serpent in a virtuous family, and a profligate who knew not what it was to have an honorable sentiment or exalted feeling. With all his talents, he groveled in the slime of licentiousness and met the fate due to his crimes."[14]

Early in June, General Rosecrans began to position his army for his campaign to capture Chattanooga. Among the units moved was the First Cavalry Brigade, from Franklin to Triune. General Granger's corps also moved to this area, leaving only a garrison and heavy siege

[14] Jordan, "The Battle of Thompson's Station," pp. 308–309.

guns at Franklin.[15] William Thomas wrote of the move on June 2, "Struck our dorg tents and Marched through Nolinsville and reached Triune in the affternoon and camped there A great many troops are stationed here."

Three Confederate cavalry brigades under Nathan Bedford Forrest, Frank C. Armstrong, and J. W. Starnes struck at Franklin on June 4.[16] General Granger sent the First Brigade of cavalry to relieve the danger to Franklin. Shortly before dark these cavalrymen ran into Armstrong's Rebels about a mile and a half east of Franklin. In the ensuing fight General Armstrong, his escort, and his battleflag were captured and the rest of the enemy driven from the field. In the confusion, however, Armstrong escaped but his escort and banner were secured. Colonel Archibald Campbell, in charge of the expedition, claimed that he could have captured all of Armstrong's brigade if there had been another hour of daylight.[17]

Again, on June 7, a report of an attack on Franklin sent the Ninth Pennsylvania and Sixth Kentucky riding from the camp at Triune. They found a detachment of Forrest's cavalry near Franklin and drove it south toward Lewisburg. The Ninth camped for the night where the Triune and Eagleville roads come together.

About eight-thirty in the evening, an orderly from the picket post on the Triune road approached Colonel Jordan's tent with two officers who had come to the post with the request that they be taken to the commanding officer. Without examining the officers, Colonel Jordan sent them on with the orderly to the headquarters of Colonel John P. Baird of the Eighty-fifth Indiana Infantry, who commanded the garrison at Franklin. At eleven o'clock Jordan was awakened and told that Colonel Baird wanted to see him immediately; he was soon mounted and riding into Franklin.

When Jordan reached headquarters, Baird told him that he suspected the two officers were spies, although their papers seemed to be in order. These papers included orders, apparently genuine, signed by James A. Garfield, Rosecrans's chief of staff. At Baird's request, Jordan

15 *Ibid.*, p. 309.
16 Armstrong and Starnes commanded brigades in Forrest's division, Army of Tennessee.
17 O. R., Ser. 1, XXIII, pt. 1, pp. 359–62.

picked up a candle and visited the prisoners. When he asked them to sit up, he immediately recognized one of them as a Captain William Orton Williams, whom he had met in Washington during the early days of the war when he had carried dispatches from Governor Curtin to General Winfield Scott. Williams was an officer on Scott's staff, and he and Jordan had eaten together at Willard's Hotel on several of Jordan's subsequent trips to Washington.[18]

As soon as he recognized the man, Jordan called him by name. Finding that he was known, Williams admitted to Jordan that he had resigned from the U. S. Army and had joined the Confederacy. The men were dressed in Union forage caps, overcoats with regulation brass buttons, and U. S. Army trousers. When Jordan asked them to unbutton the overcoats, they revealed dress coats of Confederate officers. A telegram was sent to General Rosecrans, and no time was lost in taking the actions prescribed for such a situation, as will be seen from the record of the Military Commission. The court, with Colonel Jordan as president, had met and had found the prisoners guilty as charged by 3:00 A.M.[19] During the trial, the prisoners gave the following statement of their activities:

> That they came inside the lines of the United States Army, at Franklin, Tenn., about dark on the 8th of June, 1863, wearing the uniform they then had on their persons, which was that of Federal officers; that they went to the headquarters of Col. J. P. Baird, commanding forces at Franklin, and represented to him that they were Colonel Auton, inspector, just sent from Washington City to overlook the inspection of the several departments of the West, and Major Dunlap, his assistant, and exhibited to him an order from [Assistant] Adjutant-General [Edward D.] Townsend assigning him to that duty, an order from Major-General Rosecrans, countersigned by Brigadier-General [James A.] Garfield, chief of staff, asking him to inspect his outposts, and a pass through all lines from General Rosecrans; that he told Colonel Baird that he had missed the road from Murfreesboro to this point, got too near Eagleville, and ran into rebel pickets, had his orderly shot, and lost his coat containing his money; that he wanted some money and a pass to Nashville; that, when arrested by Colonel [Louis D.] Watkins, Sixth Kentucky Cavalry, after examination

---

[18] William Orton Williams was the prisoner's name in the U. S. Army. When captured, his papers listed him as Lawrence Auton. The second prisoner was Lt. Walter G. Peter, whose alias was Maj. Dunlap (Jordan, "The Battle of Thompson's Station," pp. 309–11).

[19] O. R., Ser. 1, XXIII, pt. 1, pp. 424–25; Jordan, "The Battle of Thompson's Station," pp. 311–12.

they admitted that they were in the rebel army, and that his (the colonel's) true name was Lawrence Orton Williams; that he had been in the Second Regular Cavalry, Army of the United States, once on General Scott's staff in Mexico, and was now a colonel in the rebel army, and Lieutenant [Walter G.] Peter was his adjutant; that he came in our lines knowing his fate, if taken, but asking mercy for his adjutant.

After hearing the evidence and the prisoners' statements, the court found the prisoners guilty of being spies. The finding was telegraphed to Rosecrans's headquarters. While awaiting a reply, Colonel Jordan stayed with the condemned men. They asked to be allowed to write to their friends. Lieutenant Peter wrote to his mother in Maryland. Williams wrote a letter and also sent a package containing a ring, a silver cup, and both greenbacks and Confederate money to a Mrs. Louisa Lamb in Montgomery. Williams told Jordan that this was a widowed daughter of Robert E. Lee, to whom he was engaged.[20]

Soon a telegram was received from Rosecrans's headquarters, and Colonel Baird issued the required order, as follows: "The finding is approved, and, by order of Major-General Rosecrans, the prisoners will be executed immediately by hanging by the neck till they are dead."[21]

Colonels Jordan and Baird did not witness the execution. However, three regiments were called out, assembled into ranks, and marched to the gallows where they were formed into a hollow square facing the gallows. The sentence was carried out in the presence of three regiments. The spies were buried in unmarked graves.[22]

William Thomas missed the execution because he had remained at Triune as an orderly at brigade headquarters. There was action at Triune on June 9, and Thomas reported, "the pickets near our camp Were driven in in the affternoon   the 4th Ky Cav went out but the rebs were Two Strong for them   we got the balance of the Brigade in camp and Started and Had a brisk fight for about 3 miles   the rebs were in force but they Fell Back towards Evening   2 men of the 4th Ky were severely wounded."

One last skirmish on June 11 ended this phase of the war.[23] "The rebs attacked us again today," wrote Thomas, "they were so Close that

20 Jordan, "The Battle of Thompson's Station," pp. 312–14.
21 O. R., Ser. 1, XXIII, pt. 1, p. 425.
22 Jordan, "The Battle of Thompson's Station," p. 314.
23 O. R., Ser. 1, XXIII, pt. 1, pp. 374–75.

the Shells were coming into camp   Our brigade went and Had a fight
With them   we fought most all day but the rebs Had to fall back   6
men out of our regt got wounded & 1 killed   We took a great many
prisoners." The man killed was Corporal John R. Boyd of Company C,
another of the Blain boys.

By this time, General Rosecrans was ready to march against Bragg's
defensive line. Before they began the campaign, however, the music lov-
ers and the practical jokers had an opportunity to enjoy themselves.
Thomas wrote, "passed the evening [at] Billy Sweatam Consert   awful
crowded and Some of the boys cut the ropes out side of the tent   pretty
nearly falling down."

XIV

Rosecrans's Chattanooga Campaign

Received orders to march at 2 Oclock A.M.   Started at 8.o.clock and marched through Eagleville   then we met the rebels and a Brisk Skirmish Ensued   we Drove them Slowly for about 8 miles past Eaglesville   Then they opened a battery Upon us and the fight became more earnest   We got our Battery in position and fired a few shots at them   then they were silent   Next thing they made a Charge on our Right flank   A brisk fight ensued but the rebels again fell back   Col Brownlow[1] Shot His Horse trying to Shoot a rebel that had come through our lines

On June 23, 1863 the Ninth Pennsylvania Cavalry, riding in the van of the First Cavalry Division, became the first unit of the Army of the Cumberland to engage the enemy during Major General William S. Rosecrans's campaign that ultimately captured Chattanooga and drove the Confederate army out of Tennessee. The cavalry fought the skirmishes described by William Thomas when they marched south from their camp at Triune in a diversion intended to convince the enemy command that the main Union thrust would be toward the Confederate left flank at Shelbyville. When the rest of the Union army marched the next day, the principal forces aimed for the gaps in the mountains near the center of the Confederate line.[2]

Behind the Pennsylvania cavalrymen rode the Second Michigan, First East Tennessee, and Fourth Kentucky, forming Colonel Archibald P. Campbell's First Brigade. After these men came the Second and Third Brigades of Brigadier General Robert B. Mitchell's First Division. This strong column rode as far as Eagleville without incident but

[1] Col. James P. Brownlow, First East Tennessee Cavalry.
[2] O. R., Ser. 1, XXIII, pt. 1, p. 547; Cist, pp. 155–60; National Park Service, *Chickamauga and Chattanooga Battlefields*, National Park Service Historical Handbook Series, No. 25 (Washington, D. C.: Government Printing Office, 1956; reprint ed., 1961), pp. 5–8.

met an enemy skirmish line immediately after passing through the town.

The Ninth quickly dismounted and formed their own skirmish line. They began to drive the enemy back toward the town of Rover. The fighting proved to be especially tiring because of the extreme heat and because the advance was made through dense undergrowth. As a result, the Ninth was relieved after driving the enemy two miles, and each of the other regiments of the First Brigade took its turn at fighting until they had advanced for eight miles. Here the Federal troopers came upon an outpost of the main Confederate defense line, a position held by infantry and artillery.

Soon the entire First Cavalry Brigade was engaged in a sharpshooting match with the defenders. The Confederate artillery discouraged any idea the officers may have had for an assault. At the same time, a Union battery, brought up from the Second Brigade, forced the enemy to remain in their works on the front. However, a column of Rebel cavalry suddenly appeared on the right flank of the Union line. The attack came on a road that was unmarked on the Federal officers' maps. Although surprised, the Tennessee and Kentucky regiments on the right of the Union line quickly changed front and repulsed the assault, but not until a few Rebels had broken through the line.[3]

After dark, General Mitchell noticed that his men were "almost exhausted in strength" and ordered them to ride back beyond Rover and camp. The men slept unsheltered on the ground. During the night rain began to fall.

The rain continued through the morning and, by noon, when the column began to march again, the roads had become quagmires. Again the troopers fought and marched. William Thomas wrote of the action:

> Started off again and Marched through a mud road all day   Met the enemy near Middleton   the second Brig in advance   we had a Brisk fight but drove the rebels Out of Camp   Killed and wounded unknown Burned their camp and Started Back   Marched 16 miles through awful mud   It rained all Day   Halted at 10.p.m.

At Middleton, the Second Brigade encountered enemy sharpshooters in log buildings in the town and in ravines of the surrounding area.

---

[3] O. R., Ser. 1, XXIII, pt. 1, pp. 542–44, 547.

The cavalrymen spent a few hours exchanging shots with these sharp-shooters but did not press the fight because an infantry column was reported to be coming up to assist in assaulting the place. However, when the infantry had not appeared by late afternoon, General Mitchell struck with his cavalry alone.

Once again, the First Brigade was called upon for the attack. The Ninth Pennsylvania and Second Michigan advanced on foot and drove the Rebels from their strong positions. A battalion of the Ninth was commended for bravery by Colonel Campbell for their part in the action.[4]

After dark, the cavalrymen retired to Salem and bivouacked. Here they remained during June 25 and 26. By this time, the Army of the Cumberland was marching, and William Thomas noted, "Rosencranz whole army are making an Advance." He also wrote, "Troops are advancing on every road and through the woods."

General Rosecrans had planned a brilliant campaign by which he hoped to block Braxton Bragg's retreat to Chattanooga and to force the Confederate army to fight in Tennessee. He nearly succeeded. While his cavalry was demonstrating in front of Shelbyville and skirmishing toward the Confederate main defenses in that area, he started his infantry marching for Hoover's and Liberty gaps through the mountains to the east. After forcing the gaps, the infantry and cavalry were to march rapidly to the Elk River and cut off the Confederate army's retreat.[5]

Rosecrans could have succeeded had the weather been normal. However, rain fell for seventeen consecutive days beginning on June 24, the very day his army began to march. Major General David S. Stanley, chief of cavalry, wrote, "The rain ... converting the whole surface of the country into a quagmire, has rendered this one of the most arduous, laborious, and distressing campaigns on man and beast I have ever witnessed."[6]

The campaign began auspiciously. On June 24, Colonel John T.

4 *Ibid.*, pp. 544, 547.
5 Guernsey and Alden, II, 530–31.
6 O. R., Ser. 1, XXIII, pt. 1, p. 538.

Wilder's brigade of mounted infantry moved so quickly into Hoover's Gap that they found few enemy ready to meet them. They surprised the Rebels a second time when superior forces attempted to drive them from the position. Wilder's men gave the first real demonstration of the fire power of the new Spencer repeating rifles and successfully defended the gap until General George H. Thomas's corps could come up.[7] Wilder, an Indiana industrialist, had quickly seen the value of the repeaters and had purchased the rifles with his own funds. His soldiers gladly repaid him in installments on paydays.[8]

General Thomas's corps, moving through Hoover's Gap, flanked Bragg's position at Tullahoma, and Bragg ordered a retreat. The 18,000 infantry at Shelbyville were among those Confederate troops who started to march toward Chattanooga. Major General Joseph Wheeler's cavalry corps was left in front of Shelbyville to cover the withdrawal. On June 27, Stanley's Union cavalry began to campaign again, and William Thomas wrote:

> Started off early in the morning and marched towards Shellbyville   Skirmishing the whole Road   reached the fortifications in the affternoon   our 2 Division of Cav are Here under Gen Stanley   1st Brig 2 Division Charged on the fortifications and took a few Hundred prisoners   we pushed them slowly till near town When they opened one of their battries upon us   then our Brig Charged On one road into Shellbyville and the 2d Brig on another   We routed them completely out of the place   there was a general Stampede of rebels at the bridge   they could not get Across fast Enough and a great many Jumped into duck river   We captured in the fight 4 pices of artillery an about 900 to 1000 prisoners   Killed unknown   the 7 Pa Had Lead Of the Charge on one road and the 9th Had Lead On the Other   Capt [Gilbert] Waters Co L Got Killed today   Horse fell in the Charge and broke the Capt neck.

General Rosecrans had ordered the cavalry to drive the enemy from Guy's Gap north of Shelbyville, but when the Federals reached the vicinity and deployed for an attack, the Rebel force retreated to fortifications four miles north of Shelbyville. Against this position the Seventh Pennsylvania and Fourth Regulars, of the Second Division, made a

[7] *Ibid.*, pp. 457–58.
[8] Henry Campbell, "The War in Kentucky-Tennessee As Seen By a Teen-Aged Bugler," *Civil War Times Illustrated*, II, No. 7 (Nov. 1963), p. 28.

mounted charge through the abatis, drove the enemy from the fortifications, and chased them toward Shelbyville. By the time they reached the outskirts of the town, the Union troopers had become strung out; and when they encountered artillery fire, they fell back out of range to reorganize.[9]

While these troopers were regrouping, General Robert Mitchell moved the entire First Division up in support. Then, in a simultaneous assault, the Second Division drove over the works in front of the town and chased the Rebels down the main street while the First Division, with the Ninth Pennsylvania in the lead, charged on the left of Shelbyville. Thus, when the enemy, fleeing the charge down the main street, congregated at the bridge across Duck River, they made an inviting target for the troopers of the Ninth Pennsylvania. After charging into the mob and engaging in hand-to-hand combat, the Pennsylvanians took possession of the bridge, pushing into the river any Rebels who refused to surrender. General Mitchell estimated that 175 to 200 of the enemy were killed on the riverbank or drowned in the river.[10] Cornelius Baker received a flesh wound in the fight at the bridge but proudly reported that he remained on duty.

The cavalrymen encamped on the battlefield that night. The next day, William Thomas reported, "The boys found the rebel Gen Wheeler and Beauforts Horses drowned with some of their papers in the Sadlebags." The same day, Mitchell's cavalry division marched back to Guy's Gap and then rode as rapidly as they could on the muddy roads through Hoover's Gap and Manchester. They reached the Elk River on July 2, forded the river and, because the Rebels were nearby, lay in line-of-battle all night.[11]

On July 3, the cavalrymen marched to Decherd and along the railroad to Cowan's Station. Thomas commented, "the roads are awful bad   a great many teams are sticking in the mud." He also observed, "Rebel Deserters are coming over to our lines pretty thick."

Foraging in the area was good, and on July 4 Thomas wrote, "We

9 O. R., Ser. 1, XXIII, pt. 1, pp. 539–40, 544–45.
10 *Ibid.*
11 *Ibid.*, p. 545.

Had a Feast to day on geese and Chickens." For several days thereafter he wrote, "the boys are out foraging." On July 7, news reached this victorious army that Vicksburg had been captured and that "the rebel forses under Lee are drove out of Pa."

On July 10, the cavalry began to ride again, and on July 13 "Crossed the line into Alabama   Marched through Some beautiful Country pass the place where McCoock [Brigadier General Robert L. McCook] was Shot by a Bushwhacker." General McCook was shot by guerrillas while ill in an ambulance.[12]

On the fourteenth, the cavalry marched through Huntsville and encamped in some woods near the town. During their stay, the soldiers had a chance to visit Huntsville. "i was Sporting Around Huntsville to day," wrote Thomas on the fifteenth. He said it was a beautiful town. The men had work to do around Huntsville. They foraged through the countryside. An additional chore was "pressing in the niggers and all kinds of cattle." A few days later Thomas added, "Pressed in all the mules and negroes along the road."

On July 21, General Mitchell marched his division north to Fayetteville, Tennessee, in an effort to control lawless elements of the population. The bushwhackers remained active after the cavalry arrived, and William Thomas reported, "Some men of the 1st Tenn Got Captured by Guerrillas to day [July 23] near the picket post." The next day he wrote, "report of a man of the 4th Ohio Cav being Hung outside of our picket Post By Guerrillas."

To combat the bushwhackers "Gen Mitchell is Bringing in all the citizens Around Here into camp and making them Take the oath of Alleigance to the U S Gov." A short while later, Colonel Edward M. McCook, commanding Mitchell's Second Brigade, took sterner measures. He ordered that all captured bushwhackers be hanged and also ordered the destruction of all property in areas where bushwhackers attacked Union soldiers. With these penalties, bushwhacking became a less popular activity, and incidents became less frequent.[13] By August

---

[12] Guernsey and Alden, I, 224. Robert McCook was the brother of Maj. Gen. Alexander McD. and Col. Daniel McCook, mentioned in chap. 10.

[13] O. R., Ser. 1, XXX, pt. 3, p. 106.

3, relations with the people of the area had improved sufficiently that William Thomas could report "the Citizens are beginning to bring eatables to camp to sell."

The next day camp was moved from the north bank of the Elk River and a new camp made in the yard of a large, brick house on the bluff on the south side. Thomas pitched his tent on an Indian mound. He wrote about the people living in the house: "the man that lives here is a rank rebel and all the family." On August 18, the cavalrymen marched toward Huntsville. "marched to The Rebel Sectary of war plantation Sectry [Leroy P.] Walker," wrote William Thomas. The next night, the cavalrymen were encamped on "the old ground" at Huntsville.

General Rosecrans was now preparing the second move of the campaign. He had flanked the Confederate army out of Middle Tennessee; now he would fake them out of Chattanooga. His principal problem was logistics. He had to supply his army, deep in eastern Tennessee and northern Alabama, by means of a single railroad that extended back to Louisville, 300 miles away. However, by late August, adequate supplies were on hand to allow the resumption of the offense.

Rosecrans first sent a small part of his army north of Chattanooga, and this body of troops made a most conspicuous demonstration, convincing Bragg that the blow would come from the north. Meanwhile, the bulk of the Union army was concentrating along the Tennessee River west of Chattanooga in the general area of Stevenson and Bridgeport, Alabama.[14]

As a part of this assemblage, Stanley's two divisions of cavalry began to march east from Huntsville on August 12. Some regiments were left at various points along the railroad, and the Ninth Pennsylvania marched on alone beyond Stevenson and camped near General Phillip H. Sheridan's headquarters at Bolivar on August 15. William Thomas was able to visit Bolivar and Stevenson on successive days. On August 19, he reported that General Rosecrans and General Stanley had arrived in this forward area and established their headquarters near the camp of the Ninth Pennsylvania.

By August 28, pontoon bridges were completed across the Tennessee River. On this day, the Second Michigan crossed the bridge at Caper-

14 National Park Service, pp. 8–9; Guernsey and Alden, II, p. 537.

ton's Ferry. The First East Tennessee crossed on the following day, and the Ninth Pennsylvania on the 31st. By September 2, the entire First Cavalry Division was across and, on September 3, began to ascend Sand Mountain.[15] Thomas described the march: "Very steep for two miles Marched on the mountain all day   Descended into Wills Valley in the evening   Davis Division is Here."[16] On September 4, the Ninth marched southwest toward Rawlinsville, Alabama, and on the following day reached Lebanon, Alabama. "Met only a small squad of Rebs," noted Thomas, "passed a saltpeter Cave and Burned the works and the Salt peter Mills."

The Army of the Cumberland was entirely across the river on September 4 and, as they began to cross the mountains and threaten the railroad from Atlanta, General Bragg in Chattanooga had a choice of being trapped in that city or retreating quickly into Georgia. He chose to retreat. By September 8, all the Confederate army was out of the town and retreating southward. Federal troops entered the city the same day and remained in control of Chattanooga for the remainder of the war.[17]

15 O. R., Ser. 1, XXX, pt. 1, pp. 890, 894, 899; Cist, pp. 179–80.

16 The division referred to was the 1st Div., XX Corps, commanded by an Indiana officer with the unlikely name of Brig. Gen. Jefferson C. Davis.

17 Guernsey and Alden, II, 537; Cist, pp. 184–85.

XV

Started off at 9. A.M. And marched towards Lafayette Skirmished with the rebel pickets within 3 miles of town Then the 9th Pa made a charge And Run into a Hornet Nest of rebels they Checked our Charge 3 times We had to Fall Back When they Opened their Battries Upon us but we captured all their Skirmishers and pickets outside the Main line Braggs whole forse was Laying at Lafayette Withdrawn from Chatta- nooga they had a regular V formed for us and we ran into it when they poured it into us Heavy for a while drawed back to Alpine and camped

Chickamauga

The charge by the Ninth Pennsylvania on September 13 that carried nearly to La Fayette was the deepest Federal penetration into Georgia during the 1863 campaign. The charge changed the course of the campaign because the captured men belonged to Major General John C. Breckenridge's division that had recently moved from Mississippi to Georgia to reinforce Bragg's army.[1] The capture of these pickets was the first definite information General Rosecrans received to confirm that Bragg was being strengthened and that he was preparing to launch an attack instead of retreating toward Atlanta. Rosecrans began to concentrate his army, which had come through three widely separated gaps in the mountains and was vulnerable to defeat in detail by the now numerically superior enemy.

When the Confederate army left Chattanooga, Major General Thomas L. Crittenden's XXI Corps moved in. George H. Thomas's XIV Corps and Alexander McCook's XX Corps were south of Chattanooga between the Tennessee River and Lookout Mountain. Rose-

---

[1] O. R., Ser. 1, XXX, pt. 1, p. 892; National Park Service, p. 12, states Bragg's reinforcements as Maj. Gen. Simon B. Buckner's corps, 8,000 men, from Knoxville; two divisions under Maj. Gen. John C. Breckenridge and Maj. Gen. W. H. T. Walker, 9,000 men, from Mississippi; plus two brigades, 2,500 men, also from Mississippi. Later 15,000 men of Lt. Gen. James Longstreet's corps arrived from Virginia.

crans, convinced then that the enemy was in full retreat, had Thomas cross the mountain into McLemore's Cove while McCook crossed to the town of Alpine, near present Menlo, Georgia, farther south. Crittenden's and McCook's corps were separated by forty miles of mountainous country. The cavalry marched in the van of McCook's corps.[2]

At daylight on September 9, the First Cavalry Division began to ascend Lookout Mountain. On the top they met enemy skirmishers and drove them eastward across the mountain and down the steep slope into Broomtown Valley. Progress was slow on the mountain, and when the Union troopers reached Henderson's Gap "we had to Cut our way Down with axes   the rebs Had Felled trees across the road" according to William Thomas. Again they met Rebel skirmishers in the valley but outflanked them and drove them through Alpine. That night the Yankee cavalrymen bivouacked at Alpine, formed in line-of-battle, and were up again and standing to horse at 3:00 A.M.

On September 10, the First Cavalry Division, including the Ninth Pennsylvania, made a reconnaissance toward Rome while the Second Division scouted along the roads toward La Fayette. The former group went as far as Melville without meeting the enemy and returned to Alpine in the evening. The following day the First Brigade, First Division, alone returned to Melville and scouted to within twelve miles of Rome learning that heavy enemy forces were encamped north of the town. They bivouacked at Melville that night.[3] Rations were scarce. "Lived on Sweet potatoes the last 3 days," wrote William Thomas.

The brigade returned to Alpine on September 12, and after stopping only long enough to feed their horses, marched toward La Fayette to assist Brigadier General George Crook's Second Division on a reconnaissance. They encamped that night at a place known as Valley Store, ten miles south of La Fayette.[4]

At about this time, command changes in the cavalry became necessary. General David S. Stanley became so ill that he could not sit astride his horse and had to be sent to the rear. Brigadier General Robert B. Mitchell took command of the Cavalry Corps, and Colonel Edward M.

[2] Cist, pp. 180–84; National Park Service, pp. 9–10.
[3] O. R., Ser. 1, XXX, pt. 1, pp. 891–92, 895.
[4] *Ibid.*, pp. 899–903.

McCook moved up to command the First Division. On the night of September 12, all of McCook's division except the First Brigade was on the La Fayette–Summerville road while the First Brigade was with Crook's division on the La Fayette–Alpine road.[5]

On September 13, Companies A, C, and E of the Ninth Pennsylvania led General Crook's column toward La Fayette. They encountered pickets three miles from town and drove them back to a strong line. Here a volley, which killed one man, stopped the advance of the Pennsylvania troopers. The enemy then fell back to the crest of a brush covered knoll and opened a severe fire.

Colonel Archibald Campbell directed Lieutenant Colonel Roswell M. Russell to push forward a squadron to reinforce the skirmish line and clear the road. Russell ordered two companies, H and F, under Major Edward G. Savage, to charge. The charge met with a momentary check because clouds of dust concealed a deep gully running across the road. This hazard tripped the first four horses. When the debris of horses and men was removed, the charge was continued but had not advanced more than 200 yards when the enemy opened a withering, enfilading fire, killing one man, mortally wounding two others, and disabling eight horses. Captain William Shriver, of Company H, had two horses shot under him; and Lieutenants George A. Shuman and Thomas W. Jordan each one. When the balance of the regiment came up, they tore down the fences and deployed in the fields beside the road. They had just begun to drive the enemy from their cover when ordered to withdraw. Eighteen of the Rebel pickets were captured in this action.[6]

The withdrawal order came from General Crook, who saw that a large enemy force was moving around to get into the rear of the embattled regiment.[7] The Ninth had run into the main concentration point of the Confederate army. Braxton Bragg had planned to go out and strike George Thomas's big Union corps on the next day. Fortunately for the Army of the Cumberland, Bragg's subordinates failed to carry out his orders to attack giving the Federal army additional time to

5 *Ibid.*, pp. 892, 899–903.
6 *Ibid.*, pp. 903–904.
7 *Ibid.*, p. 918.

Upper left: Bugler Cornelius Baker, Company C. *Upper right*: Julia Bower Baker. *Lower left*: Private William A. Stump, Company C. *Lower right*: Saddler Leopold Miller, Company C.

Chattanooga Valley from Lookout Mountain as it appeared during the Civil War. *U.S. Signal Corps photograph, Brady Collection, National Archives.*

Trestle bridge below Whiteside, Tennessee. *U.S. War Department, General Staff photograph, National Archives.*

Midway Church, near Savannah, Georgia.

Upper left: Captain George A. Shuman, Company H. *Upper right*: Sergeant Samuel P. Gutshall, Company C. *Lower left*: Private Samuel Baker. *Lower right*: Corporal Alfred Corman.

Bennett House, where Sherman and Johnson made the
surrender at Durham Station, North Carolina.

Left: "Star" engraved by Cornelius Baker. *Right*: "Badge" engraved by Cornelius Baker. *Lower*: Stone Bible sculptured by Cornelius Baker.

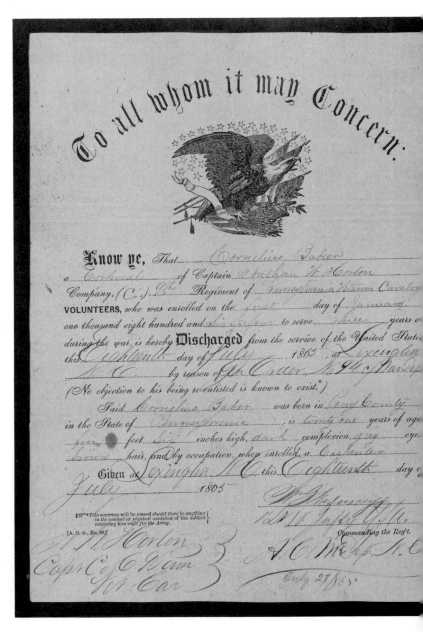

To all whom it may Concern.

Know ye, That _Cornelius Baker_
a _Corporal_ of Captain _Nathan W. Horton_
Company, (C.) _7th_ Regiment of _Pennsylvania Veteran Cavalry_
VOLUNTEERS, who was enrolled on the _first_ day of _January_
one thousand eight hundred and _sixty four_ to serve _three_ years o
during the war, is hereby **Discharged** from the service of the United State
this _eighteenth_ day of _July_, 1865, at _Lexington_
_N.C._ by reason of _Gen Order No 94 of War Dep_
(No objection to his being re-enlisted is known to exist.*)

Said _Cornelius Baker_ was born in _Perry County_
in the State of _Pennsylvania_, is _twenty one_ years of age
five feet _six_ inches high, _dark_ complexion, _grey_ eye
brown hair, and by occupation, when enrolled, a _Carpenter_

Given at _Lexington N C_ this _Eighteenth_ day o
July 1865

☞ *This sentence will be erased should there be anything
in the conduct or physical condition of the soldier
rendering him unfit for the Army.
[A. G. O., No. 99.]

W W Jennings
Lieut Col 7 U.S.A.
Commanding the Reg't.

N W Horton
Capt Co C Penn
Vet Car

A C Welsh N C

July 27/865

Cornelius Baker's discharge paper, 1865.

concentrate.[8] After the fight near La Fayette, the cavalry retreated to Alpine.

On September 14 the Union cavalry left Alpine and ascended the east slope of Lookout Mountain, camping near Little River on top of the mountain that night. The next day the Ninth Pennsylvania descended into Wills Valley and escorted the cavalry wagon train to Valley Head.

On the sixteenth the regiment recrossed Lookout Mountain, passing Jefferson C. Davis's infantry division on top of the mountain, and then descended through Dugout Gap into McLemore's Cove. They marched only four miles on the seventeenth and six miles the next day.[9] During the morning of September 19, the entire Cavalry Corps moved to Crawfish Springs, the present town of Chickamauga. William Thomas wrote:

> Warm Day and dusty   Started off again And Caught up to Davis Div they were Engaged with the rebels at Chickamauga Creek   Davis Div made a Charge and Drove them back 4 miles through Caslet Gap   Heavy fighting all along the lines   Heavy firing till Long after dark   we were engaged with the rebels all day on the flanks and gaurding the train   The rebs were trying to Capture the Ammunition train all day   we were Stationed at Crawfish Springs   the Ambulances are busy bringing in the Wounded to Crawfish Springs.

William Thomas saw only the action on his front and knew little about the course of the battle. The cavalry was at the far right of the Federal line while the most severe fighting was at the extreme left. The cavalry's assignment was to cover the upper fords of Chickamauga Creek, protect the field hospitals at Crawfish Springs, and guard the wagon trains.[10]

The Union army had succeeded in uniting before the first Confederate attack was launched on September 19. During the previous night, General George H. Thomas's corps had marched past Thomas Crittenden's corps near Lee and Gordon's Mill and had taken position across the Rossville road. Alexander McCook's corps had also arrived and began to form on Crittenden's right. Beyond McCook was John T.

---

[8] National Park Service, pp. 13–14.
[9] Col. McCook, Col. Campbell, and Lt. Col. Russell all report camp at Cedar Grove Church on Sept. 17. Campbell and Russell report camp at Bailey's Crossroad on Sept. 18.
[10] O. R., Ser. 1, XXX, pt. 1, pp. 893, 899–900, 904.

Wilder's mounted infantry. At the extreme right was the Cavalry Corps with the First Division along Chickamauga Creek and the Second Division extending west from Crawfish Springs.[11]

The Ninth Pennsylvania was assigned a sector extending from the springs to Cowan's Ford with its left in contact with Wilder's brigade. The principal action of the Ninth came when a squadron of Rebel cavalry appeared on the south bank of the creek. Two companies of the Ninth crossed and dispersed this force.[12]

Unfortunately, the Union field hospitals were located at Crawfish Springs, the farthest position from the army's operating base at Chattanooga and separated from it by Missionary Ridge. The abundance of water, required for the water-dressings then in use, was the reason for locating the hospitals at Crawfish Springs; but this decision caused one of the worst medical disasters of the war. On the first day of the battle, ambulances had to move in both directions along a single, narrow road. In spite of this restriction, some 4,500 wounded were brought to the hospitals by midnight of the nineteenth. On September 20, the error of locating the hospitals on an exposed flank became apparent when the Confederates shelled the hospitals. They said that they mistook the hospital flags for battle flags.[13]

On the morning of September 20 the Confederates again struck hard at the extreme Union left, and Rosecrans was forced to move more men from the center and right to strengthen the left until General Thomas had more than half the army under his command. When Longstreet's Confederate corps, recently arrived from Lee's Army of Northern Virginia, struck near the center of the Union line, they found a gap caused by a command error. Longstreet's men poured through the breech, splitting the Union army. Longstreet then joined the assault on the Union left. This part of the Federal line was in the shape of a horseshoe around Snodgrass Hill to fight off attacks coming from three sides. The lines held for the rest of the day and won for General Thomas the nickname "The Rock of Chickamauga."[14]

---

[11] Guernsey and Alden, II, 545; National Park Service, pp. 13–15; O. R., Ser. 1, XXX, pt. 1, p. 893.
[12] O. R., Ser. 1, XXX, pt. 1, p. 904.
[13] Adams, p. 94.
[14] National Park Service, pp. 19–23; Cist, pp. 203–15.

Of course, the cavalrymen did not know about the events on the left and center of the line, but suddenly their officers also found that they had lost contact with the rest of the army. The Ninth Pennsylvania was ordered to try to contact Major General Phillip Sheridan and to open a line of communication. The regiment had trotted back about two miles when Lieutenant Colonel Roswell Russell saw enemy troops with artillery on a hill that commanded the road. He immediately began to deploy his troopers to determine the strength of the Rebel position. However, before his men began to attack, orders came for them to return to Crawfish Springs, where the rest of the cavalry was under mounting enemy pressure.[15]

"We had to fall back 7 miles into Chattanooga Valley," wrote William Thomas, "we Had to leave our wounded In the Hands of the rebels at Crawfish Springs." General Robert Mitchell reported that all wounded able to ride in wagons were evacuated and Colonel Edward McCook wrote that all wounded cavalrymen were brought out. However, thousands of the wounded were left behind to be cared for by the enemy.[16]

When the cavalry marched away from Crawfish Springs, the Ninth Pennsylvania became rear guard of the retreating column. The column moved slowly because it included ambulances, the Cavalry Corps' wagon train, and the wagons of the XX Corps (McCook's). The column marched on the old Chattanooga road that cut behind Missionary Ridge and went down Chattanooga Valley between the ridge and Lookout Mountain.

Before they had marched many miles, the Federal cavalry was nearly surrounded by enemy cavalry and infantry. The long train of slow-moving wagons tempted the Rebel cavalry to make a dash at the column, but the Ninth Pennsylvania beat off the assault and enabled the wagons to roll unmolested to Chattanooga.[17] Signs of the defeat were spread all along the road. The cavalry recovered two guns that had been abandoned by McCook's corps and brought along nearly 1,000 stragglers from the same corps. "There was never work more opportunely

[15] O. R., Ser. 1, XXX, pt. 1, p. 904.
[16] *Ibid.*, pp. 895, 896.
[17] *Ibid.*, 905.

done on the battlefield than the work of the cavalry on the 20th of September at Chickamauga," General Mitchell wrote about the performance of his command.[18]

At midnight, the cavalry was in line-of-battle across the valley south of McFarland's Gap, through which General Thomas's tired men were then retreating. In two days of the hardest fighting of the war, Thomas's men had beaten off assault after assault. After dark on September 20, Thomas ordered them to withdraw through McFarland's Gap and to Chattanooga. The cavalry held their line all day on September 21, repulsing at least one attack, and enabled Thomas's infantry and artillery to march to Chattanooga without being molested by the enemy from the southern end of Chattanooga Valley.[19]

On September 22, the cavalry left their position and retired into Chattanooga. "Although they knew our army had suffered disaster," reported Colonel McCook, ". . . there was no wavering, no haste; they retired from the field slowly and orderly."[20] At 6:00 P.M. the Ninth Pennsylvania crossed the river under enemy artillery fire. Soon they took up a new position on Moccasin Point opposite William's Island and patrolled from that point to the sector near the town covered by the infantry pickets.[21]

Cornelius Baker missed the Battle of Chickamauga. Malaria, the second most prevalent disease of the war, was the cause. His medical record shows that he entered the general field hospital at Stevenson, Alabama, on September 18. The record lists the ailment as "intermittent fever." Very likely Cornelius had dropped out of the ranks a few days before; possibly when the regiment passed through Alpine.

Next, Cornelius was sent to General Hospital No. 12 in Nashville, arriving there on September 28. He probably made the trip on the new hospital train that had been placed in service about a month before, operating between Stevenson and Nashville. This was the first true hospital train. The Medical Director of the Army of the Cumberland, George E. Cooper, designed a new car that was very similar to the Pullman car of a later era. An arrangement of boards converted day coach

18 *Ibid.*, pp. 893–94, 900.
19 *Ibid.*, pp. 896, 900.
20 *Ibid.*, 897.
21 *Ibid.*, 905; O. R., Ser. 1, XXX, pt. 3, p. 807.

seats into lower berths, and litters slung from braces extending from the side walls formed upper berths. The train had two of these cars and several freight cars equipped with beds. The advent of the new train was timely, and it was filled to capacity every trip after the Battle of Chickamauga.[22]

In later years, Cornelius related that he thought he was going to die. Like many other soldiers he found his own medication. Somehow he found the strength to slip out of the hospital and make his way to the river, where he drank all the water he could hold. Shortly thereafter he began to recover and attributed his recovery to the river water. On October 15, he was transferred to the convalescent hospital.

Convalescence was slow. Cornelius was discharged from the hospital and returned to duty on December 18. His discharge and reenlistment papers were dated January 1, 1864, indicating that he was with the regiment at Mossy Creek (now Jefferson City), Tennessee, on that date. However, the muster rolls of January and February show him absent in the hospital. One final medical record shows that Cornelius reported into the convalescent hospital at Camp Nelson, Kentucky, from Lexington on February 22 and that he was sent to Knoxville to report for duty on the following day. Probably he did return to duty in December, but the campaigning in mud, rain, and cold brought on a relapse.

While Cornelius Baker was in Stevenson during the beginning of his illness, the Army of the Cumberland was in a desperate situation in Chattanooga. All practical routes for bringing supplies into the city had been cut by the enemy. The cavalry of the Army of the Cumberland was given the task of helping to protect the railroad lines by which reinforcements to relieve the city would come.[23]

[22] Adams, pp. 107–108.
[23] National Park Service, pp. 27–30.

XVI

A Chase Across Tennessee

Wheeler with His Cavalry Made a raid Down through Sequatch valley and Burned One of our trains with forage provisions and ammunition of 500 teams[1] Crossing Waldon Ridge going to Chattanooga   the 2nd Brig had a fight with them and took 61 prisoners   Killed unknown   We reported to McCoock and camped for the night   Some of our Cav Still in pursuit

The action described by William Thomas on October 3 was the end of one of the desperate attempts by the Federal command to get provisions to the beleaguered Army of the Cumberland. The occupation of Lookout Mountain by the enemy prevented all transportation into Chattanooga by rail or water. The wagon train destroyed by Major General Joseph Wheeler had come from the railroad in Alabama by a circuitous route up the Sequatchie Valley.[2]

While the army was pinned down in Chattanooga, Wheeler with a force of 5,000 to 6,000 cavalry was turned loose on "an extensive plan of destruction to our communications, and plunder, rapine, and murder throughout Middle Tennessee and Northern Alabama," as Major General George Thomas expressed it.[3] The hard, relentless pursuit of Wheeler prevented the Confederate cavalry from accomplishing the objectives of the raid and also prevented additional forces under Brigadier General P. D. Roddey and Brigadier General S. D. Lee from joining Wheeler.[4]

[1] Guernsey and Alden, p. 551, indicate that the train was 10 miles in length; Cist, p. 231, says 300 wagons were burned.

[2] Cist, pp. 230–32; National Park Service, pp. 24–27.

[3] The Army of the Cumberland was in a desperate situation in Chattanooga. The men were resolved to starve before they surrendered, and they very nearly did starve before a way was opened to move quantities of supplies into the town.

[4] Gen. Roddey commanded a brigade of Wheeler's cavalry; Gen. S. D. Lee commanded all cavalry in Mississippi (O. R., Ser. 1, XXX, pt. 2, p. 644).

The Ninth Pennsylvania Cavalry had reached Chattanooga on September 22, and the next day William Thomas wrote, "to day the two opposing armies Lay in line of Battle Only a short distance apart   it is reported that Burnside is coming with reinforcements."[5]

On September 24 the cavalry was forced to move six miles out of Chattanooga to obtain forage for their horses. At midnight the men were called out and the horses were saddled. The reason, according to William Thomas, "The rebs Charged the breasworks at Chatanooga Twice in massed column But were repulsed with Heavy loss."[6]

During the evening of September 25, the cavalry moved from the Chattanooga area and marched to positions where they could protect the railroad from Nashville. The Ninth Pennsylvania camped near Caperton's Ferry on the Tennessee River in Alabama. Some Confederate cavalry forded the river on September 28 but recrossed before the Pennsylvanians could come up to them.[7] On September 30, William Thomas reported one of the outstanding logistical achievements of the war when he wrote, "Troops are passing through Stephenson to Chattanooga From the Potomac."

On the night of September 23, when word reached Washington that the Army of the Cumberland was besieged, Secretary of War Stanton immediately invited President Lincoln and several army officers to an emergency council meeting. That night a decision was reached to detach two corps from the then inactive Army of the Potomac, place them under the command of Major General Joseph Hooker, and send them as quickly as possible to Chattanooga. The troops began to entrain at Manassas Junction in Virginia on September 25; and the first soldiers detrained at Stevenson, Alabama, on September 30, after traveling 1,157 miles. By the middle of October, the entire two corps of 20,000 men, 3,000 animals, and all equipment had reached Bridgeport, Alabama, in the fastest time for a troop movement of such magnitude in the history of warfare. The route took the soldiers through West Virginia,

[5] Reference is made to Maj. Gen. Ambrose Burnside, whose Army of the Ohio was in Knoxville. Thomas's information, however, was incorrect; Burnside's army was not marching to relieve Chattanooga.
[6] This comment appears contrary to the general opinion that Bragg made no serious attempt to capture Chattanooga.
[7] O. R., Ser. 1, XXX, pt. 2, p. 675.

across Ohio, through part of Indiana, and across Kentucky and Tennessee into Alabama, in spite of a need for frequent detraining because the railroads used different gauge track.[8]

One danger of Wheeler's raid was the possible disruption of this troop movement. The Union cavalry began to pursue him on October 1 and made their first contact with Wheeler's force near Dunlap the next day.[9] The same day, the Ninth Pennsylvania broke camp at Caperton's Ferry and marched up the Sequatchie Valley. By halting for only two hours during the night to feed their horses, the regiment reached Dunlap and joined the rest of the First Division on the evening of the third.

The division left Dunlap during the evening of October 4 and began to cross Cumberland Mountain. They halted for the two hours necessary to feed on the mountain at a place where Wheeler had struck a second wagon train.[10] The scene was described by William Thomas: "The Mountain was Strewn with broken botles an Boxes were the rebs had robed the Sutlers That were in the train   Laying full of dead mules that the rebs Shot   Could not take along."

After robbing the train, Wheeler had continued across the mountain and had marched to McMinnville. Here, General George Crook with the Second Division of Union cavalry and John T. Wilder's brigade of mounted infantry caught up to Wheeler's rear guard. A brief skirmish ensued about which Crook reported, "They were charged with the saber, before which they could not stand."[11]

The First Division reached McMinnville at eight o'clock on the morning of October 5 shortly after Wheeler and Crook had passed through. William Thomas observed, "the rebels Had burned all our commissary Stores And All Gov property and took 400 of our men prisoners   4th Tenn regt that were Stationed there." After a short stop in McMinnville, the division rode on through Woodbury and camped

---

[8] Guernsey and Alden, pp. 555–56; National Park Service, pp. 27–30; Hooker's command consisted of the XI Corps, under Maj. Gen. Oliver O. Howard, and the XII Corps, under Maj. Gen. Henry Warner Slocum.

[9] O. R., Ser. 1, XX, pt. 2, pp. 675, 679.

[10] Guernsey and Alden, p. 551, indicates there were 800 to 1,500 wagons in the two trains destroyed by Wheeler on Walden's Ridge and Cumberland Mountain.

[11] O. R., Ser. 1, XXX, pt. 2, p. 644.

at midnight on Cripple Creek between Woodbury and Murfreesboro. The troopers had ridden fifty-two miles in twenty-four hours.[12]

While McCook's division was going into camp on Cripple Creek, General Crook's division had started to draw rations in Murfreesboro. Thus, when McCook's troopers reached Murfreesboro at nine o'clock the next morning, Crook's men had all been provisioned and had resumed the chase. The First Division stayed three hours in Murfreesboro to draw rations and to feed horses.[13] William Thomas wrote, "The rebels did not Enter Murfreesboro   they passed within 3 miles and burned a bridge on the railroad and took 1 company prisoners that were guarding it." Wheeler also managed to destroy three miles of track, but the close pursuit had forced his men to flee before large-scale destruction of the railroad could be accomplished.

When they left Murfreesboro, McCook's men rode hard to overtake the Second Division. Along the way, the cavalrymen met "parties of bridge guards whom Wheeler had captured, but had not time or means to take along, as his movements were very precipitate," according to General Robert Mitchell, who commanded the Union cavalry corps.[14] Mitchell's command was united for the first time when McCook's men caught up with Crook about eight miles from Shelbyville.

On October 7, the Union cavalry marched into Shelbyville. The city had been sacked by Wheeler's men. Upon leaving Shelbyville, Wheeler's force was split, with the main body marching toward Farmington and a second column moving toward Unionville. The Federal column also divided, with Crook's Second Division and Wilder's brigade pursuing the main body and McCook's First Division chasing the smaller party. McCook's troopers crossed Duck River at dusk and encamped.[15] William Thomas commented, "Our horses are giving out very fast."

Also on October 7, Crook came upon Wheeler's men at Farmington and routed them "although his number far exceeded ours." In this fight, Wheeler lost 2 guns, 150 killed, and 300 prisoners. After this skirmish, "Wheeler's retreat was a rout and his command was running all

12 *Ibid.*, pp. 688–89.
13 *Ibid.*
14 *Ibid.*
15 *Ibid.*

day for the river, every man for himself, and hats, canteens, coats, guns, and broken down horses are strewn along the whole route."[16]

The First Division recrossed the Duck River on October 8 and passed through Lewisburg toward Pulaski. They encamped at 9 P.M. on the plantation of Messrs. Laird and Woods ten miles from Pulaski. Starting again at daylight the next morning, the troopers rode as fast as their tired horses could carry them. William Thomas wrote, "went on a charge from Pulaski to Rogersville [Alabama]." However, the enemy had managed to cross the Tennessee River before the Federal troopers could catch them. The First Cavalry Division had ridden more than 100 miles in the last two days of the chase and had covered 250 miles in six days. The horses were "terribly jaded."[17]

General Mitchell wrote that his two divisions were reduced to 2,400 effective men "simply because we have no horses fit for service." He complained, "It was not the hard marching that ruined our stock but the worthless, murderous saddles that dig holes into the backs the first day and break them down." The new saddles, he explained, were made of green hide that pulled off at the first rain, green wood that warped, and weak iron that allowed the saddles to spread.[18]

Although they did not catch Wheeler's force, the energetic pursuit by the Federal cavalry had prevented any extensive destruction in Middle Tennessee and interruption to the movement of Hooker's relief expedition. Wheeler lost, according to Union reports, 2,000 men and 6 guns. Wheeler said that he had fewer than 60 killed, 200 wounded, and 200 captured. A few days later, a Union scouting party captured one of Wheeler's couriers with a copy of Wheeler's report "in which he forgets to mention the loss of four of his guns at Farmington," as Major General George H. Thomas sarcastically commented. He continued, "His report is probably equally true in other respects."[19]

On October 10 the Ninth Pennsylvania began to march back toward Huntsville with the rest of the First Division. Arriving that same day, they learned that another Confederate cavalry force of 2,000 men and 4 artillery pieces was across the line in Tennessee and was retreating to-

16 *Ibid.*
17 *Ibid.*, p. 668.
18 O. R., Ser. 1, XXXI, pt. 1, p. 835.
19 O. R., Ser. 1, XXX, pt. 2, p. 644.

ward the Tennessee River crossings. This was Brigadier General P. D. Roddey's division, which had failed in an attempt to join Wheeler.[20]

The Union cavalry force immediately rode north from Huntsville. In the advance the Ninth Pennsylvania suddenly came upon the enemy rear guard as dusk and rain arrived simultaneously. Upon receiving a volley from the enemy who were already in line, the Ninth dismounted and deployed along the road. They then advanced toward the woods in which the Rebels had their line. Upon reaching the edge of the woods they were fired on "at short pistol range," but as they took cover quickly, only one man was killed. Then the Pennsylvanians fired all their pieces, killing three and wounding eleven. The enemy broke off the engagement and retreated.[21] William Thomas wrote, "it was so dark our men and the Rebs Came together and could not see one another." The pitch darkness with "rain pouring down in torrents" made pursuit of the enemy impossible, and the troopers went back a mile and set up camp.

The next day, William Thomas reported, "Started early and passed through New Market [Alabama]   we Fowlled the rebs till Evening   could not get up to them   we then gave up the chase." He also reported, "Our command are all out of rations and A Great many walking."

On October 14 the men marched to Salem, still without rations. From Salem they marched on to Winchester, arriving on October 16. Here, Thomas wrote, "Detail went Out of Each Regt to Dechert Station to fetch rations for the command." On October 18, details were sent for clothing. William Thomas "Seen the boys of the 46 Pa inf from the Potomac" when he was in Decherd on October 20. On October 22, the entire command went to Decherd Station "To see Gen Rosencrans pass through from Chatanooga   we were disappointed   He did not pass through till next morning." "Old Rosey" was a favorite of the soldiers of the Army of the Cumberland, but he had lost a battle. As was usual with Union generals who lost, he was replaced.

Rosecrans's replacement by George H. Thomas was part of a change of command in the Union forces. Major General Ulysses S. Grant was

---

20 *Ibid.*
21 *Ibid.*, pp. 669, 677, 680.

placed in over-all command of the Western armies and moved to Chattanooga to take charge. Directly affecting the cavalrymen was the assignment of Brigadier General Washington L. Elliott to the leadership of the Cavalry Corps, with Colonel Edward M. McCook remaining in command of the First Division.

On October 25, William Thomas wrote, "there was a heavy explosion during the night." Later they learned that the explosion had been a mine placed on the railroad but "It did not cause much damage." On November 11, Thomas observed, "part of Grants Army arrived at this place [Decherd]." The next day "more of Grants army Passed through here today." Like Hooker's force, this army, now under the command of Major General William T. Sherman, was marching to the relief of Chattanooga. Unlike Hooker, who was rushed with all speed possible to Chattanooga, Sherman had been ordered to repair the railroad from Memphis as he marched. As a result, Sherman required two months to march from Vicksburg and Memphis in contrast to two weeks to get Hooker's men from Virginia.[22]

While Union soldiers were marching to Chattanooga and soon would number 80,000 men, General Bragg weakened the Confederate force by sending General Longstreet with 17,000 men to Knoxville in what proved to be an unsuccessful attempt to drive Burnside's Army of the Ohio out of East Tennessee.[23] Thus, Bragg was short handed when Grant moved against his position on November 23, and the Army of the Cumberland made up for the loss at Chickamauga by storming the steep slope of Missionary Ridge, without orders, and breaking the Confederate line. The enemy retreated into Georgia and never again threatened Chattanooga.

Only after he had broken the Confederate army in front of Chattanooga did Grant move to relieve Burnside. When he acted, he sent General Sherman, with 25,000 men, toward Knoxville and ordered General Elliott, with the First Cavalry Division, to the same place.[24]

---

[22] National Park Service, p. 27.
[23] Guernsey and Alden, II, 552.
[24] O. R., Ser. 1, XXXI, pt. 3, p. 257.

XVII

A Winter in East Tennessee

Cold day   Started away this morning at 2 A.M.   Accompanied by 2 other Brig in Command of Col Wolford [Garrard]   Arrived at Dandridge Where we Had a Hard fight with them   they Surounded our Brig and we Had to fight Our way out   they were pouring it into us on All Sides the other Brigs did not come to Our Releif till we were out of the muss They made a charge upon us to day and took 2 pice of our artillery   the 9th Charged upon Them and retook it again   [Then] our boys Turned the guns upon them and Commenced Pouring it into them heavy for a while   We then fell back to New Market   The Loss in our Brig 59 men   rebels unknown

In this diary entry, William Thomas tells how the transplanted troopers from the Army of the Cumberland spent Christmas Eve of 1863 helping the Army of the Ohio's cavalry fight General James Longstreet's corps in East Tennessee. This was only the first of several sharp actions when the Union and Confederate cavalries tried to occupy the same ground for forage and supply. After failing in his siege of Knoxville, Longstreet had retreated to Morristown, which he fortified.[1]

Colonel Edward M. McCook's First Cavalry Division, Army of the Cumberland, was encamped at Alexandria, Tennessee, on November 27 when ordered to march to Knoxville to support General Sherman's relief column that was enroute from Chattanooga to break Longstreet's siege of Knoxville. McCook's division had two brigades. As in past campaigns, the First Brigade, commanded by Colonel Archibald Campbell, included the Ninth Pennsylvania, the Second Michigan, and the First East Tennessee Regiments. The Second Brigade, under Colonel

[1] Seymour, p. 217; the Army of the Ohio Cavalry, commanded by Brig. Gen. Samuel D. Sturgis, consisted of two divisions commanded by Brig. Gen. Frank Wolford and Col. Israel Garrard.

Oscar LaGrange, was made up of the Second Indiana, the Fourth Indiana, the Seventh Kentucky, and the First Wisconsin Regiments. The Eighteenth Indiana Battery, commanded by Captain Eli Lilly, also was attached to the division. Brigadier General Washington L. Elliott, chief of cavalry, Army of the Cumberland, was with his First Division and accompanied it on the march to East Tennessee.[2]

The first obstacle in the march was the crossing of Caney Fork, then at flood stage and too deep and swift for fording. On November 28 the Ninth Pennsylvania crossed on the single ferry available, and the remainder of the First Brigade ferried across the next day. By November 30 crossing was made more difficult and hazardous when water froze on the pull ropes. On one trip, the horses became frightened and unmanageable, upsetting the boat. Eight men of the Second Indiana were drowned.[3] A sergeant, able to swim, had an oar and would have reached the bank; however, he gave his oar to a comrade who could not swim, saving the soldier but drowning himself.[4]

Ahead of the column a scouting party made up of Pennsylvania and Tennessee troopers, under Colonel Brownlow of the First East Tennessee, encountered a party of guerrillas near Sparta and put them to rout. The scout killed one, captured ten, and wounded two of the guerrillas.[5] The main column left the bank of Caney Fork on December 1 and marched to Sparta. Ahead of them, Colonel James P. Brownlow's scouts again were assaulted by guerrillas commanded by the same Hamilton, Bledsoe, and Champe Ferguson who had given the Ninth Pennsylvania trouble in the Tompkinsville, Kentucky, area during the spring of 1862. Four of the East Tennessee troopers were killed, and Captain Thomas S. McCahan of Company L, Ninth Pennsylvania, was severely wounded. Once again the guerrillas were routed.[6] William Thomas reported that eleven "bushwhackers" were killed.

The main body remained in Sparta until December 7 awaiting the

2 O. R., Ser. 1, XXXI, pt. 3, pp. 257, 556.

3 O. R., Ser. 1, XXXI, pt. 3, p. 320; Henry Campbell, "Campbell's Diary-Part 5," *Civil War Times Illustrated*, III, No. 6 (Oct. 1964), p. 46.

4 John H. Rippetoe, letter to his wife, Mary, dated Dec. 4, 1863. He said there were two boats (Vigo County Historical Society, Terre Haute, Ind.).

5 O. R., Ser. 1, XXXI, pt. 3, p. 257.

6 O. R., Ser. 1, XXXI, pt. 1, pp. 436, 591. Col. Brownlow claimed 9 guerrillas killed; 15 to 20, wounded.

supply wagons that were having a difficult, muddy march from Nashville. The cavalrymen lived comfortably, being quartered in the houses of the town.

On December 7 the column left Sparta and began to march up Cumberland Mountain. Because the wagons were repeatedly stuck in the mud, the march was slow and the command did not reach Crossville at the top of the mountain until December 9. On this same day the sutler train, marching at the rear and guarded by Company G of the Ninth Pennsylvania, was attacked by the guerrilla band. The wagons were looted. Eight soldiers and the Ninth Pennsylvania sutler were killed in this attack.[7]

The muddy march was resumed on December 9, and two days later the troopers encamped within four miles of Kingston. On December 14, orders arrived instructing Elliott to march on to Knoxville and join the cavalry of the Army of the Ohio. Elliott's column marched before noon and reached Knoxville on December 15.[8]

Major General John G. Foster, who had replaced Burnside in command of the Army of the Ohio, gave Elliott verbal orders to cross the Holston River and attack the enemy cavalry that was operating between Morristown and Knoxville.[9] On December 16, Elliott's cavalry division marched up the left bank of the Holston, and on the following day the First Brigade forded the rapidly rising river at Armstrong's Ford. By the next morning the river was too high to allow the battery to ford, and the division remained separated nearly two days when the First Brigade recrossed at McKinney's Ford above Strawberry Plains. When Elliott learned that the intent of his orders was to have his force operating south of the river, the First Brigade again forded the river during the evening of December 18. By the next morning the river had risen four feet, making it impossible for the remaining troops to cross. The division remained divided by the high water until December 23, when the Second Brigade found a boat and crossed. The reunited force marched to New Market this same day and chased a small band of Rebels out of the town.[10]

7 *Ibid.*
8 *Ibid.*
9 O. R., Ser. 1, XXXI, pt. 1, p. 631.
10 *Ibid.*, pp. 631–32; Henry Campbell, diary, No. 6, p. 46.

At 3:00 A.M. on December 24 the First Brigade, with four guns of
Lilly's battery, marched to Dandridge and the engagement that Wil-
liam Thomas described in the chapter's opening quotation. The First
Brigade was to work with Colonel Israel Garrard's Division of the
Army of the Ohio Cavalry, but as Thomas reported, the Army of the
Cumberland troopers received no help from this force when it was
needed.[11]

An hour after the First Brigade reached Dandridge at 9:00 A.M.
Colonel Campbell received a request from Garrard, who had preceded
him through town, to come to his support east of Dandridge where his
skirmishers were engaged with the Rebels. The First Brigade rode east
on the Bull's Gap road until they met the enemy near Hays's Ferry,
about four miles east of town. The Ninth Pennsylvania and First East
Tennessee made a mounted charge on the Rebel skirmishers, killing
three and capturing fifteen before precise artillery fire from three Confederate guns stopped the attack.

About the same time, an order from Colonel Garrard told Campbell to advance on the Bull's Gap road, advising that he "would move
on a side road to my left, and be not more than 2 miles distant at any
time." In response, Campbell sent the Ninth Pennsylvania forward in
column on the road and the First East Tennessee in a line on the right
of the road. Two guns of the battery were placed on a hill near the
ferry with the Second Michigan in support. When the forward regiments had advanced about half a mile, Colonel Campbell received an
order from Brigadier General Samuel D. Sturgis, chief of cavalry, Army
of the Ohio, who had command of all cavalry in the area, to return to
New Market. He sent the order on to Garrard and recalled his advanced
regiments.

A brigade of Rebel cavalry pressed the retiring troopers while another slipped around into the rear of the Yankee cavalry. A sudden
charge from the rear captured the two guns of Lilly's battery that were
not engaged. When he learned of the attack, Colonel Campbell ordered the Second Michigan and Ninth Pennsylvania to charge and re-
capture the guns. The order was executed "with great promptness and

[11] O. R., Ser. 1, XXXI, pt. 1, pp. 631, 635–36, 636–39. John H. Rippetoe to his
wife, Mary, Dec. 30, 1863.

gallantry, the guns recaptured, and the enemy driven nearly one mile, with heavy loss in killed and wounded and 14 prisoners in our hands."

Now surrounded, except for a path through woods on the left of the original line, Colonel Campbell sent a message to Colonel Garrard asking for support "which he did not send." Campbell also started his artillery and ambulances, and had the horses of his dismounted men led along the path that wound its way to the New Market road. When these were well on the way, the Tennessee and Pennsylvania troopers followed, leaving the dismounted troopers of the Second Michigan to fight a rear-guard action.

The enemy soon began pressing along the left flank, and the Pennsylvanians formed a skirmish line to protect the left while the Michiganders continued to cover the rear. The battery was emplaced on a commanding hill and the cavalry skirmishers retreated slowly, drawing the enemy toward the artillery. When the enemy came into range "a withering fire" from the guns temporarily checked their advance. When the Johnnies began to come on again, Campbell "ordered the First Tennessee Cavalry to charge with sabers, which they executed most nobly, driving the enemy's line over a fence with severe loss to their ranks; . . . Accompanying this charge the Second Michigan and Ninth Pennsylvania Cavalry opened a galling fire, which closed the fight. The enemy seeming to be satisfied with what they had received, fell back, and I marched to New Market at dark."[12]

Campbell's casualties were sixty-one killed, wounded, and missing about equally divided among his three regiments. One of Captain Lilly's Rodman guns had to be abandoned when the axle broke during the retreat. Campbell claimed eighty to one hundred of the enemy were killed and many more wounded in the fight.

Also on December 24, the Second Brigade repulsed an attack by two enemy cavalry brigades at New Market, forcing the Rebels to retreat beyond Mossy Creek. On Christmas Day, the Cumberland troopers rode out of New Market and established a new camp half a mile east of Mossy Creek.[13]

The Union commanders wanted to bring on a general engagement

[12] O. R., Ser. 1, XXXI, pt. 1, pp. 636–39.
[13] *Ibid.*, pp. 632, 636.

on December 26, but heavy rain prevented it. However, skirmishers exchanged shots, and Lilly's battery dueled with the enemy's artillery until the Rebels pulled their guns back. Next day, Elliott's cavalry drove the enemy three or four miles eastward, nearly to Talbott's Station, with the First Brigade making the last charge of the day. General Sturgis remarked, "Our troops went forward through rain and mud in fine spirits."[14]

During December 28 the First Brigade remained in their forward position with action only on the picket lines. Henry Campbell of Lilly's battery said that the opposing cavalry pickets fired only often enough to keep each other awake.[15]

On December 29 the Battle of Mossy Creek was fought, with the hardest fighting being done by the First Brigade of the Army of the Cumberland cavalry and three guns of Lilly's battery. William Thomas wrote:

> Cold Day   3 Brigades of Cavalry left Here this morning Before Day to come around on the right   our Brig Left [remained]   the Rebs attacked us at Daylight when we Had to fall back   we fell Back Slowly Fighting all the time   we fell Back to Mossy Creeck where the fighting became Heavy
>
> We had one Brig of infantry Stationed in the woods   when the rebels Charged through and came onto them the infantry opened onto them and poured Into them awhile   when they turned Back we followed them up and camped on the Old ground   the Brigs Came in on the right   Our Artillery Suffered to Day   the rebs captured one of our batteries when the 9th Charged upon them and retook it   Our Brig Lost 40 men killed [and] wounded   the other part of the Comman[d] unknown   The infantry Suffered Considerable and also Capt Lilleys Battery.

During the night of December 28, General Sturgis heard that a brigade of Rebel cavalry was at Dandridge and decided to pick them off. To accomplish his plan he sent both of the Army of the Ohio cavalry divisions and also sent the Second Brigade of the Army of the Cumberland cavalry about halfway to Dandridge as support in the event that the large force got into trouble.[16] The strategy almost proved disastrous.

There were no enemy forces at Dandridge. Instead, the entire Rebel

14 *Ibid.*, pp. 630–31, 636.
15 Henry Campbell, diary, No. 6, p. 46.
16 O. R., Ser. 1, XXXI, pt. 1, pp. 632, 648, 652.

cavalry, 6,ooo strong, with infantry support and four batteries of artillery came down the Morristown–Mossy Creek road. Only the First Brigade of cavalry, three guns of Lilly's battery, the One Hundred Eighteenth Ohio Infantry, a section of the Fifth Illinois (Elgin) Battery, and a few small detachments stood between the Confederates and Mossy Creek. The Union force totaled about 2,500 men.[17]

At nine o'clock in the morning, Colonel Campbell saw the enemy advancing toward his pickets in "several" battle lines crossing the Morristown road. Against the vastly superior force, he dismounted the Second Michigan and the First East Tennessee regiments and ordered them to give ground slowly while the Ninth Pennsylvania was sent two miles to the rear to protect the battery that was positioned on a hill south of the road.

The Michigan and Tennessee troopers did retire slowly and led the enemy to a point opposite some woods on the north side of the road. Unknown to the Rebels, the Ohio infantrymen were hidden in these woods. When the Rebel line came into range, these men fired a volley at the same time that the guns of Lilly's battery opened on the advancing column. Surprised, the enemy hesitated. Campbell immediately sent the Tennessee regiment at the enemy in a saber charge that threw the Rebels into temporary confusion.[18]

Shortly after this exchange seven Confederate guns opened on Lilly's battery and the supporting cavalrymen of the Ninth Pennsylvania. Fortunately, the Union guns were behind the brow of the hill, and most of the shells passed beyond them. Even so, casualties gradually reduced the gun crews to three or four men for each gun. These men became so exhausted after two hours of continuous firing that they could scarcely move the guns back into position after recoil.[19]

During this artillery duel, the Confederates extended their line beyond the Union left, and two battalions of the Ninth were shifted from support of the battery to extend the Yankee line. When the Rebels continued to lengthen this end of the line, Campbell ordered the Ten-

[17] *Ibid.*, pp. 632, 652. The Confederate cavalry with Longstreet was Maj. Gen. Joseph Wheeler's corps of three divisions under Maj. Gen. William T. Martin and Brig. Gens. F. C. Armstrong and J. T. Morgan.
[18] O. R., Ser. 1, XXXI, pt. 1, pp. 656–57.
[19] *Ibid.*, pp. 660–61; Henry Campbell, diary, No. 6, p. 47.

nessee regiment to make a mounted saber charge while the Second Michigan attacked dismounted. The Tennesseans broke the enemy line and stopped the flanking move.[20]

Soon afterward, General Elliott noticed an enemy build-up at the other end of the line, which he correctly interpreted to be for an attack on the Elgin battery. The remaining battalion of the Ninth was ordered to leave Lilly's guns and move to the right. When the Rebel attack came, the Pennsylvanians repulsed it with their revolvers in close fighting.[21]

Steady pressure pushed back both Union flanks so that the battle line took the shape of a horseshoe. Repeated charges by the enemy on Lilly's guns, now the key to the fight, were repulsed by more than 100 rounds of canister. However, Rebel sharpshooters approached near enough through a railroad cut to begin picking off the men and horses of the battery. A desperate charge by the Union infantry regiment and dismounted cavalry on the left delayed the Rebel advance and distracted the enemy artillery fire from the Union battery long enough to allow Lilly to hitch up and retreat to another position.[22]

The exhausted artillerymen did this job too quickly, and one gun was left on the field, where it was captured. Captain Lilly and an alert group of Ninth Pennsylvania troopers quickly charged the captors, retook the gun, and hauled it to the rear.[23] The battery, the cavalry, and the infantry groups were in new positions on a high hill northeast of Mossy Creek by two-thirty in the afternoon. The situation was critical. It seemed only a question of time before the numerically superior enemy would lap around the flanks or break through a quarter-mile gap in the line.[24]

Suddenly, a cheer went up from the Union soldiers posted on high ground. On the right they saw a blue column with gleaming sabers riding toward the enemy flank. The Second Brigade had arrived. The two guns that had accompanied the Second Brigade began to fire into the enemy line at the same time the cavalrymen struck the flank and rear.

20 O. R., Ser. 1, XXXI, pt. 1, pp. 652, 654, 656–57.
21 *Ibid.*, pp. 641, 654, 658.
22 Henry Campbell, diary, No. 6, p. 47; Rippetoe to his wife, Dec. 30, 1863.
23 Henry Campbell, diary, No 6, p. 48; O. R., Ser. 1, XXXI, pt. 1, pp. 654, 660–61.
24 O. R., Ser. 1, XXXI, pt. 1, pp. 654–55, 661.

The First Brigade began to advance along their front when the Rebel line began to waver. Hit hard in front and flank, the Rebels retreated, some hastily but others fighting from the patches of woods along the road. By dark the Yankees had recovered all lost ground and camped that night "on the old ground."[25]

Thus ended the Battle of Mossy Creek. Union casualties were 109. Confederate casualties were estimated at more than 250. Citizens told Union officers that more than 20 wagonloads of dead and wounded had been taken to the rear by the Rebels.[26] Dr. Oscar M. Robbins of the Ninth Pennsylvania, then in charge of the division medical staff, was cited for the fast and expert care that both Union and Confederate wounded received during and after the battle.[27]

The cavalry division remained in camp east of Mossy Creek for several days. The afternoon of December 31 turned bitter cold. That evening the soldiers built big bonfires of fence rails and, wrapped in their blankets, slept close to them. However, Colonel McCook and the divisional staff officers were snug in a nearby house. During the night some of the troopers set fire to McCook's house, making a magnificent bonfire. The soldiers close to the house slept the rest of the night in comfort, but the officers had to turn out and find new quarters.[28]

January 1, 1864, dawned bitter cold with a sharp north wind. Men who began to ride their horses to water quickly dismounted and walked behind their steeds, using them for windbreaks. The cold was especially hard on the Army of the Cumberland cavalrymen since their overcoats had not reached them. Few men had good stockings; clothing had not been issued for a long time. They accepted the condition philosophically. "The Rebels were worse off than we were," wrote Henry Campbell of Lilly's battery, "for half of them have nothing on their feet at all."[29]

Neither side initiated any serious action for a while after the Battle of Mossy Creek, and the Union cavalry moved their camp back to the town of Mossy Creek. On January 14 the Union cavalry marched to

---

25 *Ibid.*, pp. 655, 658–59; Campbell, diary, No. 6, p. 48.
26 O. R., Ser. 1, XXXI, pt. 1, pp. 649, 653, 655.
27 *Ibid.*, p. 656.
28 Henry Campbell, diary, No. 6, p. 48.
29 *Ibid.*

Dandridge because forage was more plentiful in that area.[30] William Thomas mentioned, "Colonel Vemont of the 7th Ky Cav was shot by one of his magors on the march Whiskey the Cause." Upon reaching Dandridge, they drove enemy pickets out of town. January 15 was spent foraging. Also, on that day, clothes and boots were issued for the first time since the cavalrymen had left Middle Tennessee.[31]

On January 16, Colonel Frank Wolford's cavalry division was sent east on a road called Bend of Chucky, while Garrard's and McCook's divisions marched along Bull's Gap road that paralleled the first road to the north. Garrard and Colonel Campbell, who commanded Mc-Cook's division that day, had orders to march nine miles east.[32]

Wolford met a heavy concentration of the enemy and soon asked for help. Campbell's division was ordered to his aid. Because of the condition of the fields, the division could not cross directly over to the Bend of Chucky road and were obliged to countermarch toward Dandridge. The Ninth Pennsylvania, having been at the rear on the eastward march, became the advance on the countermarch. About two miles from town, a crossroad connected the two roads and the Ninth swung south on it. As they neared the Bend of Chucky road, Colonel Thomas J. Jordan saw Wolford's division galloping in full retreat past the intersection.[33]

Now in danger of being flanked, Jordan had the Second Michigan dismount and occupy the brow of a hill. He asked them to hold off the enemy if possible until his dispositions were completed. Although outnumbered five to one, the Second Michigan held.

While the Ninth Pennsylvania formed a line at the left of the Second Michigan, they were subjected to "a galling fire" from enemy hidden in dense woods less than 200 yards away. The Pennsylvanians advanced into this gunfire and drove the enemy from their cover. When the Second Indiana had formed on the left of the Pennsylvanians, Jordan ordered his whole line to advance. Within five minutes, the enemy began to retire, but kept up a steady fire while retreating through the woods. Once they were driven into the open, the Rebels retreated in

[30] O. R., Ser. 1, XXXI, pt. 1, pp. 80, 81.
[31] *Ibid.*, pp. 85, 87.
[32] *Ibid.*, p. 80.
[33] *Ibid.*, pp. 81–82, 87.

wild confusion. The Federals pursued for a mile and a half, but darkness and an exposed right flank made it prudent to break off the engagement. Wolford had failed to bring his division up to cover the right flank.[34]

Enemy infantry attacked the First Wisconsin Regiment on January 17, driving them from their camp. Within fifteen minutes, the Second Brigade retook the camp and captured several of the Johnnies. These men were from three different Confederate infantry brigades and reported another full division was in the road behind them. Faced by all the Rebel cavalry and at least two infantry divisions, the Union officers decided to retreat that night. The decision was fortunate because General Longstreet had moved his entire corps to the area with the intention of fighting if he found an inferior force.[35]

The Federal cavalry left Dandridge at 10:00 P.M., January 17, and reached New Market at dawn. On January 18, William Thomas recorded, "Started off again at Daylight and Crossed the Holston river 6 miles Below Strawberry Plains at McHerd Ford   Met our infantry Coming Back to Knoxville   Camped within 6 miles of Knoxville   Marched about 60 miles."

On January 19 the cavalrymen passed through Knoxville and crossed the river on the pontoon bridge. The next day, they marched to within four miles of Sevierville and camped along the Little Pigeon River.

On January 26 the First Brigade was encamped at Fair Garden, located at the junction of the Dandridge and Newport roads, near the Middle Fork of the Little Pigeon. Wolford's division was posted between this position and the French Broad.

The same day, Armstrong's and Morgan's divisions of Confederate cavalry succeeded in crossing the river and routed Wolford's division. The troopers raced back across the Middle Fork where Colonel Campbell was getting his men into line across the road. When stopped by the First Brigade, the Confederates brought up artillery and shelled Campbell's troopers, forcing them to retire south of the Middle Fork before darkness stopped the fighting.

34 *Ibid.*, pp. 87–89.
35 *Ibid.*, p. 85.

At daylight the next morning, the Battle of Fair Garden began. Henry Campbell of Lilly's battery described it as "one of the nicest battles we ever fought."[36] Colonel Campbell had his men deployed across the road south of the creek. The Second Michigan, dismounted, straddled the road; the Ninth Pennsylvania, also dismounted, formed on their left; and the First Tennessee, mounted, took position on the right.[37] Because they were so greatly outnumbered by an enemy in a strong position on a ridge, the Union cavalrymen, according to Henry Campbell, were "strung out to look as large as possible."

The Pennsylvania and Michigan skirmish lines were advanced to the creek and exchanged shots with the enemy skirmishers for about an hour. During this action, some of the Pennsylvania troopers worked their way across the stream and occupied a hill that overlooked the Confederate position. From this position they began to rake the enemy, forcing them to retreat. The Rebels retired to a strong position on a ridge on the north side of the East Fork, leaving a covered bridge across the creek. Once again, the Pennsylvania and Michigan skirmishers fought their way across and, in a sudden charge, seized the ridge while the Pennsylvanians occupied the hills on the left.[38]

Before making this advance, Colonel Campbell had been advised that the Seventh Kentucky would advance on his right to protect this flank. However, the Seventh did not advance, and a heavy enemy force soon attacked the exposed right flank of the Second Michigan, forcing them to retreat, which caused a traffic jam at the bridge. But Lilly's battery quickly put twelve rounds of percussion shells among the pursuing Rebels and gave the Michiganders enough time to get across.[39]

The Ninth Pennsylvania was still on the opposite side of the creek and in danger of being cut off from the brigade. They fell back into heavily wooded hills. Fortunately, before the enemy could organize an attack, the Second Brigade came up on the left of the Pennsylvanians. The entire Union line then began to advance, and the enemy line "began falling back slowly at first and in good order, but as our men kept

36 Henry Campbell, "Campbell Diary—Final Installment," *Civil War Times Illustrated*, III, No. 9 (Jan. 1965), p. 37.
37 *Ibid.*, O. R., Ser. 1, XXXII, pt. 1, p. 142.
38 O. R., Ser. 1, XXXII, pt. 1, p. 142.
39 *Ibid.*, pp. 142–43.

advancing at the double-quick, they kept moving faster and faster."[40] When a force of Johnnies attempted to stand in some woods, the Fourth Indiana made a mounted saber charge into them, causing a rout. When the Federal troopers saw this happen, "Our entire line caught the infection and run right into the woods regardless of all danger or numbers."[41]

The panic-stricken Rebels fled down the road, and when a group tried to stand, mounted charges by the Fourth Indiana and First East Tennessee quickly dispersed them and caused them to rejoin the rout. This action ended the Battle of Fair Garden. Colonel McCook reported the results: "We captured two 3-inch rifled guns, with their horses; about 800 small arms, which we destroyed; 112 prisoners (12 of them commissioned officers, 2 of the latter being regimental commanders); General Morgan's battle-flag and his body servant, General [John T.] Morgan himself narrowly escaping. We also recaptured the regimental colors of the Thirty-first Indiana Volunteer Infantry, and one other regimental color (a silk American flag), which was in the possession of the rebels, and a battery guidon. Many of their killed and wounded fell into our hands, and I estimate their losses in killed and wounded, exclusive of the prisoners taken, at upwards of 200."[42] Union casualties were thirty-one, of whom twenty were in the Pennsylvania and Michigan regiments.

However, the Confederates sent strong infantry forces across the French Broad River on January 28. William Thomas wrote, "Their Cavalry was Reinforced in the evening by infantry   it is reported that a large force of Rebels infantry are across the river Between us and Knoxville."

Thomas's information was accurate, and the next morning the Union cavalry began to march out of the area. Passing through Sevierville, they moved up the West Fork of Little Pigeon River. By evening, they had reached Wear Cove, an open area of farmland at the foot of the mountains.

On January 30 the entire force rode through Wear Cove Gap and

[40] Henry Campbell, diary, No. 9, pp. 37–38.
[41] *Ibid.*; O. R., Ser. 1, XXXII, pt. 1, pp. 139–40, 142–43, 148–49.
[42] O. R., Ser. 1, XXXII, pt. 1, p. 140.

into the valley of Little River. The Ninth Pennsylvania was left at the gap in the event the enemy were following the column while the rest of the division marched to Maryville. Here they remained for ten days to rest their horses.

On February 1, William Thomas wrote, "it is reported that Longstreet is Reinforced by the Greater part of Lees Army." This rumor was false, and it was Longstreet who would reinforce Robert E. Lee in the spring before General Grant began to march south with the Army of the Potomac.[43]

[43] After the Battle of Chattanooga, Ulysses Grant was promoted to lieutenant general and to the command of all U. S. armies, moving his headquarters to be with the Army of the Potomac.

XVIII

Veteran Volunteers

the Boys are most all Enlisting in the
Veteran Service . . . I put my name
down to day in the Veteran Service
3 years longer   400 Dollars Bounty.

William Thomas stated very simply one of the most important decisions he and the other veteran soldiers were called upon to make: whether to reenlist for a second three years when their initial term of service expired. Thomas appears to have considered his decision a little longer than most others in the regiment because he did not sign until January 7.

On January 1, 1864, 397 of the 684 eligible men of the Ninth Pennsylvania Cavalry reenlisted. Among these were Cornelius and Henry Baker. According to Colonel Jordan, three-quarters of the regiment had reenlisted by January 4.[1]

The decision of these men, and others like them, to reenlist was of the utmost importance to the future prosecution of the war. The service terms of the 1861 enlistees would end during 1864, and several hundred thousand of the most experienced soldiers in the Union Army would be free to go home. If they decided to go home, the ranks would have to be filled with new recruits and draftees who could not replace the veterans in quality and experience even if an equal number were raised.

Realizing their value, the government offered the veterans a number of inducements. First, each veteran enlistee would get a bounty of

[1] National Archives, "9th Cav. Order Book"; National Archives, Col. Jordan to Gov. Curtin, March 1864, in unbound records of 9th Pa. Cav.

$400, which compared with $100 paid to new recruits. Second, all men who reenlisted would receive a thirty-day furlough at their homes. Third, they would be called "veteran volunteers" and would be authorized to wear a distinctive service stripe. Fourth, if three-fourths of those eligible enlisted, the regiment could keep its original designation and organization. These inducements, along with the patriotic instincts of the soldiers, saved approximately 250,000 veterans for the fighting that remained.[2]

On the same day that he reenlisted, William Thomas noted that the Second Ohio Cavalry started home to begin their furlough. The Ninth Pennsylvania was not so fortunate. An eager young brigadier general, James Harrison Wilson, recently named chief of cavalry of the Western armies, had big plans in mind. He refused to issue furlough orders for some of his best regiments. On April 4, he wrote Secretary of War Edwin M. Stanton that the Ninth Pennsylvania, Second Michigan, Second Indiana, and First Wisconsin "have indicated a willingness to reenlist if furloughed but can't be spared." He also said that he planned to re-equip these old regiments with Spencer repeating carbines.[3]

Wilson's letter must have passed orders of a contrary nature on its way to Washington. A few days before Wilson wrote his letter, Colonel Jordan had written to Governor Andrew Curtin advising him that four applications for furlough had been turned down. Whereas Jordan, the lawyer, admitted to Curtin that the enlistment papers bound the men so that they could be compelled to be mustered-in, Jordan, the officer, thought that "the use of force with such a regiment would destroy its usefulness."[4] Governor Curtin possibly took the complaint directly to President Lincoln because the matter was settled faster than a protest through normal army channels. General Wilson received orders on April 8 to furlough the Ninth and the other veteran regiments immediately.[5]

This event did not take place until after the regiment had marched through more of eastern Tennessee. On January 31, they had reached

[2] Wiley, *Billy Yank*, pp. 342–43; General Order No. 191, Series of 1863 (O. R., Ser. 3, III, 414–16).
[3] O. R., Ser. 1, XXXII, pt. 3, pp. 255–56.
[4] National Archives, Col. Jordan to Gov. Curtin, March 1864.
[5] O. R., Ser. 1, XXXII, pt. 3, pp. 255–58.

Maryville after the fighting near Sevierville. They remained in Maryville until February 9, when they marched south. "Forded Little Tennessee river in the evening at McGees [McGhee]   Camped in the Evening On the Bank of Chillothoe [Chilhowee] at Mr Howards House," reported William Thomas. The next day, with two other men, he enjoyed an outing on the river in one of Mr. Howard's canoes.

On February 17, the First Brigade left their camp at Howard's and marched nine miles up the Little Tennessee. Here they encamped on the Widow Morgan's farm. Thomas identified her as "Cousin of John H Morgans." On the twentieth, Thomas wrote, "A party of Cherokee Indians arrived in camp to day from the rebel Gen Thomas Command the Renegade In Smoky Mountains and gave themselves up to our forces."

On February 23, the brigade left Widow Morgan's and rode to "Preacher Scruggs farm" four miles below Madisonville. Here, eight bushwhackers were captured by the First East Tennessee. The troopers marched from Preacher Scrugg's on March 4 and followed the railroad to Calhoun. The next day they reached Columbus.

Remaining at Columbus through most of March, the soldiers had a long rest. Some men were able to catch up on their paper work. Master Sergeant George W. Sipe of Company C wrote, "made out all the death discharges and desertions in 1862."[6]

During this period, William Thomas was serving at division headquarters in Cleveland. On March 22 he recorded a six-inch snowfall throughout which he had to stand guard duty. He reported that the Ninth Pennsylvania marched into Cleveland on March 27.

On March 29 the Ninth Pennsylvania and the Second Michigan were mustered into the Veteran Service. From this time, the Ninth was officially referred to as the Ninth Pennsylvania Veteran Volunteer Cavalry.

On April 8, Master Sergeant Sipe noted, "Received orders to go home as soon as we can get ready."[7] However, before they left, William Thomas reported one last skirmish. "we were out this Morning to Have a fight with the rebels," he wrote on April 13, "The rebels made a dash

6 National Archives, "Co. C, 9th Pa. Cav. Morning Reports."
7 *Ibid.*

upon one of our picket posts and captured them   they captured 25 men   6 of them got away   When we got there the rebs had left."

April 14 was the big day. During the morning the soldiers turned in their arms. At four o'clock in the afternoon, the men of the Ninth watched while their Second Michigan comrades entrained. Then, at 6:00 P.M. the Ninth Pennsylvania boarded their cars and started the first leg of their journey home. They reached Chattanooga at 11:00 P.M. and lay over until two-thirty the next morning.

Running all the next day and through the next night, the train brought the soldiers into Nashville at daylight on April 16. The troopers marched from the depot to Number Two Barracks for breakfast. At 4:00 P.M. they left Nashville and reached Louisville at 8:00 A.M. on April 17. At Taylor Barracks, where the troopers were quartered during their stay, they met the One Hundred Ninth Pennsylvania Infantry returning to the front following their furlough.

On April 18 the cavalrymen received $100 of their bounty and $75 advance pay. William Thomas celebrated that evening by going into the city and to the theater. The next morning, the Ninth Pennsylvania marched to the wharf with the Invalid Corps Band[8] for an escort. Here they boarded the steamboat *General Lytle* for the trip to Cincinnati.

Arriving in Cincinnati at 5:00 A.M. on April 20, the soldiers were free in the city until 6:00 P.M. Then they boarded the steamboat *Mariner* for the run to Pittsburgh. Stopping only long enough to take on coal at Maysville, Portsmouth, Parkersburg, Wheeling, and Steubenville, the boat docked at Pittsburgh at 8:00 A.M. on April 24.

Once again the troopers were treated well by the people of the city. William Thomas wrote, "Went to City Hall and partook of Dinner there kept up by the Subsistence Committe of Pittsburg   Kept up by the Citizens for the Feeding of Soldiers passing through there." In the afternoon, the cavalrymen climbed aboard the Harrisburg train for the last leg of their journey. There appear to have been two sections of this troop train; Sergeant Sipe gave departure time as three o'clock[9] and William Thomas as four.

The entire regiment was in Harrisburg early on April 25. Most of

8 See Wiley, *Billy Yank*, p. 342, for description of Invalid Corps.
9 National Archives, "Co. C, 9th Pa. Cav. Morning Reports."

the soldiers marched to Camp Curtin, but William Thomas had leave to stay at the Parke House in the city. Master Sergeant George Sipe went to the Soldiers' Home to make out the required furlough papers for Company C. He completed this detail the next morning. Then he wrote, "the boys left for home." His last entry on the April morning reports was "On furlow" written large enough to fill the space provided for the remaining days of the month.[10]

William Thomas took a vacation from his diary writing and there is no personal record of the activities of the soldiers during their furloughs. The first entry in Cornelius Baker's diary was written on May 25: "Left Blain and went to Harrisburg and stoped in the union hotell and me and my wife went to the theatre in the evening at the Wite hall."

On May 17, Cornelius married Julia Ellen Bower at Loysville. Julia was the nineteen-year-old daughter of Michael Bower of that town. The only known detail of the wedding was that a Reverend P. Sawme performed the ceremony.[11] However, the Baker family probably hired conveyances from the livery stable in Blain and went in style to Loysville. Because so many men of Company C lived in the area, the audience may have looked more military than civilian.

The men must have told exciting stories about the cavalry war in the West and, as a result, 259 new recruits were enlisted while the regiment was home.[12] The effect lasted beyond the period of the furlough and another 362 men enlisted during the following three months.[13] Among these recruits was Samuel Baker, indicating that Cornelius and Henry had impressed him that the Western cavalry war was more exciting than the Eastern infantry war that Samuel had seen.

Men could be killed in peaceful Pennsylvania. Company C's descriptive roll notes that Francis A. Greenwalt was killed in a train accident while on furlough.

On May 26, Cornelius Baker wrote, "I remaind in the hotell dur-

10 *Ibid.*
11 H. H. Hardesty, ed., *Presidents, Soldiers, Statesmen* (New York: H. H. Hardesty, 1892), II, 567.
12 National Archives, Col. Jordan report July 22, 1864, in unbound 9th Pa. Cav. records.
13 National Archives, "Quarterly Returns of Alterations and Casualties for 1864," in unbound 9th Pa. Cav. records.

ing the day   it rained nearly all day   me and my wife went up in the State House in the eavning." Cornelius and Julia also stepped into A. G. Keet's photographic studio and had their pictures taken. A few days later, after returning to camp, Cornelius wrote, "I went to town and got my photographs." On May 27, Cornelius wrote, "I remaind in the tavern till 11 A.M. and went to the depo and my wife went home and i remaind in town till eavning and i went out to Camp Curtain."

William Thomas returned to Harrisburg on May 26 but left immediately. "went down To Hum[m]elstown Acompined by my Sister," he wrote, "Left the rest of the company at Harrisburg   Had a pleasant time in Humelstown." Returning to Harrisburg the next day, Thomas "put my Sister at Mrs Montgomerys with Grace   i put up at the Parke House   i was out in Camp Curtin in the Evening on Dress parade with the regt   Spent the Evening in the National Circus."

Conscientious Cornelius Baker obeyed orders to be in camp following the dress parade on Friday evening. He probably regretted that he had sent his bride home because, on Saturday afternoon, he found "the boys had nearly all left   their was but 10 or 12 in camp." William Thomas simply "took french Leave in the evening" and went home. He found that most of the other soldiers were already home. He had a pleasant time Sunday "Visiting my freinds." The same day Cornelius Baker observed, "times are prety dull in camp to day   their is but few in camp."

By Tuesday, May 31, most of the troopers had returned to camp. "we had inspection in the eavning at 5 o clock and dress pirade   their was a croud of ladies from town come out to see uss," Cornelius Baker wrote. On June 1 he continued, "we drew clothing and reseived marching orders   we got orders to bee redy to leave the next day."

At 2:00 P.M. on June 2, the Ninth Pennsylvania veterans boarded the train in Harrisburg. They reached Newport at three o'clock and stopped there until four. Then the train ran all night and arrived in Pittsburgh at ten the next morning. Once again the Subsistence Committee of Pittsburgh provided for the soldiers. Cornelius Baker wrote that they "had a fine dinner prepaird for uss and everything that we could wish for."

Instead of marching to the wharf as they had on their first trip west, the troopers went back to the depot and got aboard a train on "the Fort Wayne and Chicago Road" that left Pittsburgh at 2:00 P.M. The train reached Crestline, Ohio, at three the next morning. Here the men changed to trains on the line to Indianapolis by way of Bellefontaine. Because William Thomas reached Indianapolis at 6:00 P.M. the same day and Cornelius Baker did not arrive there until 6:00 A.M. the next morning, it is apparent that the regiment rode different sections from Crestline. Thomas had supper at the Soldiers' Home in Indianapolis and "Slept Out in the Commons all night." This same night, Cornelius Baker wrote, "The cars run all nite   we passed threw union city w[h]ere the ohio and indanna line runs along   their the ladies had pies and kakes at the station for uss   we stoped their an hour."

This part of the regiment rejoined the earlier arrivals at the Soldiers' Home in Indianapolis for breakfast and then, according to Cornelius Baker, "got on other cars and left and passed threw Franklin Columbus and Semore and reached Jeffersonville at 7:00 p.m. and crossed the river to Louisville." William Thomas noted, "Great cheering as we entered Taylor Barracks as the 2d Michn Had Arrived a few Days before us." The trip illustrates the ability of the Northern railroads to move bodies of troops quickly. The Ninth Pennsylvania had traveled 850 miles in three days.

The Ninth Pennsylvania Cavalry spent a few lazy days in Louisville before resuming the war under unexpected circumstances. On June 7, both Cornelius Baker and William Thomas noted the departure of the Second Michigan for Nashville and "the front." "I went to the sircus in the eavning," wrote Cornelius, while William said, "I was out in the City in the Evening at the Louisville Theatre."

On June 8, Cornelius wrote, "I went to the river with Henry [Baker] and berier [John Berrier of Blain] to fish but as our luck was poor we retirnd with out any." William Thomas went to "James Robisons" circus in the afternoon and attended the Louisville Theater once more in the evening.

XIX

Morgan Raids Again

About 5 o'clock in the afternoon, the Ninth Pennsylvania Cavalry, Colonel Jordan commanding, arrived, and reinforced by this fine body of men made me feel that we were saved.[1]

Colonel George W. Munroe of the Twenty-second Kentucky Infantry and the people of Frankfort, Kentucky, had good reason for their feeling of relief when the Ninth Pennsylvania rode into town on June 12, 1864. For two days, 150 men had fought off attempts by nearly 1,200 of John Hunt Morgan's raiders to capture the fort and city. Except for twelve soldiers, all the defenders were members of the civilian Home Guards. Colonel Munroe, who commanded this little force, was on leave from his regiment and visiting in Frankfort when the town was besieged.[2]

Although the siege had ended the evening before, the people of Frankfort expected a renewal of the enemy effort. "Their was a saloot fired for uss by the sitisans from the fort," reported Cornelius Baker, thereby confirming Colonel Munroe's feeling of salvation when the relief column came into sight.

Union strength and aggressiveness brought on Morgan's fourth Kentucky raid. During May two large Federal cavalry forces began to move toward Saltville, Virginia, site of strategic lead mines. One force, commanded by Brigadier General W. W. Averill, was approaching

---

[1] O. R., Ser. 1, XXXIX, pt. 1, p. 55.

[2] Lorine Letcher Butler, *John Morgan and His Men* (Philadelphia: Dorrance & Co., 1960), p. 301.

through West Virginia, while the second, commanded by Brigadier General Stephen G. Burbridge, had started moving through the mountains from Kentucky. Morgan, defending Saltville with a comparatively weak force, decided that a raid into Kentucky would prove to be the best defense. A raid would compel Burbridge's force of 6,000 to turn around and chase him through Kentucky. Knowing that Kentucky had been stripped of fighting men to supply Sherman's army and Burbridge's expedition, Morgan wrote, "There will be nothing in the state to retard progress but a few scattered provost guards."[3]

Before marching for Kentucky, Morgan revealed that Frankfort and the L & N Railroad were his targets. To General Braxton Bragg, who now was in Richmond, he wrote, "I hope, General, that in a short time you will hear of our boys being in the capital of Kentucky."[4]

On June 1, the day before the Ninth Pennsylvania Cavalry left Harrisburg, Morgan, with 900 cavalrymen and 1,200 unmounted men, began his 150-mile march through the mountains. On June 7, the day after the Ninth had reached Louisville following their 850-mile railroad trip, Morgan came out of the mountains and captured the Federal supply depot at Mount Sterling.[5] That same day, he sent a small party ahead to destroy the railroad bridges between Frankfort and Louisville to prevent Indiana troops from reinforcing the former town. He also sent a force to cut the Cincinnati to Lexington railroad to prevent Ohio soldiers from coming to the relief of the bluegrass area.[6]

By the night of June 8, Morgan's main body was only eleven miles from Lexington. That same morning, however, his rear guard had been surprised at Mount Sterling by the advance units of Burbridge's force. Burbridge had moved faster than Morgan had anticipated, and his march of ninety miles in only thirty hours caused anxiety and some grudging admiration among Morgan's officers. Basil Duke, Morgan's brother-in-law and second in command, described the Union march as "wonderful."[7] Burbridge's men and horses were too tired to pursue

3 *Ibid.*, pp. 296–97; Duke, pp. 519–20.
4 Butler, p. 296.
5 Duke, pp. 520–24.
6 *Ibid.*, pp. 522–23.
7 *Ibid.*, p. 524; O. R., Ser. 1, XXXIX, pt. 2, p. 82.

Morgan's main body, and the Rebel raider was free to move on toward his objectives. He also had time to forage and steal horses in bluegrass Kentucky.

The next morning, Morgan's force rode into Lexington, burned a government depot, captured enough horses to mount most of his dismounted men, failed to capture the fort from the Home Guards, and rode off toward Frankfort.[8]

Lieutenant Colonel Thomas B. Fairleigh of the Twenty-sixth Kentucky Infantry had been left in command of Louisville and central Kentucky by General Burbridge. On June 9, Fairleigh telegraphed a request for troops to Governor Oliver Morton of Indiana. He advised Morton of Morgan's position the previous evening. Fairleigh also told him that he was retaining the Ninth Pennsylvania and was organizing the convalescents among the 8,000 sick and wounded soldiers then in Louisville hospitals. The only other soldiers in the Louisville area were the 400 men assigned to man the blockhouses on the L & N Railroad.[9]

Louisville must have been as destitute of weapons as of soldiers. On June 9, Cornelius Baker wrote, "We remaind in the baricks and sind [signed] the Pay rols and our Sabers and guns came   the guns was old belgamun rifels with bayonets." These were the same poor weapons that the regiment had discarded in 1862, preferring to fight with revolver and saber. Fortunately, some companies drew better weapons this time. Company B was armed with Enfield rifles.

On June 10 the troopers were issued horses, saddles, and horse equipments. Four companies, including B, rode toward Shelbyville at five in the afternoon. According to William Thomas, this scouting party marched a few miles beyond Middletown that evening and went into camp for the night. The next day, they marched through Shelbyville and on to Hardinsville before returning to Shelbyville to await the rest of the regiment.

The main body of the Ninth left Louisville at 3:00 P.M. on June 11 and, by marching all night, reached Shelbyville at dawn. After feeding their horses, the reunited regiment rode toward Frankfort.

---

8 Duke, p. 526; Butler, p. 301.
9 O. R., Ser. 1, XXXIX, pt. 2, p. 94.

While this relief column of 500 men was marching, the defenders in the fort at Frankfort were having a difficult time repulsing several attacks by the 1,200 besiegers. At one time the attackers captured the one cannon available to the defenders, but it was immediately recaptured.[10]

A novel weapon used by the defenders was one of the earliest machine guns. This was a twenty-four barrel weapon that was placed at the end of the covered bridge across the Kentucky River. This gun stopped, or at least discouraged, any attempts by the Rebels to cross through the bridge.[11]

Elsewhere, Morgan won his one real victory of the campaign. During the night of June 10 a second party of Morgan's men ambushed two trains that were rushing two regiments of the Ohio National Guard toward Lexington from Cincinnati. The surprise was so complete that all 1,600 guardsmen were captured.[12]

Morgan did not have much time to reflect on his victory because, by the evening of June 11, Burbridge's superior force was closing in on him at Cynthiana. Probably the need to get his full force of about 2,000 men together to oppose Burbridge's 5,200 was the reason that Morgan withdrew the besiegers from Frankfort.[13] As the grand finale of the siege, the Rebels burned the barracks, and the blaze lighted the countryside for miles.[14]

On June 12, Burbridge attacked and shattered Morgan's combined party, killing 300 and capturing 400. Morgan and some of his followers escaped and rode toward the mountains. Other small parties got away but stayed in Kentucky. They began guerrilla activities that troubled the Federals in the state for several months.[15] Two hundred men commanded by a Major B. W. Jenkins caused the most concern and provided some entertainment for the Ninth Pennsylvania.

In Frankfort on June 13, Colonel Jordan, as the senior officer in town, took command of all forces. He sent Company C on a scout

[10] Butler, p. 301.
[11] This gun, which is on display at Old Statehouse in Frankfort, Ky., was manufactured by Parmenter and Bramwell, Troy, N. Y.
[12] Butler, p. 303; Duke, p. 526.
[13] Duke, p. 527.
[14] Butler, p. 301.
[15] Duke, pp. 527–28.

around the town, but they saw none of the enemy. The next day this company guarded the workers who were rebuilding the railroad bridges that the Rebels had destroyed.

On June 15, General Burbridge asked Governor Thomas E. Bramlette of Kentucky, who had remained in Frankfort during the siege, to order the Ninth to pursue Morgan toward Pound Gap in the mountains. However, the governor seems to have been more concerned about the Rebels who were staying in the state than he was with those trying to get out. He did not issue the orders requested. Actually, Jenkins's band of Morgan's men had been within nine miles of Frankfort during the previous night.[16]

The next day, Cornelius Baker reported, "We went on a scout after some of Morgans men and came in contact with them and charged them for three miles and captured 2 men." William Thomas was in another scouting party that rode toward Lexington, but this group did not meet any Rebels.

On June 17, Governor Bramlette telegraphed General Burbridge that 200 of the Ninth had started on a scout that morning to try to intercept Major Jenkins's force, which had cut the railroad at Smithfield during the previous night. Bramlette indicated that he did not expect the expedition to return for three or four days. He also reported that other bands of Morgan's men were marauding in Shelby, Spencer, and Nelson Counties.[17]

Both Cornelius Baker and William Thomas were with the force that tried to catch Jenkins's band. They marched west beyond Taylorsville but failed to catch the raiders. One squad went on some distance and destroyed two ferryboats. The entire scouting party returned to the camp in Frankfort at midnight on June 19. Another group was sent out during the morning of June 20. The men appear to have enjoyed this activity, and Cornelius Baker wrote, "the regiment is in fine fettle and spirits."

On June 21 both Baker and Thomas went into Frankfort. Thomas was "visiting out in town in The Frankfort Odd Fellows Lodge." Baker

16 O. R., Ser. 1, XXXIX, pt. 2, p. 119.
17 *Ibid.*

had more serious business. "I went to town and got 2 teeth poold."

"times are brisk," wrote Cornelius Baker on June 24, "we drew rashens and we were preparen for a march." At five o'clock the next morning the regiment moved out on the road that is now called "the old Bardstown road." After reaching Bardstown, they turned south and crossed the Green River at Munfordville on June 28. The next day, they continued through Glasgow. On June 30 Baker wrote, "reached Bowling green at 1 a clock and encamped 1 mile from town back of Colage hill   Colage hill is fortifide and lyes very hy."

On July 1, the soldiers turned in their muzzle-loading Belgian and Enfield rifles and were issued Starr breech-loading carbines and new sabers. Cornelius Baker expressed the attitude of all the men when he wrote, "then we thot we were armed again."

Cornelius Baker told of the Fourth of July celebration: "the sitisans of Bowling Green had a picknick long side of our camp   it was made their for our regiment   their was lots of ladies their   it was a big day for them   their was a saloot fired from the fort at 1 a clock of 36 guns." William Thomas added, "Had a Small fight at the Picnic in the evening Between the Pa Boys and some of the Kentuckians."

On July 6 the regiment resumed the march toward Nashville. The next day, William Thomas reported, "Very Warm Day   reached franklin this morning   Turned over our Horses and Horse Equipments and sent them to the Front on the train to Nashville." On July 9 he wrote, "The Sun was scorching Hot today   Had drill on foot this morning [from four to six according to Baker]   Received marching Orders to march to Nashville on foot   Marched to Mitchelsville There we received Transportation On the Cars   the Boys are pretty near Played out."

Upon reaching Nashville on July 10, Cornelius Baker and his company camped in the yard of the "Solicofer" house.[18] Thomas and his company were sent to Exchange Barracks No. 1. The next day the entire regiment moved to a camp at Edgefield "where our Brig Had

---

[18] Zollicoffer House, on the site of the present Andrew Jackson Hotel, was formerly the property of Confederate General Felix Zollicoffer, who had been killed in the Battle of Mill Springs, Jan. 1862.

camped In Jan 1863." On July 15 the regiment received their new state colors, which like their first are now displayed in the capitol in Harrisburg.

The soldiers of the Ninth expected that they would be sent from Nashville to the fighting front, but they were disappointed. The depredations of guerrillas, bushwhackers, and the groups of Morgan's men and a threatened uprising of the Rebel sympathizers known as the Sons of Liberty, or Copperheads, led to a period of martial law in Kentucky. To maintain military rule, soldiers were needed in the Louisville area. According to a report from amateur spy Felix Stidger, the Sons of Liberty planned to burn the entire city of Louisville.[19]

On July 16, Major General Henry W. Halleck, chief of staff, U. S. Army, ordered that Lieutenant Colonel Thomas Fairleigh be relieved from command in Louisville and that he be replaced by an officer of higher rank. Halleck also ordered the commanding officer at Nashville to send two regiments of well-armed dismounted cavalry or 100-day men to Louisville. Being unassigned, dismounted, and well armed, the Ninth Pennsylvania filled the specifications exactly. On July 17, Brigadier General John F. Miller in Nashville telegraphed Halleck in Washington that his orders had been fulfilled; the Ninth Pennsylvania Cavalry had left for Louisville on the 7:00 A.M. train and the One Hundred Thirty-fourth Indiana would leave on the evening train.[20] The Ninth reached Louisville at five o'clock the same afternoon and marched out to their old camp.

The veterans of the Ninth, who had expected to join Sherman in Georgia, appear to have been frustrated by the retrograde movement. "our ofisers went to town and got tite and raised a awful fuss," wrote Cornelius Baker on the following day, "the privets put them under guard till they got sober."

For the next month, the troopers were bored with their duty of guarding citizens at picnics and at the circus, of making routine scouts and not seeing signs of the guerrillas, and of pressing horses both in and out of town. This activity led the usually enthusiastic Cornelius Baker to write, "their isant much stir   it is as usial clean up for

19 McDowell, pp. 160–67, 176–81.
20 O. R., Ser. 1, XXXIX, pt. 2, p. 173.

inspection   that is our only work   we had inspection and dress pirade   uss trumpiters bload several marches on dress pirade   after dress pirade their was a cristian comishenr came out from town and distributed tracks and testaments to the soldiers." Sometimes other people visited the camp. "their is lots of wimen in camp selen kakes and other trash," Baker wrote with apparent disdain of soft, fancy delicacies.

Some days had more activity and excitement. On July 26, Cornelius Baker wrote. "We went to town at 9 Am. and escorte General Mc p[h]ersons corps[e] to the boat landing   the escort contained the 9 Pennsylvania Cavalry and two regiments of infantry   the streets was crouded." William Thomas noted, "They are Sending the remains Home to His freinds in Ohio   He was killed at Atlanta Ga." Major General John B. McPherson, who had the respect and confidence of both General U. S. Grant and General William T. Sherman, had been a casualty when General John B. Hood attacked Sherman's army and began the Battle of Atlanta.

On July 30 unfortunate Tilghman "Toldy" Miller was mentioned in both diaries. Cornelius Baker's entry was, "Miller of Co A got kicked in the hed by a horse and dide 3 hours after he was kicked." On August 4, Baker wrote of a different excitement, "their was some of Co B men went out this eavning drest in rebel uniforms as spies and some of our Co also   S. P. Gutshall was one."

On August 6, Cornelius Baker belonged to a scouting party that found that the fears of an armed uprising in Kentucky may not have been entirely imaginary. On that day he wrote, "their was 12 men of uss went on a scout at 9 a clock this eavning and marched 6 miles and encamped long side the road." The next day he continued, "We left the pike in the morning and marched 3 miles and searched a thicket w[h]ere their was some bushwhackers hid in   their wasant any About   we went to Middleton and captured a lot of shot guns and muskets and retirnd to camp in the eavning."

For some reason, the Federal command and the citizens of Louisville became fearful during the summer of 1864. During 1862, when the Confederate army had marched in strength nearly to the outskirts of the city, no one seemed to have considered fortifying the place. Now, with the nearest enemy army fighting for its life in Georgia and with no forces threatening Louisville except some guerrilla bands, the U. S. Army and the citizens began to spend time and effort building a ring of permanent forts around the city.[21] Fortunately, no one considered retaining the Ninth to man the forts, and they finally moved to the active war theater.

[21] McDowell, pp. 170–76.

"A Grand Success of Surprising a Rebel Camp"

at Criple Crick old dibler with 1500 men was camped their and at day lite the regiment charged him enrouted them and took 150 prisners 50 of them was wunded with the saber and a lot we dident get.

The action near Readyville, Tennessee, on September 6, 1864, described by William Thomas in the chapter title and by Cornelius Baker in the quotation, was an exhilarating experience for the troopers of the Ninth Pennsylvania after their dull tour of police duty in Louisville. This was the kind of action the men had come for; a complete surprise and rout of the enemy with few casualties among themselves.

The veterans of the Ninth left Louisville for the front on August 13. They marched "with everything," including tents, wagons, and forges. They followed the road through Shepherdsville, Belmont Iron Works, Rolling Fork, Elizabethtown, Bacon Creek, and Munfordville —the same route that the Kentucky Turnpike and Interstate highway 65 follow today. Marching with expectations of getting to the area where the fighting was taking place raised the morale of the cavalrymen. Cornelius Baker observed, "the boys is in good spirits."

On August 18, the regiment reached Mammoth Cave where they had a three-hour layover. Cornelius Baker wrote of his experience, "i was in the cave a mile and came out   it was very cool in the cave their was some went in 5 miles   they said it was a nise cave." William Thomas was one of those who explored deeper. He wrote, "i was inside the Cave When the Officers came in with guide and lamps   We visited the cave and traveled 3-¾ Miles and Saw 25 Different Sights of note Some splendid views of the works of Nature."

Upon leaving the cave, the soldiers resumed their march through Dripping Springs and Bowling Green where they "camped in the old camps of the Fourth of July." After a day's rest here, they passed through Franklin and encamped "on an old rebels farm." On August 16, they rode to Tyrene Springs, at that time a famous spa, sixteen miles from Nashville. The next day they marched to Edgefield on the north bank of the Cumberland River opposite Nashville and encamped "w[h]ere we were camped in february 1863."

On August 24, William Thomas wrote, "Marched to the Murfreesboro Depot Unsadled our Horses and put them in the cars Our Sadles in Separate Cars." Cornelius Baker added, "We slep on the top of the cars during the nite." For nearly twenty-four hours through the next day and night, the cavalrymen rode on top of the cars. They passed through Stevenson, Alabama, at 10:00 P.M. and reached Chattanooga at four the next morning. Here the men unloaded their horses for the first time since loading them in Nashville. The horses were unruly after the long ride and Company C's morning report noted, "private [Henry] Baker lost his horse at the depot."

The soldiers enjoyed a few leisurely days in their camp at the foot of Lookout Mountain. On August 27, Cornelius Baker reported, "The balance of the regiment came from Nashville and they brot a lot of new recrutes along our Co got 17 new recrutes." The following day, he served "as an escort on the top of look out mountain with a lot of ofisers."

On this same day, William Thomas took a stroll on Lookout Mountain and had his picture taken on Point Lookout. On August 29 he and twenty-eight men of Company B "had our Potograph taken on one plate on Point Look out." Upon returning to camp, he heard a report that "the rebel raiders [are] in Sequatch Valley."

The raiders mentioned by Thomas were Colonel George G. Dibrell's brigade of Wheeler's cavalry. In typical American fashion, both Baker and Thomas simplified name pronunciation and called the colonel "Dibler." With General William T. Sherman closing in on Atlanta, Confederate General John B. Hood sent Wheeler's cavalry to cut Sherman's supply line between Nashville and Chattanooga. This was the same road over which the Pennsylvania cavalrymen had so recently ridden. While Wheeler's main body was operating south of the railroad, Dibrell, a native of Sparta, Tennessee, was combining raiding and recruiting in his home country to the north.[1]

On August 31, 560 Pennsylvania cavalrymen started after Dibrell's brigade.[2] First they had to ride into town and draw saddles for the recruits. Then Companies A, B, and C crossed Walden's Ridge near the Tennessee River while "the balance of the regiment crossed 5 miles firder up," according to Cornelius Baker. The three companies reached Dunlap on September 1, two hours ahead of the main column. Here they learned that Dibrell's force had left for McMinnville several days before.

To assure a fast march, Colonel Jordan sent all wagons, teams, and extra baggage back to Chattanooga. The men then rode up Cumberland Mountain and encamped after marching for several miles on top of the mountain.

On September 3 they rode hard for the forty miles to McMinnville in an effort to catch the Rebels in the town. William Thomas was one of twenty men in a flying column that rode in advance. This detail reached McMinnville only three minutes after the enemy had left. The Union troopers "followed up 6 miles Charging Scattering their rear gaurd." The rest of the Union column rode into McMinnville soon afterward, and Cornelius Baker noted, "the rebels had been their and ransacked the town."

The next day the Ninth marched westward to Woodbury. William Thomas, now a part of the rear guard, wrote, "Green corn for our horses." During the afternoon of September 5 they rode into Murfreesboro. Here they learned that Atlanta had been occupied by Sherman's army, that Wheeler was near Tullahoma, and "that the rebs was in our rear."

"At midnight," wrote William Thomas, "the Bugle sounded to horse and in 10 minutes we were Sadled up and marching on the Woodbury pike to Surprise a Rebel camp."

Dibrell's brigade had camped that night near Readyville, where

[1] O. R., Ser. 1, XXXIX, pt. 1, p. 496.
[2] Col. Jordan report Aug. 24, 1864, in the unbound records, 9th Pa. Cav., National Archives, tabulated the strength as 28 officers, 560 men, and 666 horses.

Cripple Creek flows into Stones River. Dibrell had planned to cross the railroad near Murfreesboro. However, when his scouts reported that Federal cavalry had reached that town, he decided to attempt the crossing farther to the southeast and rejoin Wheeler. Dibrell went into camp at Readyville resolved on this action. He reported that his force numbered 1,000 to 1,200 men, many of whom were recruits and that only 300 were armed.[3]

"As Daylight was peeping in the Horizon," William Thomas wrote, "We came in sight of the rebel camp at Reedyville." Colonel Jordan made his dispositions quickly. Three companies, commanded by Major Charles A. Appel, were dismounted and deployed as skirmishers on the left of the Rebel camp. Major David H. Kimmel, with four companies, was ordered to make a mounted charge on the right of the camp, and Major William H. Longsdorf's three companies were ordered to support Kimmel's charge.[4]

At a quarter past five, when there was enough light, Jordan ordered the attack. The mounted men charged past the enemy pickets, who were completely surprised and surrounded. The charge continued into the center of the enemy camp. There was little gunfire. The Yankees did their work with sabers. The rout was complete. Dibrell reported, "I used every effort to rally the men, but owing to the large number unarmed, quite a stampede took place and it was with difficulty that they could be rallied and checked."[5] Part of Longsdorf's battalion pursued the "mass of fugitives" through Woodbury, five miles away.

William Thomas, like Cornelius Baker, commented on the effectiveness of the sabers. He noted that many prisoners were "badly cut up with sabers" and that "many rebels made their escape after being taken and cut with sabres." The attack captured 200 horses and a large number of Enfield rifles. Because Colonel Jordan had no wagons to transport the rifles, he had them destroyed. William Thomas recorded, "Their Loss in Killed as far as we can Learn 74." Colonel Jordan reported 130 prisoners taken and stated the Ninth's losses as 1 killed, 6 wounded, and 5 missing.[6]

[3] O. R., Ser. 1, XXXIX, pt. 1, p. 496.
[4] *Ibid.*, p. 495.
[5] *Ibid.*, p. 496.
[6] *Ibid.*, p. 495.

The Union troopers completed their job quickly and were back in their camp at Murfreesboro before ten o'clock. Among the wounded were two lieutenants of the Ninth Pennsylvania. Casualties among the higher officers were as great the next day while the men were supposedly safe in town. "Magor Apple craked His Skull and Magor Longsdorff Broke Both His Legs," William Thomas wrote, "a Horse runing away with a Carriage with Both of them in."

After rallying his men near Woodbury and waiting for stragglers to come in, Dibrell began to retreat toward the mountains. However, he did send a party of 150 men west in an attempt to contact Wheeler. On September 10 this scout ran into the advance of the Ninth Pennsylvania. Cornelius Baker wrote, "We left Murfersborough and marched to Woodbury and run in 100 of Diblers men and run them over the hills and killed 2 and wunded 4 and took 3 prisners." From the information the prisoners gave him, Colonel Jordan deduced that Dibrell had found himself cut off at the south and that he would retreat eastward out of Tennessee.[7]

On September 12 the Ninth Pennsylvania reached McMinnville, and when Company C went on picket they found "the peaches is ripe and we helped ourselves to them." At McMinnville, the Ninth was strengthened with 230 men from the Fifth East Tennessee and Second Kentucky Cavalry Regiments. The combined force then marched to Sparta. As a member of a scouting party, William Thomas rode north of Sparta. About twelve miles out they met a Union patrol that had come south from Cookeville. From them Colonel Jordan learned that Dibrell was moving fast and that the Union force would not be able to catch up. Jordan made preparations to return to Chattanooga and sent the detachments of Tennessee and Kentucky cavalry back to their regiments at Tullahoma.[8]

On September 18 the Pennsylvanians left for Chattanooga. Late that day they marched through Spencer and "encamped at dark on the top of the mountain at a run." Upon reaching Pikeville in the Sequatchie Valley, Jordan learned that Dibrell was beyond Strawberry

---

[7] *Ibid.*, p. 501. Col. Jordan wrote that prisoners said they were of the 8th Tenn. Cav. (C.S.A.) and part of William's division.
[8] O. R., Ser. 1, XXXIX, pt. 2, p. 391.

Plains, east of Knoxville, and obviously headed for Virginia. With no possibility of meeting the enemy, he apparently let his regiment get strung out. On September 19, Cornelius Baker encamped at the foot of Walden's Ridge, while William Thomas camped five miles north of Dunlap. Baker reached "our old camp at the foot of Missionary ridge" on the twentieth. Thomas did not reach camp until late the next day.

In a memorandum, William Thomas noted, "The Diblers Raid was Hard and Fatiguaging march   Suffered mostly For Rations both men and Horses Lived on Green Corn   in 22 days we marched 341 miles   Had 2 Engagements with Diblers Command which was 1800 Strong."

On September 21, Cornelius Baker wrote, "We remaind in camp and struck our tents on the old ground and made ourselves comfordable   their was some new recrutes came for the regiment." The next day, he continued, "their was a lot of new recrutes came   My brother [Samuel] was along with them   He got in our company."

For the first time since 1861, the regiment was being brought up to its full strength of 1,200 men. Neither Baker nor Thomas mentioned their opinions of the new soldiers. Some probably were green boys fresh from a month or two in training camp. Others, like Samuel Baker, were veterans who had enlisted for a second hitch.[9]

There is evidence that the veteran volunteers formed a closed club that the "one year men" could not break into. Even a close blood relationship could not get Samuel Baker into the same mess with Cornelius and Henry. Although Cornelius mentioned Henry and other old soldiers with some frequency in his diary, he did not mention Samuel again until the day Samuel was mortally wounded. They were a proud group, the veteran volunteers. They had a right to be.

When General William T. Sherman's army occupied Atlanta on September 2, the strategies of the opposing generals changed. Until then, Sherman's orders from General Grant had been to destroy the Confederate army. Now his imagination took hold, and he began to dream and scheme a plan for a march through the heart of Georgia. His opponent, General John B. Hood, had had the defense of Atlanta

[9] Samuel Baker had served earlier in Co. G., 133d Pa. Inf., a six months' regiment (National Archives, service record).

as his primary objective. Now that Atlanta was lost, he had to try to find an effective way to use his army.

Upon evacuating Atlanta, Hood's army had dug in at Lovejoy's Station, south of the city. Before the end of September, he decided to put his army across Sherman's railroad from Chattanooga. To accomplish this objective, he circled around Atlanta and struck at the garrisons at Big Shanty and Allatoona. Sherman moved too quickly, however, and before Hood could beat the garrisons into submission, the Union army was closing in.

Following this aborted strategy, Hood decided to march into Middle Tennessee. He thought that this threat would draw Sherman's army out of Atlanta to defend Nashville. For this purpose, Hood began to march toward Alabama, south of Chattanooga, planning to turn north after by-passing this city. Hood's march became known as The Forlorn Hope. At this stage of the game, the Union had too many pieces on the board. Instead of following Hood, Sherman created a new army at Nashville that was capable of dealing with Hood while he took his own army on a march in the opposite direction. Ultimately, the new army at Nashville, commanded by Major General George H. Thomas, shattered the Army of Tennessee.

Even before the Confederate army began to move around Chattanooga, the Pennsylvania cavalrymen had work to do. On September 25, Cornelius Baker wrote, "We reseived marching orders to bee redy to leave at a moments notis." Leaving their dismounted men and recruits in camp, the veterans of the Ninth marched into Wills Valley, west of Lookout Mountain. William Thomas stated the reason for the move: "it is reported that Forrest is in the neiborhood of Huntsville With a strong cavalry force."

On September 27, Cornelius Baker wrote, "their was one batallion went on a scout and the balance went back to Witesides and encamped on the signal hill[10] to guard the bridge." This was the long, tall trestle bridge over Running Water Creek, one of the most vulnerable structures on the rail line between Huntsville and Chattanooga. General

---

[10] Signal Hill is about half a mile west of Whiteside, Tennessee. The hill was fortified during the war to protect the trestle bridge. It should not be confused with Signal Mountain, north of Chattanooga.

Sherman, who respected Forrest and called him "that devil Forrest," began to send troops to Nashville to guard against Forrest. William Thomas at Whiteside noted that trainloads of soldiers were moving west.

On October 1 six companies of the Ninth went on a scout toward Lebanon. The next day Cornelius Baker wrote, "We marched within 13 miles of Belmont and we hird of a brigade of rebels on the other road trying to get in our rear and we tirnd back 6 miles and encamped." This half of the regiment marched all day on October 3 through heavy rain. Baker reported, "We left camp and hadent any rashens   We had noan to take along." The following day, the scout returned to the camp at Whiteside. "We got in camp and drew rashens and then we had to give the half to the scout that was going out," wrote Cornelius Baker. "We done 4 days without any rashens."

The other six companies formed the new scouting party. William Thomas was a member. On October 5 the scout marched six miles beyond Trenton and camped in Lookout Valley. The next day they marched twenty miles, "Fording a Great many Deep Creeks" and camped in Wills Valley. On October 7 William Thomas wrote, "Started Early and Made a Charge into Leabonan [Alabama] at noon on a small party of rebs   Co G In the Advance Captured 2 prisoners   Released one of them on account of Being Insane." The scout marched back toward Trenton the next day.

Of the activity on October 9, Thomas reported, "Started early and Went Back 6 miles to attack a party of Bushwhackers That were Anoying A party of Refugees that were moving   They Left Before we got up to them." That night, this scouting party reached the camp at Whiteside.

Meanwhile, the soldiers who stayed at Whiteside had been working on the camp. They had moved the camp off Signal Hill and into Murphy's Hollow, below the hill to the east. Cornelius Baker wrote, "we dug a dich on each side of the picket line and put troves up for the horses."

On October 10 Baker wrote, "our company went on a scout on Sand Mountain and retirnd at 6 PM. Co E went to guard the wood chopers   the state comishiner came in to day." The commissioner had come

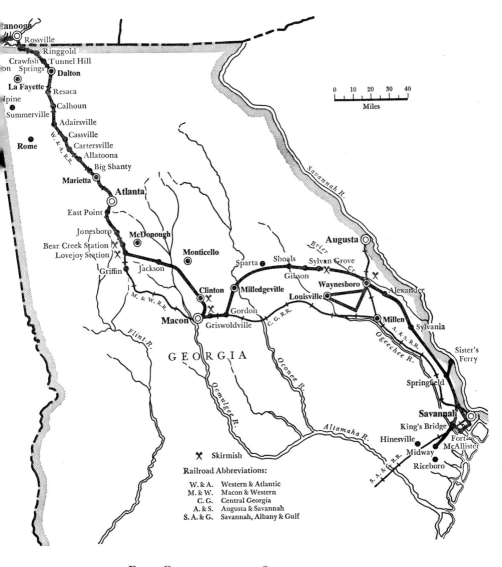

anooga

Rossville
Ringgold
Crawfish Tunnel Hill
on Springs
La Fayette ◉ **Dalton**
pine Resaca
Summerville Calhoun
Adairsville
Cassville
Rome Cartersville
Allatoona
Big Shanty
Marietta ◉
Atlanta
East Point
Jonesboro **McDonough**
Bear Creek Station ✗
Lovejoy Station ✗
Griffin Jackson
Monticello

Sparta ● Shoals
Gibson
Sylvan Grove ✗
Clinton ✗ **Milledgeville**
Gordon **Louisville**
Macon Griswoldville
Waynesboro
Alexander

Augusta ◉

Brier Cr.

G E O R G I A

Flint R.
Ocmulgee R.
Oconee R.
Altamaha R.

Millen Sylvania
Sister's
Ferry
Springfield

Savannah
King's Bridge
Hinesville Fort
Midway McAllister
Riceboro

✗ Skirmish

Railroad Abbreviations:

W. & A.	Western & Atlantic
M. & W.	Macon & Western
C. G.	Central Georgia
A. & S.	Augusta & Savannah
S. A. & G.	Savannah, Albany & Gulf

0   10   20   30   40
Miles

Savannah R.

FROM CHATTANOOGA TO SAVANNAH

for the purpose of voting the soldiers for the Pennsylvania state election on Tuesday, October 11. On election day, Cornelius Baker observed, "the poles of the Election were opend at every companys quarters at 7 A.M. till 7 Pm. the election went of[f] plasable every body appears to agree." William Thomas appears to have had less interest in the election. His diary entry for this day reads, "Laying in camp today   nothing of importance."

By October 13 the Confederate Army of Tennessee had started to march toward the Alabama line south of Chattanooga. William Thomas wrote, "Some of Co D Boys Came into camp after getting Away from the rebs at Lafayette Ga   They made a Charge Into the town and Were Repulsed   16 arrived in camp and 15 of the company were captured."

On this same day, Cornelius Baker and an unknown number of other troopers "marched to Chatanooga with Captain [George A.] Shuman for scouts." They camped in front of the hospitals. That evening, a scout was sent out, but Baker did not go because "my horse was unfit."

"the troops is coming in to Chatanooga by the car loads," Cornelius Baker recorded on October 15, "their was 8 train loads came in today." These were soldiers of Major General John M. Schofield's Army of the Ohio coming up from Georgia. Soon they would march south to try to catch up to the enemy army. The next day, Baker got his geography confused but told the significant fact correctly when he wrote, "it is reported that hood is in tenessee and he is marching torge [toward] lafiett [La Fayette]." On the seventeenth he continued, "their was a scout of 12 men went on a scout up Chatanooga valey and retirnd and also a scout went torge [toward] Crawfish Springs   they report the rebels at the Mills [Lee and Gordon's] in large forse."

On October 18, Baker wrote, "We left with 10 men to report to General [Elliott W.] rice as ordaleys   Mager General Schofield came and he ordered uss with him   the hoal armey left Chatanooga this morning   they moved out at day lite." That night Schofield's camp was near Lee and Gordon's Mill. Next day the army marched to La Fayette. Baker wrote, "remaind their during the nite   the infantry camped around the town."

The officers, at least, had some excitement on the next day's march. Cornelius Baker commented, "We left Lafiett at 6 Am and marched to the cross roads and encamped   in the way General Schofield met a drove of tirkeys and him and his staff empyed their revolvers at them i carried a dispatch to General [James D.] Morgan in the nite."[11]

The next day, Cornelius Baker went from serving the general to about the lowliest duty in the army. "We were relieved from Schofield on account of our horses was run down," he wrote. "We were detailed to drive cattle." However, they were relieved from this duty on October 22. "we went back to Alpine and joind Captain Shuman with his company," Baker wrote.

While Cornelius Baker was accompanying General Schofield east of Lookout Mountain, William Thomas was scouting down the west side. On October 16, Company B left Whiteside, and that night camped at Trenton, Alabama. The next day they "Marched on top of Lookout Mountain By a very Steep and rugged path   Descended the Mountain again on the Same Side and [marched] sever[al] miles on the Leabonan Road."

On October 18 Company B continued on toward Lebanon. "After marching 7 miles we came on the advance Of The rebel Column," Thomas wrote, "drove them 3 miles then Countermarched Back Within 4 miles of Trenton." The scout returned to Whiteside the next day.

At this time the Confederate army was marching into Alabama. General Sherman, tiring of a chase that could lead across Alabama and Mississippi, halted the Union army at the Alabama line. Although General Grant had been reluctant to approve the plan for the March to the Sea, he finally consented when Sherman convinced him that General Thomas would have adequate forces in Nashville to handle Hood. Upon receiving Grant's approval, Sherman turned his back on the enemy army and returned to Atlanta. However, he did take the precaution of sending Schofield back to Nashville to assist Thomas.

While this grand strategy was being developed, William Thomas had remained in camp at Whiteside. However, on October 24, he wrote,

[11] O. R., Ser. 1, XXXIX, pt. 1, p. 627. The dispatch carried by Baker was the only message from Schofield's headquarters "Near Valley Store" to Morgan on Oct. 20 and was an order for the next day's march.

"Started for Lafayette and Capt Riley [Michael O'Reilly, Co.D] for the wounded of Co D   Marched to Crawfish Springs." The next day they went on to La Fayette and "Got 2 wounded then Started on the Back road   Had to Leave one of the wounded on the road at a House on account of His Sufferings." Thomas also reported that "Bushwhackers Are Numerous through this Country."

On October 25 a detail of ten men accompanied the ambulance to Chattanooga "while the rest of the Co Crossed Lookout Mountain Through Nickajack Gap   reached Whitesides at dusk   found the regt gone." They found the regiment at Rossville on October 27. The following day the regiment began a march to Marietta, Georgia. They rode through Ringgold, Dalton, and Resaca that day. Thomas observed, "The Railroad Had been torn up from Tunnel Hill to Resaca   The road was Torn up by Hood." As they marched on through Calhoun, Adairsville, Cassville, Cartersville, Allatoona, Acquaville, and Big Shanty, Thomas noticed "Breastworks thrown up Everywhere." These were remainders of Sherman's Atlanta campaign during the spring and summer.

On November 3 most of the Ninth Pennsylvania reached their new camp at Marietta. Here the "nonveterans" rejoined the regiment. These were the men who had not reenlisted during the previous winter. They had been on detached duty since April when the veteran volunteers began their reenlistment furloughs.

Cornelius Baker did not reach Marietta as quickly. He remained at Alpine for a few days. One day he foraged in the direction of Summerville. "We got potatoes and molases," he wrote. On October 27 he reported, "the 4 coar [corps] is going back to Chatanooga   they passed here this afternoon and encamped a half mile from here." The next day, Baker continued, "We left Alpine at 8 Am. with the 4 coar   General [George D.] Wagner has comand of the 4 coar[12]   Captain Shuman and his squad was detailed as ordalies for Gen Wagner." On October 29 the column passed through the Chickamauga Battlefield and marched into Chattanooga. The next day, Cornelius Baker observed, "a part of the infantry got on the cars and went to Huntsville Alabama

[12] Brig. Gen. Wagner commanded the 2d Div. IV Corps.

it is reported that Hood is striken for their." The cavalrymen moved to Rossville that day and remained there "waiting for the balance of the feloes that is at bridgeport." On November 2, Baker wrote, "Capt Shuman went to town and drew rashens and clothing for his company he woodent draw any clothing for uss ony for his company."

The next day the detachment set out for Marietta. They had a hard march in the rain and cold. They marched to Calhoun but found that they could not ford the river there and had to back track to Resaca. On November 6, Baker wrote, "My horse gave out and i got a nother horse." The next day he wrote, "marched to Marietta and joind the regiment   it is camped 1 mile from town   i found all the boys well and in good spirits."

The next day was National election day. Cornelius Baker described it: "the election poles were opent at every companys quarters at 7 Am. and closed at 2 Pm.   Everything went of[f] quiet   the regiment caried 160 majority for lincon." William Thomas was more precise. He wrote, "Cast 439 vote in the Regt of which Lincoln received 303 votes   McClenan [McClellan] received 136 votes."

The nationwide count of the soldier vote gave Abraham Lincoln 119,754 votes to 34,291 for George B. McClellan.[13] Although most states tabulated the soldier votes separately, there was no uniform system. New York allowed the soldiers to vote in the field but had the ballots brought back and tabulated in the home districts with the civilian votes. Indiana's Democratic legislature would not pass a law to permit soldiers to vote in the field. Lincoln reacted by ordering furloughs for all Indiana troops on garrison duty in Kentucky and Tennessee.[14]

As the election drew near, Lincoln was confident that he would win. He was concerned about New York, where the race was close, and Pennsylvania, where he anticipated that the soldier vote would give him the state but was unsure of the home vote. He believed that if he lost both New York and the home vote of Pennsylvania, it would be a blow to morale and to the war effort.

Just before the election, Lincoln asked Generals George Meade and

[13] Guernsey and Alden, II, 669.
[14] Sandburg, III, 280–81.

Phillip Sheridan to furlough a total of ten thousand Pennsylvania soldiers so they could vote at home.[15] Lincoln had it figured with amazing accuracy. He carried the state by twenty thousand votes, 296,389 to 276,308. Of the twenty thousand plurality, fourteen thousand came from soldiers voting in the field (26,712 to 12,389).[16] Assuming that the ten thousand furloughed soldiers voted like those in the camps, they were the votes that carried the home vote and produced the six thousand plurality.

[15] *Ibid.*, pp. 287–88; Meade commanded the Army of the Potomac, and Sheridan, the Army of the Shenandoah.
[16] Guernsey and Alden, p. 669.

Marching Through Georgia

We went to burn the railroad and destroy it and we had to fite Wealers forse day and nite   in the day as we were marching along we had to build baricades every half mile to cover our rear and and at nite w[h]en we went in camp we had to baricade our selves and lay in line of battle   every 4 man had to hold our horses and the rest lay behind baricades and about every hour the rebels would charge on our lines but they would go back faster than they came.

As indicated by Cornelius Baker, the Union cavalry's March to the Sea was different from the frolicsome, carefree campaign experienced by the usual infantry soldier of General Sherman's army. While the infantry foraged freely and carried out their work of destruction with little enemy interference, the Federal cavalry fought on eleven days between November 15 and December 4. The actions were not small skirmishes between patrols and scouting parties but were fights involving all of Brigadier General Hugh Judson Kilpatrick's Third Cavalry Division and Confederate Major General Joseph Wheeler's cavalry corps. The Federal infantry marched unmolested principally because Kilpatrick's 5,500 men kept Wheeler's 11,000 fully occupied.[1] "Kilpatrick had the laboring oar," Horace Greeley wrote about the cavalry's role on the march.[2]

Kilpatrick's orders required him to feint toward Macon in a manner that would lead the enemy to believe that this city was Sherman's objective. This threat would force the only soldiers capable of interfering with the army to remain in Macon until the Union infantry and wagon trains had passed. Then Kilpatrick was to make the same sort of move

[1] O. R., Ser. 1, XLIV, 362; Jacob D. Cox, *The March to the Sea* (New York: Chas. Scribner's, 1898), p. 24. Wheeler reported that his force did not exceed 3,500 men (O. R., Ser. 1, XLIV, 411).

[2] Horace Greeley, *American Conflict: A History of the Great Rebellion in the United States of America, 1861–65* (Hartford: O. D. Case & Co., 1866), p. 690.

toward Augusta. Additionally, his force was ordered to keep Wheeler's men away from the infantry columns and the wagon trains.[3]

Hugh Judson Kilpatrick was one of the "boy" generals developed by the Union cavalry as the war progressed. An 1861 graduate of West Point, he was destined to become a major general in 1865, at the age of twenty-seven. Depending upon the authority referred to, he had established a reputation either as a daring and dashing officer or as a wild and reckless man during his service with the Army of the Potomac. While in Virginia, Kilpatrick had led a raid within sight of Richmond, and is credited with forcing Lieutenant General J. E. B. Stuart's Confederate cavalry corps into such a wide detour during the Gettysburg Campaign that this important element of Lee's army did not reach the battlefield until after the issue had been settled.[4]

"Little Kil" was transferred to the Western army during the spring of 1864 and was able to demonstrate his ability to General Sherman during the Atlanta Campaign. Although Sherman called him "a crazy damn fool," he was exactly the kind of officer needed for the work ahead. He drove his men so hard that he earned the nickname "Kill Cavalry." However, because he acted like a winner, his men rode hard and with enthusiasm. Before the end of the war the cavalrymen adopted their leader's attitude, and Kilpatrick's cavalry became the cockiest outfit in an army that came to believe it was the world's greatest.

The young general demonstrated administrative skill; he assembled and equipped his division in the two weeks between receipt of his orders and the beginning of the march. He organized the division into two brigades. The First Brigade, commanded by Colonel Eli H. Murray, was made up of the Ninth Pennsylvania, the Eighth Indiana, the Second, Third, and Fifth Kentucky Cavalry Regiments, and the Tenth Wisconsin Light Artillery. The Second Brigade, commanded by Colonel Smith D. Atkins, consisted of the Ninety-second Illinois Mounted Infantry, the Fifth, Ninth, and Tenth Ohio Cavalry Regiments, the Ninth Michigan Cavalry, and a squadron of the First Ohio Cavalry.[5]

3 Guernsey and Alden, II, 686; O. R., Ser. 1, XLIV, 362.
4 James Moore, M.D., *Kilpatrick and Our Cavalry* (New York: Hurst & Co., 1866), pp. 73–75; Rhoades, p. 285.
5 O. R., Ser. 1, XLIV, 362.

Following election day, the cavalry spent a week preparing for the march. All extra supplies were sent back to Chattanooga. The cavalry, like the rest of the army, would travel light. Only one wagon and a few pack mules were allowed for each regiment. These were to carry the spare ammunition, twenty days' rations of hardtack, forty days' rations of sugar and coffee, and salt. All other supplies needed by the army were to be foraged from the country.[6]

"the infantry is busy tairing up the railroad and burning the ties and the town was a fire," Cornelius Baker wrote on November 12, "they are burning every thing." The next day, William Thomas recorded, "The work of Destruction still goes on   The railroad is Burning and Houses all around wherever you Look   Everything in Atlanta is Destroyed." The entire railroad from the Etowah River to Atlanta was taken up, and all the rails were destroyed by bending and twisting. All machine shops and other structures of military value along the road were demolished. According to plan, this severed Sherman's communications with the North. Until contact was made with the Navy near Savannah a month later, no one in the North, not even Lincoln or Grant, knew where this army was. All the government knew was what they could deduce from the Southern papers.[7]

On November 13 "the Cavalry comand was reviewed by General Shirman" and the cavalrymen received "order to March to Morrow and Carry 11 Days Rations."

At seven the next morning, Kilpatrick's cavalry began their march. Leaving Marietta, they rode through what remained of Atlanta, headed south, and camped at East Point on land that now is a part of Fort McPherson.[8] The area had been fought over and foraged clean during previous campaigns, and William Thomas remarked, "no feed for our horses."

At 7:00 A.M. on November 15 the cavalry began to march along the west bank of Flint River. They were screening the right wing of the army, commanded by Major General Oliver O. Howard, then

---

[6] Guernsey and Alden, II, 685–86.

[7] James Moore, *Complete History of the Great Rebellion 1861–1865* (Philadelphia: W. S. Burlock, 1881), p. 444; Guernsey and Alden, II, 685.

[8] Historical marker on circle of Fort McPherson.

marching toward McDonough. The cavalry advance soon ran into pickets and skirmishers of Brigadier General Alfred Iverson's brigade of Wheeler's cavalry. They drove these men six miles through Jonesboro and encamped at that place.[9] The Ninth Pennsylvania, acting as rear guard, was not involved in the skirmishing.

The Rebel cavalry retreated to Lovejoy's Station, where 3,000 Georgia militiamen occupied the earthworks built by Hood's army after it evacuated Atlanta. Finding that this small force was facing the entire right wing of the Union army, the Confederate officers wisely ordered a retreat to Macon. Iverson's cavalry, with two rifled Rodman guns, were left in the works to cover the retreat.

When the First Brigade of Union cavalry came upon this position, Colonel Murray had the Eighth Indiana and the Third Kentucky dismount and attack the earthworks on foot. They drove the enemy from the position after a brief fight. Then the rest of the brigade attacked the Rebels, who were now in the open, in a mounted saber charge that captured the two guns and forty prisoners. The remainder of Iverson's brigade rode south toward Bear Creek Station.[10]

At noon, the Second Brigade took the advance. Iverson had rallied his force at Bear Creek Station behind some hastily built barricades. Led by the Tenth Ohio, the Federal cavalry charged over this defense line and captured twenty of the enemy. The gray horsemen scurried southward again, passing through Griffin. Beyond this town, the Union cavalry gave up the pursuit.[11]

"i went out and captured a rebel horse sadle and gun," wrote Cornelius Baker on November 17, the first full day devoted to foraging. That morning the two brigades began to march eastward on parallel roads to destroy as many cotton gins and as much cotton as possible. "Marched through a very rich Country," wrote William Thomas, "Our Brig in advance   foraging parties out pressing all the Horses Mules and Burning all the Cotton Gins through the Country." That night, the Brigade encamped four miles southwest of Jackson.[12]

[9] Cox, p. 26; Hardesty, I, 322.
[10] O. R., Ser. 1, XLIV, 362–63, 368, 386; Cox, p. 26; Hardesty, p. 322.
[11] O. R., Ser. 1, XLIV, 363, 368.
[12] *Ibid.*, p. 368.

On November 18 the cavalry marched to the Ocmulgee River. The First Brigade stopped at Cork and waited until General Howard's engineers could complete pontoon bridges. Howard put two bridges over the river at the ferry crossing on the Jackson-Monticello road. The first bridge was completed at midnight; the cavalry then rode from Cork and crossed at 3:00 A.M.[13]

During the evening of November 19, Kilpatrick and a part of the Second Brigade reached Clinton. The First Brigade camped fourteen miles north of the town. They rode into Clinton the next morning, about the same time that the rear guard of the infantry was crossing the river far in the rear.

Clinton's previous bad fortune was the town's salvation when the Union army passed through. Until about 1850, Clinton had been the leading city in central Georgia. Samuel Griswold had built a foundry in the 1820's and produced 1,000 cotton gins a year. However, the railroad, built in the late 1840's, by-passed the town; and in 1849, Griswold moved his factories to the Macon and Atlantic Railroad, a few miles east of Macon. Here he built a new town named Griswoldville, or Griswold Station. Because Clinton no longer had factories or other structures of military importance, the soldiers did not start fires, which in other towns usually spread to the houses. Thus, Clinton was spared to die a slow death.[14]

At Clinton, Companies B and L of the Ninth Pennsylvania were detached and assigned to cover the direct road from Clinton to Macon while the rest of the cavalry division marched down a more easterly road. According to Colonel Jordan, the two companies held off two regiments of the enemy for two days, screening the infantry column and wagons that were marching through Clinton.[15]

William Thomas, a member of this small force, wrote on November 20, "Marched to Clinton   Here our Co and Co L went out On the Macon road   Drove the Rebel pickets in   the rebs charged us But were repulsed By Co L   We Then fell Back one miles And stopped as picket Two Miles From Clinton."

[13] Cox, p. 26; O. R., Ser. 1, XLIV, 368.
[14] O. R., Ser. 1, XLIV, 368; historical markers in the town of Clinton.
[15] O. R., Ser. 1, XLIV, 386–87.

The next day, William Thomas's adventures nearly ended. He reported:

at 2 PM The pickets Commenced firing   They Fell Back on the reserve
The Rebs Advanced on foot and Drove us away from our position   We
Had a Skirmish Line formed and when they came to[o] close The Capt
Gave Orders to mount Our Horses   We made for our Horses and the man
That Had mine Run Back with the Company and Left Me in the Lurch So
i Had to Run about a Mile on foot and The rebs pepering me   when i
Came over a Hill and Jake Weaver Came to me with my Horse   When i
mounted Him I then Caught up to the Company   Then we Charged the
rebs But They were to[o] much for us   We then fell Back on our Infantry
     When the infantry opened On Them They fell Back at Dusk   We
Then Camped for the night

Thomas concluded this episode the next day. "We lost all our provisions Yesterday," he wrote. "The rebs Had a feast On What we Had to Leave."

Meanwhile, the remainder of the Ninth Pennsylvania had an even harder time. On November 20, Cornelius Baker wrote, "We left camp and marched to Macon   We met the enimy 6 miles from town and drove them into town and fot them till dark and we burnt the railroad bridge and fel back   our co remaind on picket 1 mile from town   the nite was awful disagreeable."

According to Kilpatrick, the Second Brigade was in the advance during the drive on Macon and the Tenth Ohio and Ninety-second Illinois were credited with most of the fighting. These regiments drove across Walnut Creek into East Macon, captured Old Fort Hawkins, and chased Wheeler's cavalry across the river into Macon proper.[16]

The Ninth Michigan, also of the Second Brigade, struck the railroad at Griswold Station. Here they destroyed Samuel Griswold's pistol factory and soap plant and captured a train of thirteen freight cars.[17] The Second Brigade then fell back toward Gordon, leaving the Ninth Pennsylvania nearest to Macon and the enemy. "the 2 batallion was on picket during the nite," Cornelius Baker wrote on November 21, "the rebels attackd uss in the morning and we had a smart fite with them and we fell back to Griswold Station to the balance of the coar

16 O. R., Ser. 1, XLIV, 362–63; Cox, p. 27.
17 O. R., Ser. 1, XLIV, 362–63; Cox, p. 27.

[division] and had a smart skirmish their before we left   We went 5 miles and camped."

General Wheeler had come out of Macon early in the morning with a part of his cavalry and attacked the Ninth Pennsylvania pickets. The Ninth, now rear guard for the cavalry division, and actually for the entire right wing of the army, retreated slowly along the Macon and Atlantic Railroad. They made a stand at Griswoldville, repulsed the enemy, and then marched unmolested across Little Sandy Creek where they camped at the rear of the cavalry division. Colonel Jordan posted pickets at the creek. During the night the Rebels made several attempts to drive the pickets from the stream. Colonel Jordan called one of these assaults "a heavy charge;" all these attacks were repulsed.[18]

"the pickets were attacted at day lite and our company and co E was sent to their suport," Cornelius Baker wrote about the start of the fight that developed into the Battle of Griswoldville. By morning of November 22, Wheeler had a strong force probing the rear of the Union cavalry. Behind Wheeler's force, 3,000 Georgia militiamen had started to march out of Macon.

Cornelius Baker wrote briefly about the cavalry skirmish, "the rebels charged uss and we fel back and then we charge them and drove them for a mite and they charge uss again and they were repulsed and then the infantry came up and fot them for 3 hours."

According to Colonel Jordan, the pickets and the two companies that were sent up as reinforcements did not fall back until they were nearly surrounded. As a result, one man was killed, two were wounded, and eighteen were captured. However, when the enemy came out onto open ground east of the creek, Major David H. Kimmel, with four more companies, made a saber charge that drove the enemy back three-quarters of a mile to their main battle line. Here Wheeler counter-charged with a stronger force, and the Pennsylvanians retreated to the creek. By this time the battery had been placed to cover the crossing of the stream, and the Confederate charge was stopped. During the charges and countercharges, four more men of the Ninth were killed, nineteen were wounded, and twenty-five were missing and presumed

---

[18] O. R., Ser. 1, XLIV, 386.

captured. Having done all the fighting so far, the Ninth was relieved from further action that day.[19]

During the skirmish, Brigadier General Charles C. Walcutt's brigade of Union infantry had come up and, with them behind him, Colonel Eli Murray moved out with the First Brigade of cavalry. He drove Wheeler through Griswold Station. Here Walcutt's infantry relieved the cavalry.

From Griswoldville, Walcutt's men fell back one mile and had entrenched in a strong position with swamps on both flanks when they saw what appeared to be Confederate infantry marching along the railroad. These were the 3,000 "old men and boys" of the Georgia militia. Wheeler's cavalry retired from further action. They knew better than to attack entrenched infantry. However, the militia did attack, not just once but seven times. They succeeded in inflicting 92 casualties on the Federals, among them General Walcutt, who was severely wounded. The militia paid with 523 casualties.[20]

After the final repulse, the militia marched back to Macon and the Union soldiers let them go. Killing boys was an experience that Sherman's hardened veterans did not want to continue. "I hope we never have to shoot at such men again," wrote an Illinois captain. "They knew nothing at all about fighting and I think their officers knew as little."[21]

After the battle, the Union cavalry marched to Gordon, already occupied by General Oliver O. Howard's troops, and rested there on November 23. The next day, William Thomas wrote, "Marched to Millidgeville   Drove the rebel Legislature out   Stoped a while In the Capitol ground and Drawed rations   The first Since Leaving Marietta." James Moore, assistant surgeon of the Ninth Pennsylvania, added more details of the visit in Milledgeville. He wrote, "The soldiers had taken possession of the State Capitol, from which the legislature had fled in dismay on the approach of the army. A mock legislature was now improvised and the forms of debate gone through, when a soldier ap-

19 *Ibid.*; Moore, *Complete History*, p. 446.
20 Guernsey and Alden, II, 688; Cox, pp. 30–31.
21 Wiley, *Billy Yank*, p. 352.

peared at the door shouting, 'the Yankees are coming.' The assembly dissolved in laughter."[22]

The cavalrymen were allowed only a couple of hours for fun and games in Milledgeville. At 2:00 P.M. they took up their march again. Crossing the Oconee River, they headed northeast in the direction of Augusta. They camped about ten miles from town that night. At Milledgeville, Kilpatrick had received new orders from General Sherman. In addition to the feint toward Augusta, he was to try to destroy the railroad bridge across Brier Creek between Augusta and Waynesboro and then continue on to Millen in an effort to release prisoners of war from a camp there.[23]

Meanwhile, Wheeler had determined that Sherman was not going to attack Macon and he led his entire corps around the front of the Union army to get into position to defend Augusta.

Although Sherman's maps show that the cavalry route took them through Sparta, it appears that a road farther south called County Line road was the actual route followed on November 25.[24] Possibly different routes were taken because the soldiers seemed to disagree on the nature of the country. Cornelius Baker commented, "the forage is plenty for horses and men," indicating a march through rich country, whereas William Thomas wrote, "Marched 30 miles Through Dismal Swampy Pine Woods." That evening the cavalry reached Ogeechee Shoals and destroyed a woolen mill and a grist mill.[25]

On November 26, the cavalry began marching toward Waynesboro by way of Gibson. General Wheeler had posted his men on the road from the Shoals to Augusta in hopes of catching the Union cavalry when they came out of the swamps bordering Brier Creek. The change of direction of the Federal cavalry placed Wheeler in their rear instead of in front, and he marched to catch up.

"We were attacted in the nite at 1 a clock and firing was kept up

---

[22] Moore, *Complete History*, p. 447.
[23] Cox, pp. 32–33; Guernsey and Alden, II, p. 688.
[24] Library of Congress, "Military Map Showing the March of the United States Forces Under Command of Maj. Gen. W. T. Sherman, U.S.A. During the Years 1863, 1864, 1865"; Col. Allen P. Julian to author, Aug. 26, 1963.
[25] O. R., Ser. 1, XLIV, 368.

till morning and our Co relieved the 5 kantuckey and we drove the rebels back and we left at 8 Am," Cornelius Baker wrote about Wheeler's attack on the rear guard of the Union cavalry at Sylvan Grove on the morning of November 27. The Confederate attack drove the men of the Eighth Indiana and Second Kentucky from their camps. However, the regiments quickly reformed their lines, recaptured their camps, and began to withdraw slowly. While these men were retreating, the next regiment in line, the Fifth Kentucky, erected barricades. Beyond them, the Ninth Pennsylvania was doing the same. The rear regiments retreated through those ahead, with each regiment holding the enemy at its barricade until the next regiment was prepared to do the same. In this manner, each regiment took its turn as rear guard and the units of the First Brigade moved from the rear of the column to the van.[26] Because the Union cavalrymen were moving steadily toward their objectives, *retreat* may not be the correct description of the movement.

Colonel Murray's men partially destroyed the bridge over Brier Creek on the twenty-seventh, but did not have enough time to do a thorough job. They passed through Waynesboro in the evening and erected barricades in a strong position a mile and a half south of town. One flank of the line rested on the railroad embankment and the other on a pond. The Second Brigade, who had been rear guard most of the day, passed through the barricades and the First Brigade was in the rear once more. Except for a part of the Ninth Pennsylvania who were engaged in tearing up the railroad, all of the brigade manned the double line of barricades during the night. Several times the enemy attacked the position but was always repulsed.[27]

At Waynesboro, Kilpatrick learned that the prisoners had been moved from the camp at Millen. He therefore changed plans, deciding to march southwest and rejoin the Union infantry columns. On the morning of November 28, Kilpatrick ordered Colonel Smith Atkins to wait at the intersection of the road from Louisville and there allow Murray's brigade to pass through. Somehow the order miscarried, and

[26] *Ibid.*, pp. 368, 387; Cox, pp. 32–33.
[27] Moore, *Complete History*, p. 447; Cox, pp. 32–33; O. R., Ser. 1, XLIV, 368.

Atkins's brigade continued to march. Assuming that the Second Brigade had stopped, Kilpatrick camped with the Ninth Michigan a short distance from the intersection.

Leaving their barricades at 3:00 A.M., Murray's brigade soon passed through the intersection. The Rebels in their rear quickly discovered Kilpatrick's camp, now isolated from the rest of the Union cavalry, and surrounded it. When he realized the situation, "Little Kil" quickly got his men mounted and personally led a charge intended to break out of the encirclement. Fortunately, the Eighth Indiana, at the rear of the First Brigade, also launched a charge at the circle when they heard firing in their rear. The simultaneous charges at the inside and outside of the ring opened a path, and Kilpatrick and most of the trapped men escaped.[28]

Shortly after this incident, the Ninth Pennsylvania became rear guard. William Thomas wrote, "We Halted a while to Feed at a plantation when the rebs Charged us But were Repulsed." This skirmish took place at Bellevue Plantation and the plantation house, thought to have been built in the 1770's, still has bullet holes from this action.[29] Following this skirmish, the Ninth Pennsylvania marched toward Buckhead Creek, three miles south. By the time they reached the stream, the main body of Kilpatrick's cavalry had crossed.

"the rebels charge on our rear w[h]en we were crossen a run and we drove them back," reported Cornelius Baker of the skirmish at Buckhead Creek. William Thomas added, "The rebs trying to cut Our regt of[f] from the Command." Here, Wheeler swung strong flanking columns out in an attempt to cut the rear elements of the Union cavalry off from the bridge and causeway. Colonel Murray seemed to be pleased with his own reaction to this attack, but his report is not clear about his successful tactic. Evidently, he attacked Wheeler's center and drove it to the vicinity of Big Buckhead Church, a mile from the creek. Covered

---

[28] O. R., Ser. 1, XLIV, 362–67; Cox, p. 33; Guernsey and Alden, II, 688.

[29] Historical marker at site. Porter Carswell, owner of Bellevue Plantation, told the author that Confederate and Union dead from the skirmishes at the plantation and at Buckhead Creek were buried behind the house. The Confederates were re-interred, but Union soldiers remain. Graves cannot be identified because the field was plowed and planted in cotton for many years.

by artillery at the bridge, the Union rear guard then fell back and crossed over the bridge. After all were across, they dismounted and burned the bridge.[30]

Because swamps extend some distance on both sides of the creek, the destruction of the bridge delayed Wheeler's crossing for two hours. One report tells that he took the pews from Big Buckhead Church and used them for bridge planking.[31]

Meanwhile, the Union cavalry halted on rising ground on Reynolds's Plantation, two miles south of the creek and near the Louisville-Millen road. Here they erected a line of barricades. Kilpatrick wrote that he had decided to give Wheeler a severe repulse. After the delay in crossing the creek, Wheeler brought his entire corps of three divisions into position before the barricades.

All three divisions charged the Federal barricades in what Kilpatrick described as "one of the most desperate cavalry charges that I have ever seen."[32] The Federals, armed with repeating and breech-loading carbines, put out such an intense and rapid fire that the charge was broken before it reached the barricades. Two more charges were made, but each with less spirit than the first charge and more easily repulsed. Cornelius Baker wrote, "their ded was laying in front of the baricade we gave them a warm Exception   they dident folow uss any firder i guess they got a nuff of Kilpatericks Cavalry by this time." All reports agree that the Union cavalry marched unmolested during the night to Louisville.[33]

On November 30 the cavalry had a day of rest, and Cornelius Baker reported, "No rebels to bee hird of   their is four coars of infantry here   their is foragers sent out this afternoon   We are all in fine spirits."

Kilpatrick's cavalry took up the march again on December 1; they rode out of Louisville on the Waynesboro road. A few miles from town they encountered Wheeler's pickets, whom they drove across Rocky Creek. The next day, working with Baird's infantry division of the XIV Corps, they drove the Rebels out of their position and along the road.[34]

30 O. R., Ser. 1, XLIV, 368.
31 Historical marker at site.
32 O. R., Ser. 1, XLIV, 362–67.
33 *Ibid.*, pp. 362–67, 386–89.
34 Moore, *Kilpatrick*, p. 34.

Cornelius Baker wrote, "marched to a crick and encamped for the nite
our regiment went on picket   our company was on the advance
our advance post was at the crick."

On December 3, Baker continued, "We left camp and marched to
the railroad and encamped   their was 2 coars of infantry came up
they marched on the railroad." The cavalry had reached Thomas's Station on the Augusta and Savannah Railroad. They encamped a mile
north of the station. General Absalom P. Baird's division occupied
Thomas's Station while the XIV Corps was spread along the track for
miles, with headquarters at Lumpkin's Station, four miles south of
Thomas's.[35]

That night the infantry and part of the cavalry went to work de-
molishing the railroad. To do this work, a company and often a full
regiment formed into a single line along one side of the track. At the
first command, the entire line would bend and take hold of the rail. At
the next command, they would raise the side of the track—rail, ties,
and all—breast high. Then they would stand the ties on end. At the
final command, they would push the entire section over; the impact
usually broke rails loose from the ties. Next, the men piled the ties,
added whatever other wood was available nearby, placed the rails on
top, and lighted the mass. In about half an hour the rails were red hot
in the center. Then, two or three men took hold of the ends and walked
in opposite direction around a tree, bending the rail into what they
called a necktie. To reuse the rail, the tree had to be cut down, the rail
hauled to a rolling mill, reheated, and straightened. A corps could de-
molish ten to fifteen miles of track in a day.[36]

The cavalrymen who were not employed at this work formed a
screen to protect the workers. Wheeler brought his cavalry and some
artillery through Waynesboro in an effort to interrupt the work, and
he did manage to send a few shells in the direction of some of the working parties; but the Union cavalry kept his force at such a distance that
the destructive work went on without interruption.

On the morning of December 4 the Second Brigade of Kilpatrick's
cavalry began to march toward Waynesboro and found Wheeler's force

[35] O. R., Ser. 1, XLIV, 362–67.
[36] Cox, pp. 35–36.

behind a series of three barricades. They succeeded in capturing the two most advanced barricades, but the third position stopped them. Kilpatrick brought the rest of his force up; he did not have to hold a reserve because he had Baird's infantry division right behind him and the entire XIV Corps within a few miles. After a hard fight, Wheeler was forced from this position, crossed the creek, and took a new position in the town itself with flanks extended from some distance east of Waynesboro to a wooded area half a mile west.

The Confederate position was strong. Because of swamps on both sides, the stream could be crossed only at the road and the railroad. These crossings were covered by the Confederate artillery. The task of taking this position fell to Colonel Murray's First Brigade.

Somehow, the Third Kentucky managed to cross and rode toward the Union right; the Ninth Pennsylvania got across and moved to the left. Murray then sent the Eighth Indiana through the swamps on foot to attack the center. The Third Kentucky made the first charge but ran into a severe flanking fire that stopped the charge and pinned the regiment down. When ordered to attack on the left, the Ninth Pennsylvania made a classic saber charge in three columns of four men abreast. Two columns rode over the barricades in the center and left of the town. At the same time, the third column broke through the defenses in the woods at the far left, outflanking the Confederates in the town. With the enemy's right shattered, the Third Kentucky was relieved of the harassing fire on their flank, and they also charged into the town.[37]

"drove Him [Wheeler] Back in great Disorder," wrote William Thomas. Within twenty minutes, the town was cleared of Rebels, and the Pennsylvania and Kentucky troopers were pursuing the fugitives along the road to Brier Creek. The enemy retreated across the creek, and the Union cavalrymen finally destroyed the bridge, which had been one of the objectives assigned when they left Milledgeville.

Cornelius Baker reported, "the los of the rebs was hevy." Assistant Surgeon James Moore, who spent the night patching wounds, wrote that more than two hundred of the captured enemy had been wounded with the saber alone, indicating the power of the Ninth Pennsylvania's

---

[37] O. R., Ser. 1, XLIV, 366–67, 368, 387–88; Moore, *Kilpatrick*, pp. 188–89.

charge.[38] Of course, the Ninth had losses. William Thomas reported, "Solomon Updegrave [Updegrove] out of our Co was shot while We made a charge upon one of their Baricades." Colonel Jordan's report showed one killed and twelve wounded—a small loss considering the result achieved.[39]

James Moore summed up the result of this fight when he wrote, "The Confederate Cavalry had been severely punished, and were now so demoralized that the rest of the campaign was passed without any attack or molestation on their part."[40]

After Waynesboro, the cavalrymen fell in behind the infantry and the wagon trains instead of in their accustomed position in front and flank. They marched through Alexander, and the First Brigade marched to Sylvania, where they became rear guard of the XX Corps.[41] On December 7, Cornelius Baker mentioned crossing the Ten Mile Swamp.

On the eighth, William Thomas wrote, "i went out with Seargt [George] Shultz and Detail of 8 men AHead of the Command Foraging For Rations for the Company   Got Hogs And Sweet potatoes But our Company Did not Come up   we Camped With the 20th Corp   passed through Springfield." Thomas was ahead of the cavalry brigade, which passed through Springfield after dark.

On December 9, Thomas wrote, "We Started aHead with our Squad got aHead of the 20th Corp   We Could not get any further   The road was Blocked with trees Cut Down across The road And on the other Side of the Blockade was a fort   The 20th Corp Made a Charge upon the fort and Took it Before dark Capturing over 800 Prisoners Camped by Ourselves 10 miles from Savanah." That same night, Cornelius Baker was encamped eleven miles from Savannah on the railroad. He reported, "Canonaden was kept up all nite in front of Savanah."

The next day the cavalry division marched with the infantry to a point just five miles from Savannah, where they "encamped during the

38 Moore, *Kilpatrick*, p. 190.
39 O. R., Ser. 1, XLIV, 388.
40 Moore, *Complete History*, p. 488.
41 Moore, *Kilpatrick*, p. 190.

nite in a splendid pine grove." On December 11, Cornelius Baker wrote, "We left camp at 7 A.M. and advanced to the rite of the town and struck the Palased road and joind our infantry and encamped at 10 a clock to nite We marched round the sity to day and camped on the south side We could see the rebel Gates. "

The following day, Kilpatrick's cavalry marched to within seven miles of Fort McAllister on the south bank of the Ogeechee River. The fort prevented the Navy ships from entering the river. Kilpatrick made dispositions to attack the fort, but was ordered to make contact instead with the Navy ships that were standing offshore.[42] This he accomplished, and the cavalry command marched to Midway Church,[43] seventeen miles south of Savannah. Cornelius Baker commented, "My horse gave out and i walked to camp i was prety tird We marched 18 M."

William Thomas and his foraging detail remained separated from the regiment while these moves were taking place. On December 11, Thomas wrote, "Heard that our Div and Co Were over on the right with the 17th Corp We crossed over there with our wagon train Came to the place where They Were Camped last night but they had left Camped by ourselves in an old House." The next day he reached a canal and camped where "17th Corp Train are Passing all night." The next day, Thomas reached the area of Fort McAllister and there learned that the command was at Midway. He reached Midway Church on December 14 but found that his company had gone south to destroy a bridge over the Altamaha River.

For some reason, only 120 men were sent with Captain Elisha A. Hancock to destroy this bridge. Thomas recorded the failure on December 15, "our Company Arrived in camp at noon Bringing in 17 prisoners Captured at Sand Hill where they Had a Skirmish But they Failed to Burn the Bridge The rebs were to[o] Strong they only Suceeded In Burning Part of the trestle work to the Bridge."

---

[42] O. R., Ser. 1, XLIV, 367.
[43] Midway Church, a colonial church built in 1792, replaced a meeting house that had been burned by the British in 1778. Organized in 1754, the congregation produced many of Georgia's colonial leaders, including Button Gwinnet and Lyman Hall, signers of the Declaration of Independence. Early ministers included the fathers of Oliver Wendell Holmes and S. F. B. Morse.

For the cavalry the March to the Sea ended when they went into camp at Midway Church. Here the officers wrote their reports; Kilpatrick commented that they marched 541 miles and crossed in front of the army 3 times. He reported that his command had destroyed over 14,000 bales of cotton and 271 cotton gins. He claimed 500 prisoners captured and estimated 1,500 enemy killed and wounded. The cavalry losses were 4 officers and 34 men killed, 6 officers and 153 men wounded, and 2 officers and 166 men missing.[44] Colonel Jordan's report showed that the Ninth Pennsylvania had more than its share of the casualties with 6 killed, 33 wounded, 42 taken prisoner, and 38 foragers missing.

Marching through a rich rural section, the Ninth captured 440 horses and mules. However, 532 horses were abandoned or lost in action. Jordan concluded his report: "My officers have all done their duty with commendable alacrity, and my men have born the hardships of the campaign without a murmur, rendering prompt obedience to the orders of their officers and displaying a patience and bravery truly commendable."[45]

Fort McAllister was captured by the infantry on December 13, and Savannah was occupied on December 21. After the fall of Fort McAllister, some time was required to clear the river and get supply ships to King's Bridge, which became the supply center for the army. Before supplies were unloaded in large volume, rations became scarce, and much of the army went hungry.

The cavalry was more fortunate than the troops in Savannah, since Midway Church was in the center of what then was a fertile rice-producing area. On six days between December 17 and December 24, Cornelius Baker went on foraging expeditions. He ranged widely, going twenty-five miles from Midway one time and beyond Riceboro and Hinesville on other trips.

"We remain in camp   the boys is all in fine spirits as it is cristmas," Cornelius Baker wrote, "We had inspection at 8 AM. We had a fine crismas roast   We had hard tack and fride pork." Perhaps, he really did think that he had fine fare because of the scarcity of food on other days. A few days later he wrote, "I went out for forage with a de-

44 O. R., Ser. 1, XLIV, 367–68.
45 *Ibid.*, 388–89.

tail to the obeechee river and we got rise in the straw   their is the splendidist kine of rise land here   our rashens is slim   We haf to hull rise to eat   our river navagations isant open yet."

On December 26 orders came to the men to get ready for a grand review on December 28. However, because of the almost continuous stormy and cold weather, the review was postponed from day to day. Finally, on January 12, Cornelius Baker could write, "We went to the sity and was reviewed by General Shirman and the Secretary [Secretary of War Edwin M. Stanton]   We were reviewed in the streats of the sity   Every thing is cherishing ther in the sity   We retirnd to camp at 8 o clock in the eavning." With the grand review, the Georgia campaign ended, and the army began to prepare for the next march.

South Carolina Reaps the Whirlwind

Mee and 10 men went on a scout and we captured 29 State Malishia flag and brot it to camp and presented [it] to Cornal Cimbel [Kimmel].

Cornelius Baker deserved more recognition than he received for his exploit of February 18, 1865. Generally, the capture of an enemy battle flag was the high point in a soldier's career. By law, enemy colors were supposed to be sent to the War Department with a history of the flag, including by whom, where, and when it was taken. Unless Baker's trophy happened to be *"No. 535 South Carolina State flag; no history"* in the list published by the Secretary of War,[1] his officers failed to send these colors to Washington. Even if this was his flag, Cornelius Baker's name was not included in this select list of heroes.

Leading scouting and foraging parties, as Cornelius Baker frequently did during the Carolina campaign, required alertness, knowledge, and judgment. At the end of the campaign Colonel David H. Kimmel reported, "The great loss [of soldiers of the Ninth Pennsylvania Cavalry] . . . was occasioned by foraging, where my men would rashly contend with superior numbers of the enemy."[2] Baker's new responsibility began while the cavalry was preparing for the march. "Corporal blain was reduced and I was permoted corporal," he wrote on January 16. William Thomas and Henry Baker also were named

---

[1] National Archives, "Captured Battle Flags: Letter from the Secretary of War . . . ," Feb. 16, 1888, *House Exec. Doc. No. 163*, 50th Cong., 1st sess.

[2] O. R., Ser. 1, XLVII, pt. 1, p. 876.

corporals while the regiment was encamped at Midway Church.

Scouting and foraging were more dangerous in South Carolina than in other areas where the soldiers had marched. In Tennessee there were pro-Union people who might warn them of the approach of Rebel patrols. Even in Georgia some citizens were not unfriendly. But in South Carolina the entire population seemed hostile. Also, the Confederate cavalry was scouting and foraging in the same areas, and chances of meeting strong Rebel parties were greater. Three days after the expedition mentioned by Cornelius Baker, other Union cavalry scouts found eighteen Federal soldiers, foragers and scouts, who apparently were murdered after they had surrendered to parties of Joseph Wheeler's cavalry. Two had their throats slit, and most wore signs lettered, "Death to all foragers."[3]

Kilpatrick and Wheeler exchanged notes over this incident; Kilpatrick threatening to execute an equal number of Wheeler's troopers whom he held as prisoners. He also threatened, "if my people when taken are not treated in all cases as prisoners of war should be . . . there shall not be a house left standing within reach of my scouting parties along my line of march, nor will I be responsible for the conduct of my soldiers, who will not only be allowed but encouraged to take a fearful revenge."[4] Fortunately, Kilpatrick's temper had cooled by the time he received Wheeler's reply, which denied that his troopers were responsible for these murders, and reprisal executions were not carried out. Even before this incident, Kilpatrick's men had been doing a quite thorough job of destruction and the difference in numbers of houses burned before and after the incident could not have been many.

During the campaign, more than half of the Ninth Pennsylvania's numbers were one-year men, the recruits who had joined the regiment at Chattanooga only a few months before. Additional recruits joined at Savannah to replace the three-year nonveterans whose terms of service had expired. "Their was 80 recrutes came for the regiment," Cornelius Baker reported on January 26, "our Co got 6 of them."

---

3 John G. Barrett, *Sherman's March Through the Carolinas* (Chapel Hill: University of North Carolina Press, 1956), pp. 104–105.
4 *Ibid.*

The Third Cavalry Division was reorganized for the new campaign:[5]

First Brigade	*Second Brigade*
Col. T. J. Jordan	Brig. Gen. S. D. Atkins
Ninth Pennsylvania	Ninety-second Illinois
Eighth Indiana	Ninth Ohio
Second Kentucky	Tenth Ohio
Third Kentucky	Ninth Michigan
Third Brigade	Third Indiana (6 cos.)
Col. G. E. Spencer	*Battery*
Fifth Kentucky	Tenth Wisconsin
Fifth Ohio	
First Alabama (squadron)	

The six companies forming the left wing of the Third Indiana and the squadron of the First Alabama were reinforcements received at Savannah. Following Colonel Jordan's promotion to command of the First Brigade, Lieutenant Colonel David H. Kimmel became leader of the Ninth Pennsylvania.

Immediately after the grand review of the army in Savannah, preparations for the coming march began. On January 15, Cornelius Baker wrote, "the condemned horses was sent to town this eavning   they took my horse for artilary." Of course, the artillery had top priority for horses. Being next in importance, the cavalrymen were authorized to take horses away from the infantry foragers. However, there were not enough horses to go around, and Kilpatrick began the march with 400 dismounted troopers. He armed these men with infantry weapons.[6]

"We received orders for to prepair for a long march and our train was loadent with rashens," Cornelius Baker wrote on January 18. The next day he continued, "our company and Co D went to a rise mill at the obeechee river for rise with 6 wagons   We loadent them with sheld rise   [I] was out 1 mile firder and got sheaf rise   it comenced raining and was verry disagreeable."

On January 22 he commented, "We remaind in camp   it raind nearly all day and times are dull   The mail went out for the last time."

[5] Cox, p. 249.
[6] *Ibid.*, p. 180; Robert Hale Strong, *A Yankee Private's Civil War*, ed. by Ashley Halsey (Chicago: Henry Regnery Co., 1961), p. 173.

In this mail, Baker sent home two small cards and photographs of his friends. One card gave mailing directions:

Addres comencing 1 25
Co. C 9th Pa Cavalry
Savannah Georgia
In care of Kilpaterick
Comanding Cavalry

One side of the second card noted, "Here are the names of the photographs" and listed the names of the soldiers whose pictures appeared in the photographs. Baker wrote a tune and verse on the opposite side of this card:

for right is might an God is God
and right the day must win

During the last half of January torrential rains began to fall, making quagmires of the roads and causing the rivers to overflow in the area through which Sherman's army would campaign. A less daring general would have postponed the march; a less self-sufficient army would have bogged down in the swamps. Groups from each brigade were organized into pioneer corps and were assigned the task of keeping the roads passable. Often they had to maintain road surfaces that were under water. They did this by laying tree trunks and fence rails transversely on the road, a procedure known as corduroying.[7]

While preparing for the campaign, Kilpatrick's cavalry camped at the supply base at King's Bridge on the Ogeechee River between Savannah and Midway Church. On January 27, Cornelius Baker reported, "We got marching orders and drew 5 days rashens and 2 days horse fead and was redy for the march." The next day the cavalry left King's Bridge and began to march toward Sister's Ferry on the Savannah River, forty miles above Savannah. During the first night, the cavalry-

---

[7] Barrett, pp. 36, 46–47; O. R., Ser. 1, XLVII, pt. 1, p. 221.

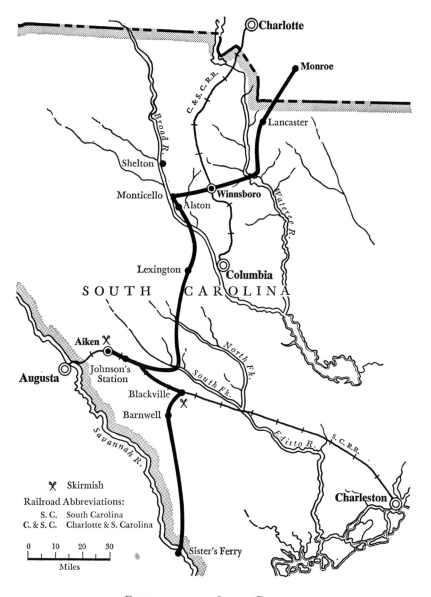

CAMPAIGNING IN SOUTH CAROLINA

223

men "went into camp along the railroad were we encamped before wen we went to Savannah."

William Thomas made the last daily entry in his diary on January 29. He wrote, "Cold Day Started Early again this Morning and Marched Back towards Springfield Marched through Swamp The roads are in an awful Condition we Have to Corderoy the roads Before we Can get our teams through Col Jordan Is in the rear all Day with His Brig Helping Teams out of the mud Camped at Dusk Marched 15 miles." The Ninth Pennsylvania reached Sister's Ferry at 11:00 A.M. on January 31. Cornelius Baker observed, "General Howard and davis and Slokem is here with their commands."

Baker's observation was only partly true. Sister's Ferry was the assembly point for the left wing of Sherman's army. This wing, commanded by Major General Henry Slocum was made up of Major General Jefferson C. Davis's XIV Corps and Brigadier General A. S. Williams's XX Corps. The right wing, commanded by Major General Oliver O. Howard, crossed the river near the coast.[8]

Before the cavalry arrived at Sister's Ferry, a pontoon bridge had been built across the river. Because high water had made the river three miles wide, long trestle bridges connected the ends of the bridge to the banks. In spite of the swift current, driftwood, and objects floated downstream by enemy cavalry, the bridge held.[9] On February 2, Cornelius Baker wrote, "We remaind in camp at Sisters ferry and drew one days rashens and a mail came for the hoal comand their was a detail went out to work on the roads on the other side of the river."

The next day the campaign began. Baker continued, "We left camp this morning at 12 o clock and crossed the river and marched 16 miles and went in camp during the nite our brigade was in the advance We passed the ripper boat [riverboat] Camden and we drew one days fead their was a detail brot it to camp We carried 2 days fead along." On February 4, the cavalry marched fifteen miles. "We got in splendid contry and their is lots of forage," commented Baker. The next day, they marched seventeen miles.

8 Cox, pp. 246–47; Barrett, pp. 44–48.
9 Barrett, p. 48; Cox, p. 168; Guernsey and Alden, II, 716.

General Kilpatrick was accused of filling his troopers' saddlebags with matches before they entered South Carolina.[10] Probably he did not have to supervise or even suggest such an activity. His cavalrymen, like the other soldiers of Sherman's army, had made up their own minds to make South Carolina suffer for having started the war. The South Carolinians had sown the wind of secession and now they would reap the whirlwind. This was the attitude of common soldier and officer alike.

After marching twenty miles on February 6, Kilpatrick's cavalry reached Barnwell. Soon afterward the place was afire and the troopers renamed the town "Burnwell." When the cavalry left, the XIV Corps moved in and completed the destruction. The only house left in the town when the army left was that of a lady who compromised her Rebel sympathies sufficiently to entertain Union officers.[11]

"We left Barnville this morning at 7 o clock," wrote Cornelius Baker on February 7, "marched within 4 miles of black ville and enguaged the enimy and charge them and drove them out of town." A part of Wheeler's Confederate cavalry was in Blackville when the Union column approached. The Ninth Pennsylvania, in the van of the Federal cavalry, made a "brilliant dash" into the town, according to Assistant Surgeon James Moore. Moore joined Colonel Jordan, Lieutenant Colonel Kimmel, and Kilpatrick's adjutant, Major L. G. Estes, in leading the charge. The attack drove Wheeler's men across the South Fork of the Edisto River.[12]

Blackville was on the Charleston and Augusta Railroad. Sherman had marked this road for destruction. The cavalry moved twelve miles west of Blackville on the eighth. On February 9, Baker wrote, "We left camp this morning at 9 o clock and marched 12 miles along the Augusta and Charlston railroad and encamped and built baricades and toar up the railroad and burnt the ties." While the cavalry marched west toward Aiken, Slocum's infantrymen spread out eastward, destroying the railroad as they marched. Beyond them Howard's wing dismantled

[10] Barrett, p. 52.
[11] *Ibid.*, pp. 52–53.
[12] Moore, *Kilpatrick*, p. 216.

the track so most of the line between Aiken and Charleston ceased to exist.[13]

The next day, Cornelius Baker reported, "The 1 brigade left camp at 7 AM and marched 4 miles   found the rebels in foarce in our front and right and the balance of our forse were imediately brot up for protection   Cornal Jordan found out their trap before he was trapped."

On February 11, Kilpatrick was less cautious than Jordan had been. Baker wrote, "the 2 brigade advanced to [Aiken] and was drove back Kilpaterick was nearly captured and his hoal staff   the rebels foloed them up to our baricades and they made several charges but were hansomely repulced   they dident even drive in our skirmishers." Although he had evidence that Wheeler's cavalry was nearby, Kilpatrick rode into Aiken at the head of his column like a conquering hero and into a trap Wheeler had set. If some of Wheeler's men had not become trigger happy and sprung the trap too soon, they might have captured the little general. As it was, Kilpatrick barely won the race back to the First Brigade's barricades at Johnson's Station,[14] sometimes referred to by the more interesting name of Pole Cat Ponds.[15]

"the skirmishin was kept up all day on the advance picket poasts," wrote Baker the next day, "We lay behind baricades all day and [slept] while we were there." He also reported, "General Kilpaterick sent a flag of truce out this eavning and our company was detailed as an escort."

At noon on the thirteenth, the cavalry left Johnson's Station and marched back to the South Edisto River. Cornelius Baker observed that the infantry was erecting breastworks at the crossing. The probable reason was that Major General Benjamin Franklin Cheatham's corps, a remnant of the Confederate Army of Tennessee, was now behind Wheeler's cavalry.[16] However, the fortifications were not needed, and Baker concluded, "the rebels haint botherd uss this eavning."

On February 14, the cavalry marched between the two infantry corps but appears to have moved ahead of the column the next day.

13 Barrett, pp. 50–52.
14 O. R., Ser. 1, XLVII, pt. 2, p. 450; Barrett, p. 56; Moore, *Complete History*, p. 484.
15 Thomas diary; Skinner, p. 340.
16 Cox, p. 169; Moore, *Complete History*, p. 484.

"Our dismounted men drove the rebels across the [North Fork of the Edisto] river," Baker reported. The cavalry and the infantry column crossed the same day.

Kilpatrick's cavalry division passed through Lexington, twenty miles west of Columbia, on February 16 and encamped nine miles north of that town. Reports indicate that they left Lexington ablaze. After they moved on, Major General John White Geary's infantry division came into Lexington for the purpose of protecting property. Geary, possibly with tongue in cheek, reported that no houses were burned while his troops were in Lexington. However, as the town was only ashes when he left, the cavalry must have done such a thorough job that Geary found no houses for his soldiers either to protect or to destroy.[17]

Columbia also burned on the night of February 17. However, the Union cavalry could not be accused of having any part in this destruction since they were riding north on the seventeenth and eighteenth through the area west of the Broad River. It was here that Cornelius Baker and squad captured the militia flag.

The task of the Federal cavalry became more difficult as they moved north. Wheeler's Confederate cavalry corps and Cheatham's Army of Tennessee infantry corps were now hurrying north from Aiken on roads parallel to those being traveled by the Union cavalry. The Confederates were trying to swing in front of Kilpatrick and reach the railroad to Charlotte. At times the Union and Confederate forces were within three miles of each other, and sometimes during night marches, details of Union troopers found themselves marching in the Rebel columns. They generally learned of their mistake and disappeared before the enemy suspected their presence.[18]

Also, because of the collapse of South Carolina's defense and morale, Lieutenant General Wade Hampton, a South Carolina hero, was released from Robert E. Lee's army and was assigned the command of all Confederate cavalry in the state.[19] General Matthew C. Butler's cavalry division also came down from Virginia. This force covered the

[17] Barrett, p. 60.
[18] Moore, *Kilpatrick*, p. 218.
[19] Cox, p. 171.

Confederate retreat from Columbia.[20] The rapid move of Kilpatrick's Union cavalry kept a wedge driven between Wheeler's and Butler's forces, and Hampton did not have a unified command until after Sherman's army crossed the line into North Carolina.

The Yankee cavalrymen continued to move north in spite of swollen rivers, muddy roads, and enemy interference. "We remain in camp till 11 and then we left and crossed Brod river," Cornelius Baker wrote on February 19, "it took uss till 2 o clock to nite before we could cross the river   The wagon train had to cross before uss   We went 6 miles and went in camp."

Kilpatrick and the Second Brigade reached Monticello during the afternoon of the twentieth. A force was sent north to Shelton where they destroyed the depot and bridges on the railroad. The First Brigade was in the rear, somewhere between Alston and Monticello.[21] Baker wrote, "I was out for horses for the batallion   We dident find any."

On February 21, Baker reported marching twelve miles east to within six miles of Winnsboro. The cavalrymen used flooring from Ebenezer Church, now called "The Old Brick Church," on their line of march, to repair a bridge that had been partially burned by the Confederates.[22] The cavalry did not have to fight for Winnsboro. Infantry foragers had forced their way into the town on the twenty-first and were followed by the left wing of the army.[23]

By February 23 the cavalry and the left wing were nearing the Wateree River. Cornelius Baker reported, "We left camp at 7 AM and marched 9 miles and we stoped and fed and cooked super and left at 7 PM and marched to the Wateree river and remaind their till half after 8 and before we could cross it was raining and verry unplesant."

The next day he continued, "We crossed the Wateree river at 9 o clock last nite and marched 4 miles and fed and breckfast their fixing gruel   we went across the river on barges   it was terrible to cross." Baker probably was referring to the canvas pontoons that supported the bridge because the cavalry did cross on them. The high water and

20 Barrett, pp. 48, 65.
21 Barrett, p. 98; Moore, *Kilpatrick*, p. 219.
22 Historical marker at site.
23 Barrett, pp. 95-97.

swift current made the crossing extremely hazardous. Other soldiers observed that the bridge heaved like a ship in a storm. After the XX Corps and the cavalry had crossed, the bridge washed out, leaving the XIV Corps on the west bank. Several days passed before the river fell sufficiently to allow rebuilding. The XX Corps on the opposite bank made little progress over the muddy roads. Thus, Sherman's army was divided and stuck in the mud.[24]

The cavalry also had trouble with mud and high water. On March 25, Cornelius Baker wrote, "We left camp at 7 Am and marched ½ mile to a crick and seein the crossing was bad we dident get across till 12 o clock   we went 3 miles and stoped till the comand closed up and then we marched to [Lancaster] and we got in camp at 11 o clock to nite." The troopers were on their good behavior in Lancaster and did little damage. The brigade commanders are generally credited with maintaining discipline. Kilpatrick had other interests. A "tall, handsome, well-dressed" woman was traveling in the general's train and occupied a room at Kilpatrick's headquarters in Lancaster, according to some reports.[25]

The Yankee cavalry feinted toward Charlotte from Lancaster. The Confederates had been unable to gather an army in South Carolina quickly enough to oppose the Union army. However, they were assembling troops in Charlotte. Almost in desperation, Lieutenant General Joseph E. Johnston was given command of all troops in North Carolina. Kilpatrick's feint toward Charlotte was intended to deceive Johnston so the growing Confederate army could be held in Charlotte while Sherman marched to Fayetteville. Either the deception worked or Johnston realized that he did not yet have enough men to challenge the Union army; for he did not march from Charlotte at this time.

The Union cavalry crossed the state line on March 1 and some part of the command reached Monroe, east of Charlotte that same day.[26] By March 3 they were farther east. Cornelius Baker wrote, "[We left] at 5 o clock on a expedition for horses   we went near Wades borough and captured a lot of horses and mules   A scout charged into Wades

24 *Ibid.*, p. 99; O. R., Ser. 1, XLVII, pt. 1, p. 421.
25 Barrett, pp. 100–101.
26 *Ibid.*, p. 114.

borough and Luitenent Grifen got kiled We went to Chesterville [Chesterfield, S. C.] to meat the comand and they dident come to Chesterville and we went out and put up at a house till the next morning." The charge into Wadesboro was made by 100 men of the Ninth Michigan.[27]

Baker's party came past an intersection called Phillips Cross Roads before the Ninth Pennsylvania reached this point. Even so, the small party was in little danger while separated from the regiment, for Chesterfield was already occupied by Union infantry.[28] The main body of the regiment did encamp that night at the crossroads, four miles north of the state line on the Wadesboro-Chesterfield road. They were the rear of the cavalry column that night.

At 7:00 A.M. on March 4 the Ninth Pennsylvania pickets at the rear of the Union cavalry were attacked, but they repulsed the enemy, who thereupon formed a skirmish line. From the extent of the line, Lieutenant Colonel David Kimmel judged that the total enemy force must be quite large and expected to be assaulted. However, the Rebels seemed content merely to exchange shots with the Federal skirmishers. This activity continued until noon.[29] By this time, Cornelius Baker's party had rejoined the regiment, after leaving Chesterfield at dawn and stopping along the way to forage.

About noon, the Rebel skirmishers moved from the rear to the right flank of the Ninth Pennsylvania. After determining that the enemy skirmishers numbered only 200 men, Kimmel sent his adjutant, Lieutenant Isaac D. Landis of Company H, with an equal number, to the left to try to flank and capture the enemy skirmishers. Landis reached high ground behind the enemy line and there saw that he was in the rear of Colonel G. G. Dibrell's entire brigade of Confederate cavalry. The Ninth was ordered to rejoin the brigade when the size of the Confederate force was learned, and the First Brigade, in turn, moved through the barricades of the Second Brigade. They marched two miles beyond and built a line of barricades at "a white house."[30]

[27] *Ibid.*, pp. 113–14.
[28] J. R. McBride, *History of the 33d Indiana Veteran Volunteer Infantry* (Indianapolis: Burford, 1900), p. 169.
[29] O. R., Ser. 1, XLVII, pt. 1, p. 876.
[30] *Ibid.*, pp. 867, 876; Barrett, p. 113.

"our company went on picket and the rebels charged them," Cornelius Baker wrote, "We lay in the baricades all nite."

The attacking force was Wheeler's entire corps of three divisions. Wheeler, having determined that Sherman was marching for Fayetteville instead of toward Charlotte, hurried eastward to get between the Union columns and Fayetteville. His advance struck the Ninth Pennsylvania at Phillips Cross Roads.

Colonel Jordan anticipated that his barricades would be assaulted by Wheeler's whole force at dawn on March 5. However, when daylight came, he found that the enemy had withdrawn.[31] Wheeler, evidently more intent on getting in front of Sherman than he was on fighting the Yankee cavalry, had marched toward Fayetteville. However, the swollen waters of the Pee Dee River stopped him for several days.[32]

Leaving their position, the Union cavalry also marched to the Pee Dee. Wheeler had moved northeast; the Federals marched southeast through Morven and struck the river one mile south of the state line. "We got to the river at 3 o clock at nite and we remain their during the day waiting till the pontoons were laid and we crossed at 5 o clock," Baker wrote on March 6.

By marching all night and stopping only to feed the horses, the Union cavalry reached the vicinity of Rockingham about midmorning. Here they found foragers already skirmishing with the rear guard of Matthew Butler's Confederate cavalry division. The Ninth Pennsylvania, a detail of the Third Kentucky, and the foragers charged into the town. In the skirmish that followed, Confederate Brigadier General Hugh K. Aiken was killed and the Rebels were driven from the town. The action was over by 10:00 A.M.[33]

The First Brigade took their turn as rear guard when the cavalry marched toward Fayetteville on March 8. This march proved to be a difficult one. During the night of the 8th, most of the brigade was dismounted to draw the wagons and artillery across Drowning Creek, which made a swamp more than half a mile wide. *Through* may be a

---

31 O. R., Ser. 1, XLVII, pt. 1, p. 867.
32 Barrett, 114–15.
33 Barrett, p. 115; O. R., Ser. 1, XLVII, pt. 1, pp. 861, 867.

more accurate term than *across* for the passage of this creek. Colonel Jordan reported, "The men were many times in mud and water to their armpits."[34]

The brigade went into camp at 4:00 A.M. on the ninth but were on the move again at 8:00 A.M. Once more, the men had to dismount and manhandle the wagons and guns through Deep Creek and Devil's Gut. They went into camp two miles beyond the latter place at 9:00 P.M.[35]

The First Brigade was now far behind the rest of Kilpatrick's cavalry. The van had come upon the rear of Confederate General William J. Hardee's column on March 9 at a place called Solemn Grove in Union reports and Solomon's Grove locally and in most Confederate reports.[36] Hardee's force consisted of the defenders of Charleston who had had to retreat when Sherman's capture of Columbia made Charleston untenable. Hardee's men had managed to stay ahead of Sherman's columns.[37] From prisoners, Kilpatrick learned that Hampton's three divisions of cavalry were to the rear and marching eastward. Kilpatrick determined to intercept this force.[38]

With Jordan's brigade on the southernmost of two parallel roads, Kilpatrick posted Atkins's brigade on the second. He then learned of a third road farther north and personally accompanied the small Third Brigade to this position. A crossroad connected the three positions so the brigades could support each other. However, events did not work out as Kilpatrick planned.

About 1:00 A.M., Jordan became aware of a heavy enemy force passing his position on a road about two and one-half miles away, thereby cutting his communications with the other brigades. Atkins's brigade also was outflanked and separated from the Third Brigade. Thus, Hampton successfully isolated Kilpatrick with his weakest brigade. At daylight, Hampton was in position and struck the Federal camp with all three of his divisions.[39]

The surprise and force of the attack drove the Federal troopers from

34 O. R., Ser. 1, XLVII, pt. 1, p. 867.
35 *Ibid.*
36 Barrett, p. 125; Cox, p. 179.
37 Cox, pp. 178–79.
38 O. R., Ser. 1, XLVII, pt. 1, p. 861.
39 *Ibid.*; Barrett, pp. 125–26; O. R., Ser. 1, XLVII, pt. 2, p. 786.

their camp and into a swamp behind it. Kilpatrick was nearly captured. He reportedly came onto the porch of the house in which he was staying, dressed in his nightshirt, just as a Confederate soldier rode up looking for a general to capture. With a "he went that-a-way" gesture, Kilpatrick sent the man away and then ran to the swamp where most of his men had fled. Kilpatrick's staff was besieged in the house that he had just left. Other reports say that Kilpatrick's lady friend appeared on the porch during the shooting and was most gallantly escorted to the safety of a ditch by a Confederate officer.[40]

The Rebels stopped to loot the camp and this delay gave Kilpatrick time to organize his force. Fortunately, his 400 dismounted men were nearby; and when they appeared with their rifles and bayonets, many of the Confederate troopers thought the Union infantry had arrived and they fled. The cavalrymen also charged from the swamp and, after a hard fight, regained their camp and drove the more numerous enemy away.[41] Surgeon James Moore of the Ninth Pennsylvania reported that more than 100 dead were left in the camp by the enemy. He also said there were 600 Rebels wounded and captured and that the houses all along the Confederate line of march to Fayetteville were filled with wounded.[42] Federal losses also were heavy. Kilpatrick reported these as 4 officers and 15 men killed, 7 officers and 61 men wounded, and 103 officers and men taken prisoner.[43] The Federal infantrymen called this action "Kilpatrick's shirt-tail skedaddle."[44]

Colonel Jordan began marching south toward the plank road in accordance with orders he had received from Kilpatrick the day before. While marching he heard the firing and turned his column toward the sound of battle. However, the fight was over before he got near.[45] His force did meet the Second Brigade and, with them, camped that night twelve miles west of Fayetteville. On March 11, the combined force

[40] Barrett, pp. 126–29; Cox, p. 179.
[41] O. R., Ser. 1, XLVII, pt. 1, pp. 861–62; Barrett, pp. 128–29.
[42] Moore, *Complete History*, p. 488.
[43] O. R., Ser. 1, XLVII, pt. 1, p. 862.
[44] Barrett, p. 130.
[45] O. R., Ser. 1, XLVII, pt. 1, pp. 867–68; National Archives, "Co. C., 9th Pa. Muster Roll, Apr. 30, 1865" lists several casualties at Solemn Grove. They probably were serving with the artillery or with dismounted men. Some reports on the fight at Solemn Grove indicate Jordan's brigade arrived on the scene of the skirmish.

marched to a place four miles west of Fayetteville on the plank road where they camped. The Federal infantry already was in Fayetteville and in touch with Navy ships. Thus, the march through South Carolina ended. However, the shooting did not stop. On March 12, Cornelius Baker recorded, "S P Gutshall and 6 men of uss went for forage and ran into a squad of rebels and Gutshall got wunded threw the arm." The next day he continued, "We remaind in camp and drew rashens   The regiments horses is orderd to bee tirnd over   washed my shirt and drawers   sent sergent Gutshall away." Samuel P. Gutshall spent what time remained of the war in the hospital in Fayetteville and returned to Blain upon discharge.

XXIII

Averasboro and Bentonville

We left camp at 7 AM and marched 2 miles and met the enimy and our brigade was sent to the right we dismounted and advanced on foot threw the swamps and relieved the 8 indiana and our regiment advanced and drove the rebel infantry one mile and held them in check 4 hours and then the infantry relieved uss and we mounted our horses and went to the left and we run into their lines and drove them from their position then we were relieved by the 2 brigade and our batallion went after the ammunition train 15 miles in our rear we marched till one o clock to nite our loss is farely hevy we had 2 wunded from our company.

Here Cornelius Baker summarized the Battle of Averasboro as he saw it. This fight on March 16, 1865, was one of the few actions in which cavalry not only fought superior numbers of infantry but actually drove them from a fortified position. "This action fully demonstrates the fact that Federal cavalry, when properly handled and led by brave, determined officers, are fully equal to rebel infantry," Colonel Jordan concluded from the battle.[1]

The brunt of the fighting at Averasboro fell upon Jordan's First Brigade and the Ninth Pennsylvania and Eighth Indiana carried the heaviest share in the brigade. One-twelfth of Jordan's brigade were killed or wounded, and most of these men were in the two regiments that did the heaviest fighting.[2] Jordan was brevetted a brigadier general for the manner in which he handled his force at Averasboro.[3]

While the Union army rested for a few days in Fayetteville, Confederate General Joseph E. Johnston was able to bring the scattered elements of his army together. Respecting the skill of his adversary and

[1] O. R., Ser. 1, XLVII, pt. 1, p. 869.
[2] *Ibid.*
[3] Amann, II, 56; *Commemorative Encyclopedia*, p. 1195.

overestimating the size of the opposing army, General Sherman became more cautious than he had been in the preceding campaign. He also wanted to reach Goldsboro as quickly as possible and join forces with the armies that Generals John M. Schofield and Alfred Howe Terry were leading in from the coast.

To effect this union, General Hugh Judson Kilpatrick was ordered to march up the plank road to Averasboro with only enough wagons to carry the bare minimum of ammunition for normal campaigning. Four divisions of the left-wing infantry, also with a minimum of wagons, were to follow the cavalry. General Henry Warner Slocum's two remaining divisions were ordered to march with the wagon train on a more direct road to Goldsboro. General Oliver O. Howard's right wing was ordered to march on a road farther south, also with four fast-moving, unencumbered divisions and two following with the train.[4]

General Johnston had just a few days available for stopping Sherman's army. Once Sherman's and Schofield's armies joined, the Union would possess such overwhelming numbers in North Carolina that the Confederate army would be little more than an annoyance.[5]

Before deciding where to fight Sherman, Johnston had to determine if the Union army planned to march to Raleigh or to Goldsboro. Once he learned the true objective, his plan was to isolate and defeat one wing of the Federal army. The major portion of Johnston's army was assembled at Smithfield, about half way between Raleigh and Goldsboro, to be in position for whichever alternate Sherman might choose.[6] General William J. Hardee's force of about 7,500 men and Joseph Wheeler's cavalry were retreating toward Smithfield from Fayetteville. Hardee was ordered to resist at Averasboro. If only the Union cavalry and a small force of infantry came up to Averasboro, Johnston could be certain that the Federal goal was Goldsboro. However, if strong infantry forces were employed, Raleigh obviously was the target.[7]

On March 15, the Federal army marched out of Fayetteville. "We left Fayetteville at day lite and crossed the Kapefear river and marched

4 Barrett, p. 149.
5 Cox, pp. 239–41, shows combined strength of Sherman and Schofield as 88,948, and of Johnston's army as 33,450.
6 Barrett, p. 149.
7 *Ibid.*, 150, 160.

15 miles and drove the rebels all day," Cornelius Baker wrote. "then the 2 brigade charged their breastworks and went 3 miles from their." Wheeler's cavalry offered only enough resistance to slow Kilpatrick's advance. When the Union column approached General Hardee's position six miles south of Averasboro, he ordered Colonel Alfred Moore Rhett's brigade to build breastworks in front of the main fortifications to delay the Yankees until he could get his wagons safely to the rear. Skirmishers were posted in front of Rhett's works.[8]

About three o'clock that afternoon, the Ninth Michigan, riding in the van of the Second Brigade, struck the Rebel skirmish line, dismounted, and drove the enemy into Rhett's breastworks. When the rest of the Second Brigade came up, they drove Rhett's men out of the forward earthworks and back to the main line.[9] In the confusion Colonel Rhett, a South Carolina aristocrat, rode near a group of horsemen who addressed him in language "more forcible than polite." When he rode up to the group threatening to report their insolence to General Wade Hampton, he learned too late that they were not Hampton's men but Kilpatrick's, and they made him their prisoner.[10]

Following Rhett's men, the Yankee cavalrymen moved close to the Rebel main fortifications and into artillery fire. All of the Second Brigade, except the Ninth Michigan, were withdrawn and ordered to build barricades some distance in the rear. The Michiganders continued to skirmish until the barricades were completed, and then they withdrew. The Confederates soon moved out of their works to probe the Union position, but the fire of the Tenth Wisconsin Battery kept them at a respectful distance.[11]

At dark, all action ceased with the Federals behind their barricades and the Rebels in their earthworks. Kilpatrick asked General Slocum for a brigade of infantry. These reinforcements arrived about midnight and manned the center of the barricades.[12]

By dawn of March 16 the Third Brigade of cavalry was in position on the left of the infantry brigade and was guarding the sector from the

---

8 *Ibid.*, 150.
9 *Ibid.*, 150–51.
10 *Ibid.*, 151–52.
11 Moore, *Kilpatrick*, p. 230; Barrett, p. 150.
12 Moore, *Kilpatrick*, p. 231; O. R., Ser. 1, XLVII, pt. 1, p. 868.

barricades to the swamp formed by a branch of the Cape Fear River. The First Brigade had moved up on the right of the infantry, with the Eighth Indiana at the front. The Second Brigade was the reserve because they had done the heavy fighting on the previous day.[13]

At 6:00 A.M. the Eighth Indiana opened the action with a mounted charge that drove the Rebel skirmishers back to the fortifications and carried all the way to the earthworks. Colonel Fielder A. Jones thought that this first line of trenches could have been captured easily if the Union infantry had advanced. However, finding that his men alone could go no farther, Jones dismounted them and sent the horses to the rear. The Eighth then formed a skirmish line connecting to the right flank of the infantry.[14]

This line had just been completed when the Rebels charged along the entire front, but hardest at the Union right. Colonel Jordan moved forward with the rest of his brigade and, upon learning from Colonel Jones that the line was in danger of being outflanked, ordered two battalions of the Ninth Pennsylvania to dismount and form on the right of the Eighth Indiana line.

"The Ninth had hardly got into position when they were charged by the enemy's infantry, and charge after charge was met by it and the Eighth Indiana in quick succession," Colonel Jordan reported. "About 10 A.M. Colonel Jones reported to me that his ammunition was giving out, and I at once sent for the ammunition train to be brought up, and as the attack by the enemy became (as they were constantly reinforced) more frequent and determined, I ordered the Second Kentucky in to strengthen the lines of Colonel Jones."[15]

Because the ammunition was far in the rear and the roads were bad, Jordan realized that a long time might elapse before the ammunition would arrive. Therefore, he ordered the Third Kentucky from their position on the extreme right and had them form a line close to the right of the infantry. Except for one battalion of the Ninth Pennsylvania held in reserve, the entire First Brigade was on the line.

"The ammunition now came up but not in sufficient quantities to

---

[13] Moore, *Kilpatrick*, p. 231.
[14] O. R., Ser. 1, XLVII, pt. 1, p. 871; Barrett, pp. 152–53.
[15] O. R., Ser. 1, XLVII, pt. 1, 868.

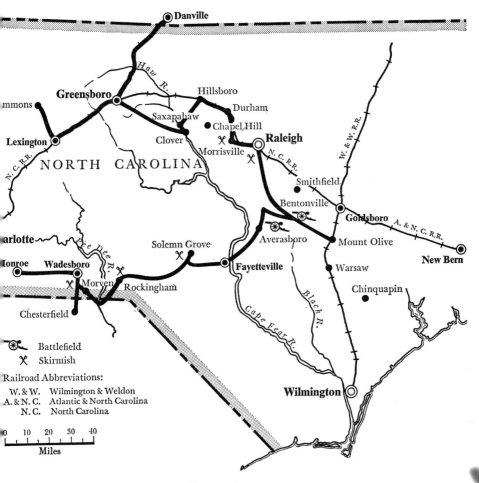

INTO NORTH CAROLINA

fill the demand," continued Jordan, "and the attacks of the enemy rather increasing than diminishing, all the ammunition was distributed and the brave fellows held their ground, finally driving the enemy back to their intrenchments."[16]

Shortly before noon, the Second Brigade came up to relieve Jordan's men. General Smith Atkins placed his Spencer carbine-equipped regiments, the Ninety-second Illinois and Ninth Michigan, into barricades

[16] *Ibid.*

behind the Eighth Indiana and Ninth Pennsylvania positions. These barricades had been built by troopers of these regiments when they came to the rear after using up all their ammunition. When the fresh regiments were in line, the First Brigade retired and mounted their horses.[17]

About 12:30 P.M. a brigade of infantry came up and relieved the Second Brigade as well. The cavalry brigades were ordered to march up a road on the right that led around the Confederate flank and behind their fortifications. The Ninth Ohio led the march along this road. Unknown to them, a Confederate infantry brigade was hidden in the swamp only a few yards from the road. When the Ninth Ohio came opposite this position, the Rebels "opened a most murderous fire upon it."[18]

"It had to fall back, the rebels following," wrote Colonel Jordan. "The Ninth Pennsylvania, being in advance was at once brought into line and, as the Ninth Ohio passed through its intervals, opened so hot a fire upon the charging line that it fell back in confusion. My command, having been in action from 6 A.M. till 2 P.M. almost without intermission, and having less than five rounds of ammunition to the man left, I was ordered to retire to the rear, to dismount the men, and allow my command to rest."[19]

By the time Jordan's men had retired, sufficient infantry had come up to mount an attack on the Confederate fortifications. A flanking column on the right, along with a frontal assault, forced the Rebels out of their forward works.[20] However, the Confederates defended their main line until evening when Hardee, having determined that the principal Federal army was not marching in the direction of Raleigh, ordered his troops to retire.[21] They left many of their wounded on the field, and the Union soldiers took them to the John Smith and Farquhar Smith houses, which still stand. Here the Federal surgeons performed all necessary operations before moving on with the army. The Federal wounded were cared for at the William Smith home and then

[17] *Ibid.*
[18] *Ibid.*
[19] *Ibid.*; Barrett, p. 154.
[20] Barrett, p. 153; Cox, pp. 183–84.
[21] Barrett, pp. 154–55.

were taken in ambulances with the army rather than leaving them to become prisoners of the Confederates.[22] Probably the badly wounded would have fared better with the enemy. The ride to Goldsboro over rough roads must have been excruciating. However, the men probably preferred staying with the army regardless of additional pain and suffering.

During the evening after the battle, William Thomas, with a squad of six men, was assigned to Kilpatrick's headquarters. He carried a dispatch to General Jefferson C. Davis.[23] "i delivered my dispatch when Gen Davis gave In my charge Genl [Colonel] Rhett of the 1st Brig South Carolina Arttillery and Lieut to Escort Back to Killpatricks Quarters," he wrote. "on our way Back Rhett told me that By His Orders the first Shot was fired upon Sumpter Had command of Fort Moultrie at The Time." This was the same Colonel Rhett who had been captured during the first day's fight. To brag or even to mention that he was responsible for firing the shot that started the war to a Union soldier who had had to fight four years because of this action seems either foolish or reckless. Maybe it was just typical of the man about whom one Union officer wrote, "From the conversation of this Rebel Colonel, I judge him to be quite as impractical a person as any in his class."[24]

On the day after the battle, Cornelius Baker's battalion brought up the ammunition so badly needed during the battle. "We left at day light and went 2 miles to our train and got breckfast and left at 9 Am with 11 wagons of ammunition and came to the battleground and encamped," he wrote. "We had a muddy time of it."

On March 18 he continued, "We left camp at 7 Am and crossed the black river with the ammunition train and me and 4 men went out for forage and we kept between the Goaldsborough and the rolley [Raleigh] road the cavalry moved on the rolley road and the infantry on the Goaldsborough the third brigade had a little fite with the rebels we went in camp at 7 Pm 55 miles from Go." The cavalry continued toward Raleigh to keep up the delusion that Sherman was marching

---

[22] *Ibid.*, pp. 155–56.
[23] Jefferson C. Davis commanded the XIV Corps.
[24] Barrett, p. 151.

that way. Instead of fooling the enemy, the Federals fooled themselves. Kilpatrick, meeting strong picket resistance, concluded that the Rebels were concentrating on Raleigh; and his report convinced Sherman that he would not have to fight before reaching Goldsboro.[25]

Johnston was getting his army positioned to strike what he hoped would be a crippling blow at the left wing of the Union army the next day. Because of the fight at Averasboro, the difficult crossing of the Black River, and the terrible condition of the roads, the left wing was strung out along the road to Bentonville. The head of the right wing, marching on a better road farther south, was nearly a full day's march ahead. Plainly, Sherman did not expect a battle.[26]

Everything seemed normal at daylight of March 19 when the foragers moved out ahead of the column and began to skirmish with Rebel cavalry pickets as they did every morning. However, on this morning, reports came back from the foragers that "they don't drive worth a damn."[27] Some foragers managed to push forward far enough to see a strong enemy force constructing earthworks. Still the Federal officers thought that they were facing Hampton's cavalry alone. Only when the lead division of the XIV Corps attacked the fortifications and was repulsed did the officers realize that they were facing most or all of Johnston's army. Then the Union soldiers also began to dig in, and General Slocum ordered the other divisions of the XIV Corps and the lead divisions of the XX Corps to hurry forward toward Bentonville.[28]

The Federal cavalry also was marching toward the sound of battle. Cornelius Baker wrote, "We left camp at 7 Am and marched on the left flank in the direction of were the infantry was fiting till we got within 3 miles and stoped and fed 2 hours then we advanced to were the fiting was going on and formed a line in the rear forming the left flank and we built baricades and remaind their during the nite the rebels charged our lines one time after an nother and still got repulced."

The battle was not that simple. At 3:15 P.M., when Hardee's corps got into position, the Rebels on the right and left attacked and soon

25 *Ibid.*, pp. 160–61, 164.
26 *Ibid.*, pp. 161–62.
27 *Ibid.*, p. 163.
28 *Ibid.*, pp. 163–68.

had the advance division of the Union army in full retreat. Some of the Federal infantry, by their own admission, showed "to the Rebs as well as the outside some of the best running ever did."[29] Finally repulsed, the Confederates fell back and struck again. They nearly succeeded in surrounding elements of the XIV Corps. General Braxton Bragg, commanding the Confederate center, did not attack at the same time as the remainder of the army.[30] Had he attacked with the rest of the Confederate army, the situation of the Federals might have become desperate.

As the afternoon wore on, the XX Corps began to arrive and stabilized the Union line.[31] Johnston had nearly succeeded. None of the Union right wing had moved to the field. Only General John A. "Black Jack" Logan of the right wing had halted his corps upon hearing the sound of battle. The head of the right wing continued toward Goldsboro and reached a point only seven miles from Mount Olive that evening. Logan's XV Corps was at a crossroad leading toward Bentonville.[32]

The Union cavalry did not get in the fighting either. However, they were in their assigned position to protect the Federal left flank in the event that Wade Hampton's cavalry attempted to ride around it. This was the infantry's battle, and the cavalry was not called upon to fight on this or the following two days. "We remain in our position till one o clock Pm and our brigade advanced 2 miles and built baricades and encamped and the third brigade took our position," Baker wrote on March 20. "Shots with the artilary was exchange all day   our hole line advanced one mile this eavning and had a small skirmish   we are 21 miles from Goaldsborough."

About noon on this day, Logan's men began to reach the field. Their road brought them up to the Confederate rear. The arrival of these Federal troops forced Johnston to realign his army and resulted in the Federal advance observed by Baker.

On March 21, Cornelius Baker continued, "We left our position and came back to inner line at 11 o clock to day and the brigade went to the right flank [where General Joseph A. Mower's division nearly

---

29 *Ibid.*, p. 169.
30 *Ibid.*, p. 171.
31 Cox, pp. 191–95.
32 Barrett, p. 176.

cut the Rebels' escape route][33]   their wasant much firing today oney [artillery]   this eavning at 5 o clock our brigade went back to our old position and Co C of our regiment and one company out of the 8 indany went out one mile for forage in the rear of the rebel lines at a house and got forage   they could be hird talk[ing] from were we were."

Because most of the Union army had reached the field on March 21, General Johnston had only one logical move for his much smaller force. "The rebbels evacuated their positions during the nite leaving a great many of their wounded on the field and at day light our infantry comenced marching torge Goldsborough," Baker wrote on March 22. "the cavalry remaind on the field and held it during the day and brot the wounded rebels in and established a hospatle for them   our foragers were sent out during the day and [we] left at 11 o clock to nite and marched in the direction of holley [Mount Olive] station and went in camp at 2 o c."

On the twenty-third he continued, "We left camp at day lite this morning and marched 12 miles and went in camp   our company went on picket on the road   this is a splendid country   their is lots of forage." The following day he commented, "i went from the picket post for forage and went 8 miles from our camp and took the road that run to [illegible] and came to within 11 miles of Mt olive Station and remaind their during the nite." Foraging was good on the twenty-fifth; "We got 6 bushels of weat and took it to a mill and got it ground and got 2 bugeys to hol our forage and we got to camp at [Mount Olive] station at sundown."

Marching into Goldsboro and Mount Olive, Sherman's infantry and cavalry were a far cry from the romanticist's ideal of a victorious army. Instead of brass bands in the van, the advance of this army was composed of herds of cattle and hogs being driven by foragers. These were followed by wagons, buggies, coaches, and other vehicles loaded with live poultry, hams, and other edibles foraged from the countryside. Few soldiers had complete uniforms, and those who did had done much patching. Hats were of every variety that were found in the houses along the line of march. Shoes and boots were worn out from two months of marching and wading through swamps. Bearded faces

33 *Ibid.*, p. 180. Gen. Mower commanded the 1st Div., XVII Corps.

were black from the smoke of burning turpentine stills and pine woods.[34]

Although they were ill-clad and dirty, the men formed one of the healthiest armies that ever marched. In spite of exposure to winter weather and frequent wading through swamps and rivers, Sherman's army had less sickness than any other Civil War army.[35] The diet of fresh meat and vegetables, instead of army rations, had much to do with this record. Also, many soldiers probably did not report sick for fear of missing some of the fun and excitement of the Carolina Campaign.

At Goldsboro and Mount Olive, the army began to receive supplies by rail from Wilmington and New Bern, North Carolina, on the coast. "We remain in camp and we got a big mail   our teams came in from the river and brot it along," Baker wrote on March 29. "we drew 3 days rashens and foragen is stoped   i rote a letar and sent a goald ring in it." No clue is given about where he got the ring. The next day "their was a train came up to here from Warsaw Station and went back this eavning." On the twenty-ninth, the men drew their first clothing since leaving Midway Church in January.

On April 1, Cornelius and Henry Baker, accompanied by ten privates, went to Chinquapin, about thirty miles southeast of Mount Olive, on a foraging expedition. On consecutive days, the troopers "got 3 horses," "got 4 horses and some tatoes flour and meat," and "got a cart and loaded it down with ham and honey." Returning to Mount Olive on April 7, they received word that Richmond had fallen.

The capture of Richmond did not bring peace in North Carolina because Johnston's army was in the field with a possibility that Lee could outmarch Grant and unite the two Confederate armies. On April 9, Cornelius Baker wrote, "We remained in camp and received marching orders and prepaird to leave on the coming morning."

[34] *Ibid.*, pp. 186–89.
[35] *Ibid.*, pp. 191–92.

XXIV

Peace

*We remaind in camp and General
Sherman Schofield and Howard and
Blair came to Durham Station and
went out to Johnson with a flag of
truce to resieve the sirender of
Johnson   they left here with a flag of
truce at 11 o clock AM and retirnd
at 5 PM   Johnsen sirendered his
hoal Armey to General Shirman to
day at 2 o clock.*[1]

In this way, Cornelius Baker told of the final surrender of the Confederate army on April 26, 1865. Generals Sherman and Johnston had negotiated a surrender earlier, on April 17 and 18. On the seventeenth, Cornelius Baker wrote, "General Sherman came up from raleigh and him and General Kilpaterick went out to meat Johnsen with a flag of truce   their was a large escort went with him   4 out of each company of different regiments   the day was verry plesant and warm." On the eighteenth he continued, "their was a detail to escort General Sherman between our lines and the rebels with a flag of truce with the pirpose of making Peas   he came in the eavning at 4 PM."

Although Lee's surrender on April 9 is popularly thought of as the end of the Civil War, Sherman's army and especially Kilpatrick's cavalry had more fighting to do and more casualties to suffer before the war ended in North Carolina. On the same day that Grant and Lee met to make terms, Sherman's men received orders to resume their campaign the next morning.

Sherman's principal concern now was that Johnston might choose to disband his army, that the men would disperse, and that a guerrilla

---

[1] The Union officers were Major Generals William T. Sherman, John M. Schofield, Oliver O. Howard, and Francis Preston Blair, Jr.

war, which might last for years, would start.² He hoped to defeat the Confederate army before this happened. However, he had small chance of catching the Rebel army if Johnston did not want to be caught. The Confederates now had the advantage of a railroad on which to retreat and could retire faster than the Federals could advance. Sherman's cavalry was his best bet to bring Johnston to bay and he told Kilpatrick, "I don't care about Raleigh now, but want to defeat and destroy the Confederate army; therefore, you may run any risk. Of course, don't break the railroad except to the rear (west) of Johnston, as we want the rails up to Raleigh."³

On April 10, the Union army marched. Cornelius Baker wrote, "We left Mount olive at 8 AM and marched in the rear and left of Goldsborough and encamped during the nite near our old battle ground [Bentonville] on the Goldsborough road." By the night of April 11, the van of the cavalry had reached a place on Middle Creek that Kilpatrick identified only as Mr. Moore's house.⁴ Because bridges over Black Creek had been destroyed, the Union cavalry had been forced to take a long detour over bad roads with no forage. Baker wrote, "We are 26 miles from rollie [Raleigh]   it is reported that the rebels evacuated the town." This rumor preceded the actual event by one day.

"We left camp at 7 Am and our brigade was in the rear," Baker continued on April 12. "the 2 and 3 brigade drove the rebels for 15 miles and encamped within 6 miles [of Raleigh]   our regiment was sent out on our right flank to charge the rebels rear   We went 3 miles and met the rebels in large forse and our company and Co E and k charged them and their forse was too heavy and we had to fall back and we ralied and turnd and drove them back to their old position   We had 7 missen out of our company 5 wunded and a liutenant [Nathan Horton] and corporal [Alfred L. Corman] taken prisner   brother Samuel was mortly wunded and left on the field."

2 Guernsey and Alden, II, 773; Barrett, pp. 209–10.
3 O. R., Ser. 1, XLVII, pt. 3, p. 172.
4 *Ibid.*, pp. 269–70.

In addition to Samuel Baker, Private David T. Dumb was killed. The capture of Lieutenant Horton left the company without a commissioned officer, and Master Sergeant George W. Sipe took temporary command. Horton and Corman returned to the company a few days after the Confederate surrender.[5]

In his summary of the campaign, William Thomas wrote, "In this Action the Assistant Surgeon Of the regiment James Moore was wounded In The Left Lung While assisting to inspire Courage into the men who were almost Worn out with Constant Engagements With The Enemy and rapid marches By day and night." Fortunately, Moore recovered.

This attack by the Ninth Pennsylvania succeeded in cutting off a large part of General Wade Hampton's cavalry, including the general himself. Hampton did not slip out of this trap until after dark.[6] The presence of Union cavalry between the Confederate cavalry and Raleigh worsened an already confused situation for the peace commissioners appointed by Governor Zebulon Baird Vance of North Carolina.

These commissioners were two former North Carolina governors, David Lowry Swain and William Alexander Graham. They had boarded a train in Raleigh at 10:30 A.M. with a letter from Governor Vance to General Sherman and a safe-conduct issued by General William J. Hardee. A few miles from town, they reached General Hampton's lines. Hampton expressed some doubt about the propriety of their mission but reluctantly let the train move on. They had gone only about two miles when a courier from Hampton rode up and told them that the safe-conduct had been withdrawn and they were to return to Raleigh. The commissioners thought that Hampton should inform them of this in person and waited until the general came and ordered them to the rear. By this time most of the afternoon had passed. After the train had moved less than two miles toward Raleigh, it was stopped by Federal cavalry.[7]

After relieving the commissioners of watches and other valuables,

5 National Archives, "Co. C., 9th Pa. Cav., Muster Roll, Apr. 30, 1865."
6 Barrett, pp. 212–13.
7 *Ibid.*, pp. 210–14.

the cavalrymen sent them on to Kilpatrick and turned their attention to robbing and scaring the conductor. The commissioners, after some discussion with the cavalry leader, including a lesson in profanity—"It is 'By God' and 'God-damn' all the time with Kilpatrick"[8]—were sent on to General Sherman.

In a letter to Governor Vance, Sherman responded that he doubted if hostilities could be ended by an agreement between them and suggested that Vance remain in Raleigh and keep the state government functioning. He also sent orders to Federal troops to respect and protect the governor, state officials, the mayor, and civil authorities. The commissioners returned to Raleigh the next morning, April 13. Kilpatrick let them pass through his lines with the warning that if his troopers met resistance in the city, "we will give you hell." As the commissioners approached Raleigh, they saw smoke and flames at the railroad station. Wheeler's cavalrymen, the last Confederates to leave the city, had plundered and fired the depot before retreating.[9]

When General Jordan's First Brigade advanced toward Raleigh soon after the commissioners had reentered the city, they met Mayor William Harrison who had come out to surrender the capital.[10] The offer accepted, the Yankee cavalrymen rode into Raleigh. "We entered the town," wrote Cornelius Baker, "and Kilpaterick's flag was hoisted on the coarthouse [State Capitol] and as his galent troops marched along they gave 3 cheers." While the staff, with Kilpatrick at its head, rode up Fayetteville Street, a straggler from Wheeler's cavalry fired five shots at them. He was caught and promptly executed.[11] Otherwise, the city was quiet, for most citizens remained in their homes.

Upon leaving Raleigh, "we imedatly forged forward and drove the rebels 18 miles beyond the town and encamped." Two miles out of town on the Durham road, Wheeler's rear guard resisted the advance of the Federal cavalry but were quickly put to flight. Sensing final victory, the Union cavalry was irresistible.

"at Morrisville He [Wheeler] again made a Stand," William

8 *Ibid.*, p. 214.
9 *Ibid.*, pp. 214–16, 218.
10 *Ibid.*, p. 221.
11 *Ibid.*, pp. 221–22.

Thomas wrote, "But the Division Soon was formed and the works Charged by The Ninth Penna Ninth [Eighth] Indiana and Ninth Ohio and Third Kentucky For Reserve and in less time than it Takes to Write it the Enemy was routed In the Wildest Confusion Broken by the Terrific fire of the Battery of the Ninth Pennsylvania Veteran Volunteer Cavalry." These were the last guns fired during the campaign. Although they actually were a part of the Tenth Wisconsin Battery, some of the men of the Ninth were serving the guns at the time so a certain amount of credit rightly belongs to them.

After the fight, the Union cavalry encamped and Company C went on picket. Baker concluded his daily entry, "Brother Samuel dide with his wund this morning in a house were the charge was made."

William Thomas continued his summary of the campaign with actions on April 14, "The column was again United and moved on after the Fleeing Enemy When a flag of Truce was Discovered approaching and was Received by the Ninth   It proved To be a Letter From Genl Joe Johnston To Genl Sherman asking Terms of Capitulalation and from this meeting Eventually The Surrender was agreed upon." Johnston's message had reached General Wade Hampton's headquarters late on the night of the thirteenth. Hampton passed it through the lines to Kilpatrick the next morning.[12] Thus, after marching only two miles, the Federal cavalry went into camp. They were not sure that the end of the fighting had arrived and built barricades as a precaution.

On April 15, the First and Third Brigades marched to Durham Station and the Second went to Chapel Hill. The Rebel cavalry had retreated beyond these towns, and the main Confederate army was at Hillsboro. The next day, Cornelius Baker wrote, "We remaind in camp at Durham Station and foraged west   went out at 1 o clock   General Sherman and staff came to the station on a train and their is a flag of truce sent out to General Johnsen this eavning." Sherman returned to Raleigh that evening.

Just before boarding the train at Raleigh on April 17, Sherman received a telegram advising him of President Lincoln's assassination. After swearing the telegraph operator to secrecy, Sherman proceeded

12 *Ibid.*, p. 228.

to Durham Station for his meeting with Johnston. Sherman feared for the safety of Raleigh if word of the assassination reached his soldiers before an adequate guard was posted in and around the city.[13]

Upon reaching Durham Station, Sherman was met by the escort of four men from each company that Baker mentioned. According to William Thomas, the escort was commanded by Major John M. Porter of the Ninth Pennsylvania. The party left Durham Station at 11:20 A.M. and rode about five miles west. Here they met General Johnston and his party. Johnston mentioned that he had passed a house a short distance back, and the generals decided to hold their meeting there. This house was the Daniel Bennett house. The generals asked and received Mrs. Lucy Bennett's permission to use it. She moved the family to one of the outbuildings.[14] The generals negotiated during the afternoon but did not reach a final agreement. Outside the house, Kilpatrick and Hampton exchanged boasts and threats.[15]

General Sherman returned to Raleigh that evening, had adequate guards posted, and then issued orders announcing Lincoln's death. Some soldiers did begin to march toward Raleigh but were dispersed and returned to their camps.[16] To the citizens of Raleigh who feared that the city would be sacked, the sound of Yankee footsteps patrolling the streets was reassuring that night.

The following day, Sherman and Johnston met again at Bennett's house and completed the surrender terms that included political as well as military settlements. Knowing that they had gone beyond their authority, they pledged themselves to obtain the necessary approval from their governments.[17] While awaiting approval, the two armies observed an armistice. Except for foraging expeditions, the troopers remained in camp.

President Andrew Johnson did not approve the surrender agreement. Some subjects covered required congressional legislation and could not be decided by the military or even by the Chief Executive. The President sent General Grant to North Carolina to make a strictly

[13] *Ibid.*, p. 231.
[14] *Ibid.*, pp. 231–32.
[15] *Ibid.*, p. 235.
[16] *Ibid.*, pp. 235–36.
[17] Guernsey and Alden, II, 773–74; O. R., Ser. 1, XLVII, pt. 3, pp. 243–44.

military agreement on the same terms he had given to General Lee.[18] Grant, not wanting to embarrass Sherman, remained in the background, and very few people knew he was in Raleigh. However, he met Sherman and passed along the President's instructions.[19]

When word that the original terms were not approved reached the army, the soldiers prepared to resume the fight. On April 24, Baker recorded ". . . the news came from Washington that Johnsens sirender wasant excepted   we drew rashens and horse equipments." The next day he wrote, "We remaind in camp and tirnd over our unservasable ordanance and preparen for a move." However, there would be no more fighting. Later that day "their was several flags of truce came in and went out."

Generals Sherman and Johnston met again on April 26 at the Bennett house and concluded the terms of surrender. Johnston was reluctant to sign without certain agreements regarding rations and transportation for his soldiers. Sherman, burned once, would not add these to the formal agreement. Fortunately, General John M. Schofield, who was to become military governor, had accompanied Sherman and drew up a separate agreement covering Johnston's objections, thus avoiding a possible stalemate.[20] The terms agreed to, Sherman returned to Raleigh and gave the papers to General Grant, who carried them to Washington.

Following the final agreement of peace terms, Sherman's infantry began their final march to Washington to participate in the grand review. The cavalry remained in North Carolina with regiments serving as garrisons in various cities to guard communications. On April 27, Baker noted, "the 8 indana left and went back along the railroad." On the twenty-eighth he wrote, "We sadled up this morning at 8 o clock for drill and the orders was countermanded and we got 5 days rashens for to go to Greansborough with a train and on our way we met a flag of truce and we halted till we reseived a retirn dispatch from Kilpaterick   then we went 9 miles from their and guarded the men while they put up a bridge on the North Carolina senteral railroad   they com-

18 Guernsey and Alden, II, 774.
19 Barrett, pp. 267–68.
20 *Ibid.*, pp. 270–71.

enced at 1 o clock P.M. and finished it at 9 Pm that eavning   then we
went back to camp and got in camp at 12 o clock to nite."

On April 30, Baker wrote, "the 3 brigade left and the 13 Pennsylvania went to Fayetteville to do garrison duty and their was 6 rebel
trains came in from hilsborough on their way to Goldsborough." The
next day, Lieutenant Horton and Corporal Corman returned to the
company. About the same time, "the pyaneers came back to the company." The men no longer lived on the fresh food foraged from the
country. "We drew 1 days rashens of salt horse," Baker wrote.

The Ninth was assigned to Lexington for garrison duty. On May 4
they "left Durham Station this morning at 8 o clock and marched to
Hilsborough and went in camp at the North Carolina Military insta-
tute." The next day, Baker's battalion marched through Saxapahaw to
Clover factory.[21] Here "Cop E and Co G went out on a scout and brot
in 16 men that had fled the factory." Baker also wrote, "i went out in
the contry for a pleasure ride."

The battalion marched toward Greensboro on May 8 and "went in
camp on a rebel Cornels farm." They reached Greensboro the next day
and then marched to Lexington with a wagon train and artillery, reaching that town on the eleventh.

On May 18, Baker wrote, "the report is that Stoneman captured
Jeff Davis."[22] On the twentieth, he told of promotions, "their was some
comishins made today liutenant hortan Capt and L A Crimian [Law-
rence A. Crinnian] 1 liutenant and ordaly [George W.] Sipe 2 liutenant of our company and I and [James] harvey ordaly Sirgant Co[rp]
A L Corman Sergant and Myars [Augustus Myers] Corporal."

On June 2, Baker wrote, "Samuel Spiren [Spohn] and I got a pass
to day to go to roley [Raleigh]   We are starting at 12 o clock to nite
We got a pass and transportation." On the third he continued, "We
went to the depo at 10 o clock last nite and the train dident come and

---

[21] Reference may have been to Clover Garden, shown on maps of the period.
The "factory" was possibly a textile mill. There was a textile mill at Saxapahaw
during this period.

[22] Jefferson Davis was captured by Col. Pritchard, 4th Mich. Cav., a part of Maj.
Gen. James H. Wilson's command, on the morning of May 10, 1865, in Georgia.
(Guernsey and Alden, II, 778).

i went in the camp and got my breckfast   At 12 o clock [noon] the train came and we left for raliegh and got their at 12 o clock to nite."

On Sunday, the fourth, "Spiren and my self stayed in raliegh in the morning and went out to Paris farm to were brother Samuel and [David Dumb] was killed and [saw the] hed boards and found their graves." The next day he wrote, "Spiren and mee went in to town and remaind their during the day and sported threw the town and viewed it   it is a splendid town and stores of all kind are opend   We got on the cars and left raliegh at 12 o clock to nite."

At the station in Lexington, Baker met the one-year men who had been mustered out and were on their way to Richmond and home. With these men gone, numbers were ridiculously low some days: "We remaind in camp and their was drill in the foarnoon   our company dident drill   their was 2 corporals and one privet [present]." He noted that "times appears verry lonesin and werey."

However, he used the dull days profitably by engraving "stars" for the other soldiers. These were silver identification pins showing name, regiment, and company of the soldier and serving the same purpose as today's "dog tags." Baker sold these for one dollar. He also wrote, "i worked at a badge for my self." This was a larger pin that identified the regiment only and a note attached to it told that he made it from three twenty-five-cent coins. He returned to carpentry and made chests for "Cap Shelp" (Captain Doctor A. Shelp, Company L) and "for the doctor," probably S. C. Walker, Surgeon of the Ninth.

There was some relief from camp life. Baker with a detail of twelve men went across Muddy Creek for forage. The next morning "6 of uss went to hear Dunkard Preachen across the Mud Crick." Two days later they returned to camp with their wagons loaded with hay. Near the end of June, Cornelius Baker and Leopold Miller went on an excursion to find food for the officers' mess. They went to Clemmons. They stayed overnight at "Mr hainses." "their was 2 of the 10 ohio boys put up at the same place   they came from Salem." The next night the soldiers attended "a picknick at halls ferry," and the following morning "we went to the preaching near hainses." Apparently Baker and Miller accomplished their mission and returned to camp with "11½ dosens of eggs 2 hams and 4 lbs of butter and a lot of unions."

On June 8, "Joans [Lawrence Jones] of our company was under guard at town and he got off the guard last nite and took Capt hortans horse and scadadled Sergant Corman and Corporal Meyers went after him they went 10 miles and came back." The next day, "Sebert [Jacob Seaberts] was out on a pass and hird were Joans was and Corporal [Jacob] Waidl[e]y and Corporal [Augustus] Molt went out after him he is beyond Silver Hill 25 miles from here." They never saw or heard of Jones again.

The Fourth of July was spent in Lexington. "the regiment went to town on review and after review we piraded threw the town and then we were pirmitted to dismount and a detail of 4 took our horses to camp and we marched out to the plase prepaird for the selibration their was a couple of speeches made and Washingtons fairwell Address was red the odde feloes were out selibraten the foarth."

Finally, on July 19, the Ninth Pennsylvania began the last leg of their circuit. "We packed up and went to town to start at 12 o clock to nite and the train dident come and we left Lexington at 12 o clock to day the 20 went to Greensborough and chainged cars and took the richmond road and left at 5 o clock and we got to danville at 1 o clock and left at 6 o clock the 21 we chainged cars we reached Sity point in the eavning at 9 o clock and took the boat on James river and left for baltimore at 10 o clock to nite We got in the bay in the morning of the 22 we stoped 25 minutes at foartras monroe we reached baltimore at 8 o clock to nite the 23 and remaind on the boat till morning We marched to the depo and left at half past 12 to day and on the 23 we reached Harrisburgh and marched out to Camp Kertain [Curtin] and we put up tents and went in camp The distance from Lexington No Ca. to harrisburgh is 630 miles."

After nearly a week spent turning in arms and accoutrements, filling out the discharge papers, and being paid, the Ninth Pennsylvania Veteran Volunteer Cavalry was disbanded. Cornelius Baker reached Blain and William Thomas arrived in Lykens on August 1. "My Freinds Were glad to see me Come," Thomas wrote of his homecoming, "But There were Some Sad faces for Them That did not Come."

During the years that followed the war, every soldier of the regiment was able to say with pride, "I was a veteran of the Ninth Pennsylvania Cavalry." Every old trooper was proud of what he and his regiment had done. In the nation's crisis, he had voluntarily done his duty twice by enlisting and reenlisting. His regiment had done more to win the war than most others. Although involved in some of the hardest campaigns and fights of the war, the Ninth Pennsylvania had never been beaten in an even fight and had never "skedaddled" in the face of superior numbers.

The Old Soldier

He was known to have been one of the most honored and faithful of all the members of our Grand Army Post, and died as he had lived—a dutiful citizen and devoted lover of his country.

Every other Tuesday for about ten years before and after the fiftieth anniversary of the Civil War, an old man left a house in the 118th block of Emerald Avenue in the farthest south section of Chicago and walked toward the 119th Street trolley line. His erect posture, steady stride, white beard, black slouch hat, and dark-blue coat with brass buttons marked him as a Union Army veteran. Just south of the house, the old soldier passed a lot which he had arranged as a military establishment, with wooden cannons and numerous American flags. A sign on a rose arbor identified the place as Ft. Baker and the former trooper as Cornelius Baker.

Cornelius made these biweekly trips regardless of the weather. Some days when he reached 119th Street, which was unpaved during most of these years, he found a quagmire. This, of course, did not hinder an old soldier who had marched through the mud of Tennessee and the swamps of the Carolinas. He crossed the street without hesitation and then walked the short block east.

Because the cars ran on a schedule, Cornelius did not have to wait very long on the street corner before one of the red- and cream-colored trolleys rattled across the railroad tracks at Halstead Street and ran the two blocks to his corner, where it stopped to let the old man board. As soon as he was safely on the rear platform, the conductor, who stood facing the rear of the car, gave two quick pulls on a rope that rang a

257

bell on the front platform notifying the motorman to proceed. After paying his fare, Cornelius entered the passenger compartment through a sliding door behind and to the right of the conductor. By this time, the car was accelerating and beginning to sway sideways most violently, forcing the old gentleman to hold onto the straps and then the backs of the seats for support. Selecting one of the forward-facing rattan seats, Cornelius fell into it or seated himself, depending upon the direction and force of the car's lurch.

The trolley continued east, stopping now and then to pick up passengers, for about a mile until it reached Michigan Avenue, where it turned north. Stops became more frequent as the car moved through the business district of Roseland. Beyond Roseland, the crew made up lost time because of a stretch of several miles through empty land. However, north of 79th Street, stops became increasingly frequent again and alerted Cornelius that he was approaching 63d Street. Just before the car reached this intersection, he joined the line of disembarking passengers at the front of the car.

Upon alighting, Cornelius crossed to the northeast corner to await a westbound car. When it came, he boarded it and rode to Princeton Avenue, about half a mile west. Here he got off, walked half a block north, and entered the two-story building that served as the meeting hall of the George G. Meade Post 444 of the Grand Army of the Republic.

The activities of this post had become the most important events of Cornelius's life after his family had been raised and his regular work ended. Although the journeys to and from the meetings were long and tiring, Cornelius seldom was absent at roll calls.

The long trolley car trips gave him a chance to think of the events of his long life. In retrospect he now realized how groundless had been his fears and those of the other veterans some sixty years earlier when the Union army was mustered out of service and returned to civilian life. Then there had been uncertainty about whether there would be work for so many men and whether they would be able to adjust to civilian life after four years of the excitement, adventure, and comradeship of war.

Indeed, the demobilization of the Union army and the absorption of the soldiers into the civilian population were remarkable because of the speed, apparent ease, and the small amount of friction with which these tremendous undertakings were accomplished. When the Confederate armies surrendered in April 1865, the Federal government had 1,034,064 soldiers scattered from the Gulf to the Ohio and from Virginia to Texas. By August, 640,806 of these men had been discharged; and by February 1866, 952,452 soldiers had returned to their homes. This demobilization amazed every civilized foreign government that had a history of disbanding large armies.[1]

Just how many are a million men? During May of 1865, when the Army of the Potomac and most of General Sherman's army were in camp around Washington, Secretary of War Stanton decided that a grand review would be in order. On May 23 the Army of the Potomac, marching sixty abreast down Pennsylvania Avenue, required six hours to pass the reviewing stand. The next day, Sherman's army marched, taking seven hours to pass the stand. And these armies were only about one-fifth of the total under arms. To most people, the U. S. Army had been a few bright-eyed boys going off to war and a few cripples coming home. Here, for the first time, they saw the army as it truly was, and they were awed by the military might that had been created.[2]

The simplicity of the government's plan for disbandment, the attitude of the Northern people, and the characters of the soldiers were the principal elements that contributed to the success of the demobilization. The army kept the individual regiments together in camp until all records and papers—muster rolls, pay rolls, discharges—had been made out. Then the soldiers were transported to camps near their homes. Only then were the men paid and discharged.[3] For many, pay was substantial. The Ninth Pennsylvania veterans received the $290 still due on their reenlistment bounties and their entire pay from August 31, 1864, which amounted to $156 for privates.[4] Most men reached

[1] Ida M. Tarbell, "How the Union Army was Disbanded," *Civil War Times Illustrated*, VI, No. 8 (Dec. 1967), pp. 4–6.
[2] *Ibid.*, pp. 8–9.
[3] *Ibid.*, pp. 4–9, 44–47.
[4] National Archives, "Co. C, 9th Pa. Cav., Muster Roll, Apr. 30, 1865."

home with their funds intact because of the government's wisdom in bringing the men close to parents, wives, and other home influences before paying them.

The civilian population had determined that the returning soldiers would have every opportunity to find work. Not only did they find jobs for the veterans in their local communities but supported policies that required the filling of government openings with veterans. They also supported those programs necessary for caring for the cripples and the handicapped and the payment of pensions to the invalids, widows, and orphans.[5]

And the soldiers themselves were determined to find work. They were confident and self-reliant men who did not expect nor desire special favors. In the expanding economy that followed the war, most men were able to return to their old pursuits or to find new occupations. Some men found work and resumed their lives in their hometowns, but many others followed Horace Greeley's advice to go west. In the resumption of their civilian lives, the veterans of the Ninth Pennsylvania also included those who stayed near home and those who moved west.

General Jordan returned to the legal profession in Harrisburg after the war. However, a few years later, he went into the lumber business in Williamsport. Possibly this business failed or became too difficult for Jordan's advancing years because he secured a position with the Post Office in Philadelphia and, still later, transferred to the Mint in the same city. He died in Philadelphia April 2, 1895, at seventy-four.[6]

William Thomas returned to Lykens and resumed his trade. He married Maria Kissley on July 19, 1868. William died in Lykens June 28, 1896, leaving Maria and two minor children. In an affidavit to the U. S. Bureau of Pensions, the Reverend P. S. Hooper, minister of the Lykens Lutheran Church, told of William's character as an adult: "He was known to have been one of the most honored and faithful of all

---

[5] Tarbell, pp. 45–47.

[6] *Commemorative Encyclopedia*, p. 1195. Jordan's children were David W., an artist, and a daughter identified as the wife of Rev. Leonard Woolsey Bacon of Connecticut.

the members of our Grand Army Post, and died as he had lived—a dutiful citizen and devoted lover of his country."[7]

Although the Baker homestead remained in the family for another hundred years under the ownership of the elder Cornelius until 1897, son Charles until 1914, and grandson Roy until 1968, the soldier sons left Blain. John and Jeremiah remained in Perry County; John at Newport and Jerry at Kistler, a few miles from Blain. Both were survived by two children.[8] Frederick's pension record shows that he became a steel worker in Lorain, Ohio. In 1903, his leg was fractured and permanently disabled in a mill accident. After the accident he lived in the Soldiers' Home of Erie County where he died on May 4, 1907. He was survived by three sons. His pension file contains the only information the author found of David, the "mere lad," mentioned on page 1, who ran away to enlist but was rejected because of his age. Frederick named him as next of kin and gave his address as Shilo, Ohio.[9]

Henry Baker, of the Ninth Pennsylvania, moved to Ottawa, Illinois, after the war. He married while there. However, when this wife died childless, Henry returned to Blain and married an Ellen Thomas in 1880. A short while thereafter he moved to Chicago. He died in 1904. A son and daughter continue to live in Chicago.[10]

Of these soldiers, Cornelius Baker had the longest and fullest life. By 1868, he and Julia had two sons, making essential the finding of steadier work than was available in the Blain area. During this year, the family moved to Chicago. Soon, Cornelius sent word back to his relatives that carpenters worked all year in Chicago, a situation that

[7] National Archives, William Thomas pension file. The minor children were Annie May, b. Apr. 8, 1883, and Benjamin Franklin, b. Oct. 17, 1885. Adult children were not listed.

[8] Roy H. Baker and Mrs. Lela Kessler, Blain, Pa., nephew and niece of John and Jeremiah Baker; National Archives, Jeremiah Baker pension file. His wife was Maggie Stroup and children were Annie S., b. Aug. 4, 1870, and Hulda J., b. Sept. 12, 1879.

[9] National Archives, Frederick Baker pension file. Frederick had three sons by his first wife, Anna Gamble. The eldest son was George C. Others were not named in the record.

[10] Letter, Arthur Baker, son of Henry, to author, Sept. 4, 1963. The daughter is Mabel Baker.

was hard for the relatives to believe. Brothers Henry and James later moved to the Chicago area and worked as carpenters.

For many years, Cornelius did well in the big city. He changed from wage earner into a building contractor. However, he became overextended and the depression of the 1890's nearly wiped him out. Because this trouble came while Grover Cleveland was president, he held the conviction thereafter that hard times came whenever the Democrats were in power. He managed to hold onto one house at the far south end of the city by finding employment at the Pullman Company, and the family moved into it.

Along with economic problems came a series of personal troubles. In 1890 Julia died. About a year later, he married a widow who brought three stepchildren into the family. She also passed away two years later. Cornelius married once again in 1895.[11] In 1898 war came again, and son Edward enlisted. He died the following year while serving in the Philippine Islands.[12] Edward's death ended the personal tragedies. The minor children grew up and left home, and Cornelius was able at last to take an increased interest in his old-soldier activities.

In his exertions to participate in the functions of the G.A.R., Cornelius Baker was typical of the old soldiers of this generation. The idea of a veterans' organization to maintain the strong spirit of patriotism of the war years came shortly after the end of the conflict, and the Grand Army quickly grew to be one of the strongest social and political forces in the United States. Through the G.A.R., hundreds of thousands of veterans became one voice in support of patriotic causes and of pensions and care for the invalids, the widows, and the orphans of the war. A measure of their political strength is the fact that five of the six presidents of the United States elected between 1868 and 1900 were Civil War veterans.[13]

---

[11] National Archives, Cornelius Baker pension file; Hardesty, II, pp. 567–68. Cornelius and Julia Baker's children were William H., b. Feb. 27, 1865; Edward M., b. June 26, 1867; Frank, b. Oct. 14, 1868; Julia C., b. Oct. 14, 1871; Florence M., b. May 2, 1876; Frederick, b. Jan. 7, 1878; George C., b. July 21, 1881; and Grace L., b. June 27, 1885.

[12] Letters, U. S. War Dept. to Cornelius Baker, May 2, 1901, and U. S. Treasury Dept. to Cornelius Baker, July 12, 1904.

[13] Presidents Grant, Hayes, Garfield, Harrison, and McKinley were Civil War veterans.

Much of the good done by the G.A.R. was social rather than political. Committees of the state organizations visited the veterans' hospitals, the soldiers' homes, and the orphanages; and by the ability of the general organization to raise finances or to apply political pressure when necessary, they maintained these institutions at high standards.

G.A.R. posts in most Northern cities and towns became recreational clubs for the members and their families. In addition to the Grand Army itself, auxiliary units included the Womens' Relief Corps, Sons of Union Veterans, and Daughters of Union Veterans. Although the veterans' civilian interests varied widely, they found a common ground socially in the meetings, encampments, and campfires sponsored by the Army. The activities gave the old soldiers a feeling of value and importance to the community and the country after their working years were over.

Having secured pensions for the invalids, widows, and orphans during the organization's early years, the G.A.R. became the principal proponent of pensions for the soldiers as they approached old age. By twentieth-century standards of government largess, the pensions drawn by the Civil War soldiers do not appear generous. For example, men who could prove service-incurred illnesses that affected their ability to work received a payment of two dollars a month from 1865 until 1890, when the government became more lenient and invalid pensions of eight dollars became available for nonservice-incurred sickness as well. From that time pensions were gradually increased to fifty dollars a month by the early 1920's.[14]

His pension permitted Cornelius Baker to participate in his old-soldier activities, and as the years passed, he was given more responsibility in his post's functions. From 1917 through 1923, he represented the post at the state encampments held in various cities in Illinois. In 1919 he was elected post commander. These positions were a significant honor and responsibility because the George Meade Post was the third largest in Chicago. He also attended several national encampments, which were the major annual events for the Grand Army veterans, attracting as many as 20,000 people as late as 1922.

[14] National Archives, pension records of Cornelius Baker, John Rowell, and others.

Second only to the national encampments in importance was Memorial Day. May 30 had been established to honor the Civil War dead, and the veterans observed it according to its original intent. Every year, Cornelius Baker and the children and grandchildren who lived in Chicago met at Oakwoods Cemetery. The graves of brother Henry, son Edward, and wife Julia were decorated with flowers. The soldiers' graves always had new flags in the bronze G.A.R. standards. Although the old soldiers were present, the younger men were more in evidence. Squads of men from the American Legion, instead of the G.A.R., passed through the cemetery firing salutes and sounding taps over the graves of their fallen comrades.

At noon, the G.A.R. members and their wives assembled at the meeting hall of the George Meade Post for dinner. From the post, the veterans went downtown for the mile-long parade on Michigan Avenue that was the spectacular event of the day in Chicago. After 1918, the veterans of three wars marched again. First came the thin ranks of the old Civil War soldiers, then the middle-aged Spanish-American War veterans, and finally the mass of young men from World War I. Many of the Civil War veterans had to ride in the automobiles provided for them, but Cornelius Baker always marched the mile, even in his eighty-third year.

Shortly before he died on September 2, 1923, perhaps Cornelius Baker expressed the sentiments of all Civil War veterans when he said, "I have done my duty as an American citizen."

Bibliography[1]

U. S. Government Publications

Library of Congress. "Military Map Showing the March of the United States Forces Under Command of Maj. Gen. W. T. Sherman, U.S.A., during the Years 1863, 1864, 1865." Capt. Wm. Kossak and John B. Muller, St. Louis, 1865. This map shows roads, rivers, railroads, and towns for the Southern states and portions of the Northern states south of 38°30′ and from the Atlantic Coast beyond the Mississippi River.

Mugridge, Donald H., comp. *The Civil War in Pictures: A Chronological List of Selected Pictorial Works.* Library of Congress. Washington, D.C.: Government Printing Office, 1962.

Munden, K. W., and H. P. Beers. *Guide to Federal Archives Relating to the Civil War.* National Archives Publication No. 63–1. Washington, D.C.: Government Printing Office, 1962.

National Archives. *Compiled Military Service Records in the National Archives.* National Archives Publication No. 63–3. Washington, D.C.: Government Printing Office, 1965. A pamphlet explaining service records and how to order them.

———. *Genealogical Records in the National Archives.* National Ar-

[1] Members of the Ninth Pennsylvania Cavalry are indicated by an asterisk.

265

chives General Information Leaflet No. 5. Washington, D.C.: Government Printing Office, 1969.

————. *Pension and Bounty–Land Warrant Application Files in the National Archives.* National Archives General Information Leaflet No. 8. Washington, D.C.: Government Printing Office, 1969.

National Park Service. *Chickamauga and Chattanooga Battlefields.* National Park Service Historical Handbook Series, No. 25. 1956. Reprint. Washington, D.C.: Government Printing Office, 1961.

Stephenson, Richard W., comp. *Civil War Maps: An Annotated List.* Library of Congress. Washington, D.C.: Government Printing Office, 1961.

War Department. *The War of the Rebellion: A Compilation of the Official Records of the Union and Confederate Armies.* 128 vols. Washington, D.C.: Government Printing Office, 1880–1901.

Military and Personnel Records in the National Archives of the United States

Alphabetical Index to Places of Interment. Washington, D.C., 1868. Relates specifically to the interment of Union soldiers, 1861–79.

Battle Book, Special Civil War Collection, Adjutant General's Office. Lists engagements in which volunteer organizations participated. There is a similar record for Regular Army troops.

"Captured Battle Flags: Letter from the Secretary of War . . . Feb. 16, 1888," House of Representatives, *Exec. Doc. No. 163*, 50 Cong., 1st sess.

Census Records for 1850 and 1860. On microfilm. Include population listing by state, county, and township or city; name of each person in the family; color; sex and age; place of birth; profession, occupation, or trade; if attended school during the year; illiteracy; physical and mental disabilities; and value of real and personal property.

Civil War Staff Officers' Papers, Special Civil War Collection, Adjutant General's Office.

Clothing Books, Regimental Records, Volunteer Regiments. Contain clothing accounts of noncommissioned officers and enlisted men.

Descriptive Books (Rolls), Company Records, Volunteer Regiments.

Contain lists of officers, noncommissioned officers, and enlisted men, including date and place of enlistment, physical characteristics (height and color of hair and eyes), occupation, and date of discharge of individuals; also contain registers of deaths and desertions.

Descriptive Books (Rolls), Regimental Records, Volunteer Regiments. Contain rosters of commissioned officers, lists of noncommissioned staff officers, and lists of transfers, resignations, and deaths.

Generals' Papers and Books, Special Civil War Collection, Adjutant General's Office. Used in compilation of the *Official Records of the Union and Confederate Armies.*

Horse Books (1862–64), Special Civil War Collection, Adjutant General's Office. 2 vols. Relate to the furnishing of horses and horse equipment for the U.S. Army.

Letter Books, Regimental Records, Volunteer Regiments. Contain letters received and sent in chronological order.

Morning Report Books, Company Records, Volunteer Regiments. List personnel strength (present and absent) daily, with space for notations.

Muster Rolls. List men present on parade or otherwise accounted for on specified days, recorded by companies. These rolls show name, rank, enlistment date, date last paid, bounty (paid and due), clothing account, and present (or reason for absence). Reverse side of the rolls recapitulates personnel strength, number of horses on hand, and other information.

Order Books, Company Records, Volunteer Regiments. Contain copies of company orders.

Order Books, Regimental Records, Volunteer Regiments. Contain general and special orders.

Pension Records. Applications for pensions and correspondence relating thereto for Civil War veterans, their widows, and dependent children are retained in individual jackets. A microfilm index is arranged alphabetically by the veteran's name, the state from which he enlisted, and the state from which the pension application was filed. Files contain proof of service for veterans, proof of marriage of widows, and other genealogical data.

Photographs. Corps of Engineers photographs of Sherman's campaign taken by George N. Bernard, official photographer of the Military Division of the Mississippi. These photographs are a part of the Signal Corps collection of approximately 2,300 items covering the period 1861–74.

Register of Captured Flags (1861–65), Special Civil War Collection, Adjutant General's Office.

Roll of Honor: Names of Soldiers Who Died in Defense of the American Union, Interred in the National and Other Cemeteries. 27 vols. Washington, D.C., 1865–71. Relates specifically to the interment of Union soldiers, 1861–79.

Service Records. Summaries of service were made for each soldier from muster rolls and other records at the time of discharge. These summaries listed whether present or absent (and reason for absence), date last paid, bounty (paid and due), clothing account, sutler's account, amounts to be deducted from pay, and other information. These records established proof of service required for pension payments.

Diaries, Manuscripts, and Letters

Baker, Cornelius.* Diaries for 1864–65, in 2 vols.; 18 original photographs of Union officers and enlisted men; 1862 New Testament; Maynard carbine; a pistol; 3 engraved items; engraving tools; official papers (2 discharges and corporal's warrant); Confederate money; and Minié balls. Letter from Deputy Quartermaster General, U.S. War Department, to Cornelius Baker, May 2, 1901, concerning reinterment of Edward M. Baker, Co. D., 45th U.S. Volunteers; letter from U.S. Treasury Department to Cornelius Baker, July 12, 1904, concerning pay due to Edward M. Baker, deceased; notification of allowance, July 28, 1904, due Cornelius Baker as father of Edward Baker. Also other postwar items, including photographs, official papers, carpenter's tools, and furniture; Grand Army of the Republic badges, ritual books, medals, and publications. Author's collection.

Baker, George C. "War Record of Cornelius Baker," typewritten copy of manuscript, Sept. 23, 1923.

Baker, Samuel.* U.S. War Department certificate of death of Samuel Baker, Dec. 10, 1865, signed by G. W. Scolly, surgeon. Author's collection.

Campbell, Henry. Diaries for 1862–66, in 3 vols., Eli Lilly Library, Wabash College, Crawfordsville, Ind. Portions have been printed in *Civil War Times Illustrated*, II and III, Nov. 1963–Jan. 1965.

Rippetoe, John H. Typewritten copies of 96 letters written to his wife, collection of the Vigo County Historical Society, Terre Haute, Ind.

Thomas, William.* Typewritten copy of Thomas's diary, Sept. 16, 1861, to July 18, 1865, and photographs. In collection of LeRoy Robert Matter, Harrisburg, Pa.

Books and Articles

Adams, George Worthington. *Doctors in Blue: The Medical History of the Union Army in the Civil War*. New York: Henry Shuman, 1952.

Amann, William Frayne, ed. *Personnel of the Civil War*. New York: Thomas Yoseloff, 1961.

Barrett, John G. *Sherman's March Through the Carolinas*. Chapel Hill: University of North Carolina Press, 1956.

Bates, Samuel P. *History of Cumberland and Adams Counties, Pennsylvania*. Chicago: Warner, Beers and Co., 1886.

———. *History of the Pennsylvania Volunteers 1861–1865*. 5 vols. Harrisburg: B. Singerly—State Printer, 1870.

Brown, Campbell H. "Carter's East Tennessee Raid," *Tennessee Historical Quarterly*, XXII, No. 1 (Mar., 1963).

Butler, Lorine Letcher. *John Morgan and His Men*. Philadelphia: Dorrance & Co., 1960.

Campbell, Henry. "The War in Kentucky-Tennessee As Seen By a Teen-Aged Bugler," *Civil War Times Illustrated*, II and III (Nov. 1963–Jan. 1965).

Cist, Henry M. *The Army of the Cumberland*. New York: Scribners, 1898.

Commemorative Biographical Encyclopedia of Dauphin County, Pennsylvania. Chambersburg: J. M. Runk & Co., 1896.

Cox, Jacob D. *The March to the Sea.* New York: Scribners, 1898.

Culbertson, John Newton. "A Pennsylvania Boyhood," *American Heritage*, XVIII, No. 1 (Dec., 1966).

Duke, Basil W. *A History of Morgan's Cavalry.* Bloomington: Indiana University Press, 1960.

Dyer, Frederick Henry. *A Compendium of the War of the Rebellion.* 3 vols. New York: Thomas Yoseloff, 1959.

Egle, William Henry. *History of the Counties of Dauphin and Lebanon.* Philadelphia: Everts and Peck, 1883.

Gibble, Abraham H.* "The Man on the White Horse," as related by Elmer E. Strong, *Civil War Times Illustrated*, V, No. 2 (May, 1966).

Greeley, Horace. *American Conflict: A History of the Great Rebellion in the United States of America, 1861–65.* Hartford: O. D. Case & Co., 1866.

Guernsey, A. H., and H. M. Alden. *Harper's Pictorial History of the Civil War.* 2 vols. Chicago: The Puritan Press Co., 1894.

Hain, H. H. *History of Perry County, Pennsylvania.* Harrisburg: Hain-Moore Co., 1922.

Hardesty, H. H., ed. *Presidents, Soldiers, Statesmen.* 2 vols. New York: H. H. Hardesty, 1891–92.

Herr, J. K., and E. S. Wallace. *The Story of the U.S. Cavalry.* New York: Little-Brown, 1953.

Horn, Stanley F. "Perryville," *Civil War Times Illustrated*, IV, No. 10 (Feb. 1966).

Hutton, Daniel M. *Old Shakertown and the Shakers.* 4th ed. Harrodsburg: Harrodsburg Herald Press, 1936.

Jordan, Thomas Jefferson.* "The Battle of Thompson's Station and the Trial of the Spies at Franklin, Tenn.," *The United Service* (Mar. 1890).

———. "Some Military Reminiscances of the Rebellion," *The United Service* (Mar. 1889).

Kelker, Luther Reily. *History of Dauphin County.* 3 vols. New York: Lewis Publishing Co., 1907.

Miller, James Cooper.* "Memoirs," reprinted in part by *Civil War Times Illustrated*, VIII, Nos. 3–6 (June–Oct. 1969), from original manuscript owned by C. Spencer Miller, Lancaster, Pa. Miller enlisted in Co. L as James Cooper.

Lincoln, Abraham. *Literary Works*. Selected and with an introduction by Carl Van Doren. New York: The Heritage Press, 1942.

Longstreet, James. *From Manassas to Appomatox: Memoirs of the Civil War in America.* Bloomington: Indiana University Press, 1960. First published in 1896.

Lustyck, Andrew F. "Civil War Carbines," *World Wide Gun Report,* 1962.

Luvaas, Jay. "Bentonville—Last Chance to Stop Sherman," *Civil War Times Illustrated,* II, No. 6 (Oct. 1963).

————. "Cavalry Lessons of the Civil War," *Civil War Times Illustrated,* VI, No. 9 (Jan. 1968).

McBride, J. R. *History of the 33d Indiana Veteran Volunteer Infantry.* Indianapolis: Burford, 1900.

McDowell, Robert Emmett. *City of Conflict.* Louisville: Louisville Civil War Round Table, 1962.

Moore, James.* *Kilpatrick and Our Cavalry.* New York: Hurst & Co., 1866.

————. *Complete History of the Great Rebellion 1861–1865.* Philadelphia: W. S. Burlock, 1881.

Neal, Mary Julia, ed. *The Journal of Eldress Nancy.* Nashville: Parthenon Press, 1963.

Pennsylvania, Commonwealth of. *Pennsylvania Today.* Harrisburg: Department of Public Instruction, 1962.

Rhoades, Charles D. *Photographic History of the Civil War.* 5 vols. New York: Review of Reviews, 1912.

Roberts, Peter. *Anthracite Coal Communities.* New York: Macmillan, 1904.

Robertson, James I. "Military Executions in the Civil War," *Civil War Times Illustrated,* V, No. 2 (May 1966).

Rogers, J. L. *The Civil War Battles of Chickamauga and Chattanooga.* Chattanooga: J. L. Rogers, 1942.

Rupp, Israel Daniel. *The History and Topography of Dauphin, Cumberland, Franklin, Bedford, Adams, and Perry Counties.* Lancaster: Gilbert Hills, 1846.

Sandburg, Carl. *Abraham Lincoln: The War Years*. 4 vols. New York: Harcourt, Brace, 1939.
Schofield, John McAllister. *Forty-six Years in the Army*. New York: The Century Co., 1897.
Seymour, Digby Gordon. *Divided Loyalties*. Knoxville: The University of Tennessee Press, 1963.
Sherman, William T. *Memoirs of General William T. Sherman*. 2 vols. New York: D. Appleton, 1875.
Skinner, Capt. George W., ed. and comp. *Pennsylvania at Chickamauga and Chattanooga: Ceremonies at the Dedication of the Monuments*. Harrisburg: Wm. Stanley Ray—State Printer, 1897.
Strong, Robert Hale. *A Yankee Private's Civil War*. Edited by Ashley Halsey. Chicago: Henry Regnery Co., 1961.
Tapp, Hambleton. "The Road Back," a reprint from *The Civil War in Kentucky*, by the *Courier Journal* (Louisville), Nov. 20, 1960.
Tarbell, Ida M. "How the Union Army was Disbanded," *Civil War Times Illustrated*, VI, No. 8 (Dec. 1967). Originally published in *McClure's Magazine* (Mar., 1901).
Taylor, Frank H. *Philadelphia In the Civil War*. Philadelphia, The City, 1913.
Townsend, William H. "The Rage of the Aged Lion," *American Heritage*, XI, No. 4 (June, 1960).
Tucker, Glenn. "The Battle of Chickamauga," *Civil War Times Illustrated*, VIII, No. 2 (May 1969).
Upson, Theodore F. *With Sherman to the Sea: The Civil War Letters, Diaries, and Reminiscences of Theodore F. Upson*. Edited by Osborn Winther. Bloomington: Indiana University Press, 1958.
Wiley, Bell Irvin. *The Life of Johnny Reb*. Indianapolis: Bobbs-Merrill, 1943.
———. *The Life of Billy Yank*. Indianapolis: Bobbs-Merrill, 1952.
Williams, Francis Trevelyn, ed. *Photographic History of the Civil War*. 10 vols. New York: Review of Reviews, 1912. See especially Vol. IV, *The Cavalry*.
Wilson, Spencer. "How Soldiers Rated Carbines," *Civil War Times Illustrated*, V, No. 2 (May 1966).
Wright, Silas. *History of Perry County*. Lancaster: Wylie and Griest, 1873.

Index

Alabama regiment (U. S. A.): First Cavalry, 221
Aleshire, Charles C., 115, 117, 119, 121
Anderson, James, 22
Appel, Charles A., 190–91
Arms and weapons. *See* individual listings
Armstrong, Frank C., 130, 167
Army, Grand, of the Republic. *See* Grand Army of the Republic
Army, Union: demobilization of, 259; enlistment of, 14–15, 18
Ashland. *See* Clay, Henry, residence of
Atkins, Smith D., 202, 210, 221, 239
Atlanta, Ga., 192–93
Averasboro, Battle of, 235–41
Averill, W. W., 178

Baird, Absolom, 115n; his infantry division, XIV Corps, 212–14
Baird, John P., 130–32
Baker, Anna M. (sister), 7n
Baker, Charles (brother), 261
Baker, Cornelius (father), 3–7, 261
Baker, Cornelius (soldier), 7, 10–13, 66, 68, 96, 108, 112, 138; in Carolina campaigns, 219–22, 224–31, 234, 237, 241–47, 249–55; in Chicago, 257–58, 261–64; children of, 262; cost of uniform and equipment, 29; enlistments, 22, 171; describes execution, 39; on furlough,

Baker, Cornelius (*cont.*)
175–77; Grand Army activities, 258, 262–64; ill and convalescent, 148–49; in Kentucky (1864), 178, 180, 182–85, 187–88; on March to the Sea, 201, 203–204, 206–207, 209–18; married, 175; at Battle of Perryville, 83, 89; in Tennessee campaigns (1864), 187–99
Baker, David (brother), 3, 7n, 261
Baker, Edward (son), 262
Baker, Elizabeth (sister), 7n
Baker, Ellen Thomas (Henry's wife), 261
Baker, Frederick (brother), 7n, 261
Baker, Henry (brother), 7, 13, 22, 29, 171, 175, 177, 188, 192, 219, 245, 261–62
Baker homestead, 6, 7, 261
Baker, James (brother), 7n, 262
Baker, Jeremiah (brother), 7n, 261
Baker, John (brother), 7n, 261
Baker, Julia Bower (wife), 175–76, 261–62
Baker, Mary Ann Mumper (mother), 5–7, 12
Baker, Roy H. (nephew), 261
Baker, Samuel (brother), 7, 175, 192, 247–48, 250, 254
Baker, Sarah E. (sister), 7n
Baldwin, William W., 106–107
Battle flags, 169, 219
Battles. *See* individual listings
Belgian rifles, 41, 180

Longstreet, James, 146, 156–57, 167, 170
Loomis, Cyrus O., 90
Louisiana regiment (c. s. a.): First Cavalry, 73, 77–79
Louisville, Ky., preparations for defense of, 80–82, 180, 184–87
Lowe, Jacob H., 56
Lykens, Pa., 8–10, 12, 30, 255

McAllister, Fort, 216–17
McCahan, Thomas S., 158
McClellan, George B., 35, 199
McClellan saddle, 35
McCook, Alexander McD., 83–84, 86–87, 89–90, 142–43. *See also* XX Corps, Army of the Cumberland
McCook, Daniel, 88
McCook, Edward M., 139, 143–44, 147, 148, 156, 165, 169
McCook, Robert L., 139
McCullough, Hugh W., 26–27, 56–57
McKinney, Edmund, 27, 90, 121
McKnight, Owen B., 85
McMillan, J. M., 58, 65
McPherson, John B., 185
Manson, Mahlon D., 75
Mark, Cyrus, 32
Marshall, Humphrey, 103, 105–108
Martin, William T., 163
Martz, Richard, 32
Massachusetts regiment: Sixth, attacked by rioters in Baltimore, 21
Matter, John L., 32
Maynard carbines, 41n, 69, 85
Meade, George G., 199
Meade, George G., Post 444. *See* Grand Army of the Republic
Memorial Day, observance of, 264
Messner, Henry, 38
Messner, Isaac, 31–32
Messner, Phillip, 32, 76
Metzer, Fred, 48
Michigan regiments: Second Cavalry, 82–84, 86–89, 96–98, 103, 112, 114, 116, 122–23, 126–28, 134, 136, 140, 157, 160–61, 163–64, 166, 168, 172, 174, 177; Fourth Cavalry, 93, 122; Ninth Cavalry, 39, 202, 206, 211, 221, 230, 237, 239; Nineteenth Infantry, 114; Loomis's battery, 90
Midway Church, Ga., 216n
Militia, Georgia, 204, 207–208
Miller, Henry, 38

Miller, John F., 184
Miller, Leopold, 254
Miller, Tilghman, 185
Minnesota regiment: Hotchkiss's battery, 89–91
Minty, Robert H. G., 122–23
Mitchell, Ormsby M., 42n
Mitchell, Robert B., 134–36, 138–39, 143, 147–48, 153–54
Mitchell's division. *See* Cavalry Corps, Army of the Cumberland, First Division
Molt, Augustus, 255
Money, Confederate, value of, 50
Montgomery, Samuel, 19
Moore, James B., 27–28, 208, 214–15, 225, 233, 248
Moore, Nancy, 35, 38, 50–54
Morgan, James D., 126–27, 197
Morgan John Hunt, 52, 62–63, 93, 95, 97; Cave City Raid, 47–48, 62; First Kentucky Raid, 62–71; Fourth Kentucky Raid, 178–81
Morgan, John T., 163n, 169
Morton, Oliver P., 68, 180
Mossy Creek, Tenn., Battle of, 162–65
Mower, Joseph A., 243
Mumper, Elizabeth, 5
Mumper, Henry, 5–6
Mumper, Mary Ann. *See* Baker, Mary Ann Mumper
Munroe, George W., 178
Murray, Eli H., 202, 204, 208, 211
Myers, Augustus, 253, 255

Negroes, 47, 69, 116, 139
Nelson, Camp, 149
Nelson, William, 74–77, 81
Ninth Pennsylvania Cavalry: arms, 29, 40–41, 46, 69, 85, 116, 180, 183; band, 28, 51–52; in Carolina campaigns, 219–21, 224–25, 230–31, 235, 238, 240, 247–48, 250, 253–56; on Carter's Raid, 95–110; casualties, 57, 60, 67–68, 120–21, 124, 128, 133, 137, 144, 155, 158–59, 169, 190, 215, 217, 248; at Battle of Chickamauga, 145–48; in Chickamauga campaign, 142–45; colors presented, 30, 184; counties where recruited, 23; deaths, accidental, 31, 48, 76, 97, 175, 185; deaths in action, 60, 67–68, 120–21, 124, 133, 137, 144, 155, 159, 190, 215, 217, 248; deaths by murder, 48,

Ninth Pennsylvania Cavalry (*cont.*)
61; deaths from sickness, 37; discipline,
37–38, 52, 76, 112; in East Tennessee
campaign, 157–61, 163, 166, 168, 172–
73; furloughed, 173–77; against guerrillas, 52–61; horse equipments, 35–36,
112; horses, 33–35, 46, 52, 63, 108, 110,
112, 180, 217, 221; impressing horses,
72, 106–107, 204; during Confederate
invasion of Kentucky, 73–82; on police
duty in Kentucky, 30, 43–48, 180–86;
in March to the Sea, 202, 204–17;
in Middle Tennessee campaigns, 111,
113–16, 122–28, 130, 132–41, 151–52,
154, 187–99; campaigns against Morgan, 47–48, 62–71, 178–82; mustered
out, 255; nationalities and occupations
of men, 23; officers of, 19–21, 25–28;
joins Army of the Ohio, 40–43; organization, 25–28; at Battle of Perryville, 83–93; recruits, 19–24, 175, 188,
192, 220; reenlists, 171–72; visits with
Shakers, 49–54; at Battle of Thompson's Station, 113–21; in training
camps, 25–30, 34–38; uniforms, 25–26,
28–29, 112; votes in state and national
elections, 194, 196, 199
Noblets, Sarah, 24

Ohio, Army of the (U.S.A.), 42–43, 79–
82, 151, 156, 159, 196; Cavalry, 157,
159–60, 162
Ohio National Guard, 181
Ohio regiments: First Cavalry, 93, 202;
Second Cavalry, 172; Fourth Cavalry,
139; Fifth Cavalry, 202, 221; Seventh
Cavalry, 96, 99, 104, 109; Ninth Cavalry, 202, 221, 240, 250; Tenth Cavalry,
202, 204, 206, 221, 254; Eighteenth Battery (Aleshire's), 115, 117; Fifty-second
Infantry, 77; One Hundred Eighteenth
Infantry, 163–64; One Hundred Twenty-fourth Infantry, 120
O'Reilly, Michael, 113–14, 198

Parole of prisoners, 60, 67, 102, 104, 114
Patriotism of Northern people, 3–4, 14–
15, 18
Patterson, George W., 26
Pay, soldier's, 15, 112, 174, 259
Pell, Henry, 32
Pennsylvania: canal system, 4; election
of 1864, 196, 199; schools, 10

Pennsylvania regiments: Seventh Cav-
alry, 62, 122, 137; Thirteenth Cavalry,
253; Forty-sixth Infantry, 155; One
Hundred Ninth Infantry, 174. *See also*
Ninth Pennsylvania Cavalry
Pensions, 260, 263
Perryville, Ky., Battle of, 83–93
Peter, Walter G. (alias Maj. Dunlap),
130–32
Peterman, William Henry Harrison, 58
Peters, Dr. (Van Dorn's murderer), 129
Philadelphia City Cavalry, First Troop
of, 20
Phillips, Joseph, 26
Pinney, Oscar, 87
Pioneer corps, 222, 253
Polk, Leonidas, 86
Porter, John M., 251
Potomac, Army of the, 151–52, 170, 259
Potter, William M., 56
Praetorious, Louis, 28
Prisoners, 43, 46, 58–59; exchange of,
78
Punishment. *See* discipline

Railroads, destruction of, 213
Rangers, partisan, 102, 106–107
Rations, 25, 46, 52–53, 203; for horses,
102
Regiments. *See* individual listings by
state
Religion, 10, 254; of Shakers, 49–51
Rhett, Alfred Moore, 237, 241
Rice, Elliott W., 196
Richmond, Ky., Battle of, 75–76
Robbins, Oscar, 27, 165
Robinson, Andrew, 38, 60–61
Roddey, P. D., 150, 155
Rosecrans, William S., 96, 121, 127, 129,
131–37, 140, 142–43, 146, 155
Rousseau, Lovell, 90–91
Rowell, John, 71n
Russell, Roswell M., 27, 60, 72, 144, 147

Sabers, 29
Saddles, 35, 180. *See also* McClellan
saddle
Savage, Edward G., 22–23, 26–27, 31, 36,
38, 43, 88, 144
Sawme, Reverend P., 175
Schofield, John M., 196–97, 236, 246,
252
Schools. *See* Pennsylvania, schools